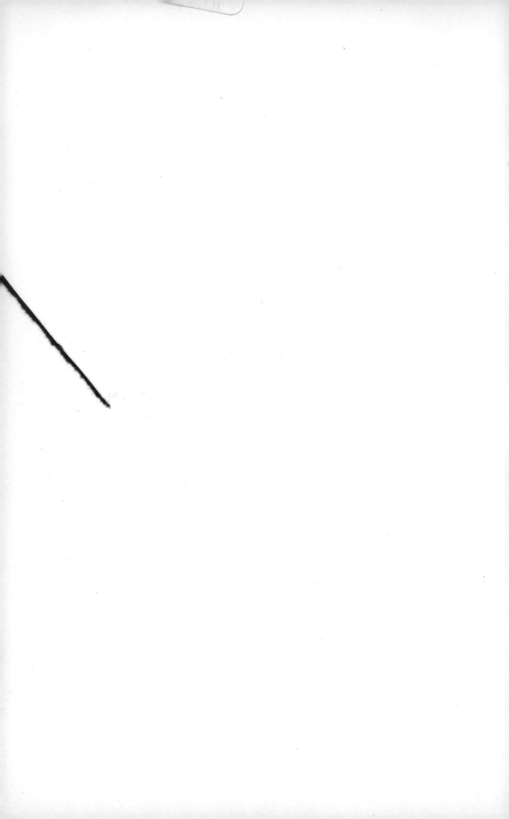

BETWEEN THE
THREE BRIDGES

by

PJ Taylor

ORIGINAL WRITING

978-1-907179-30-3

A CIP catalogue for this book is available from the National Library.

Published by ORIGINAL WRITING LTD., Dublin, 2009.

Printed in Great Britain by the MPG Books Group, Bodmin and King's Lynn

DEDICATIONS

This book is dedicated to three people. To my brother Har who wasn't around for the first half of these stories and was too young to remember the other half. This is for you Har!

To Mam and Pop or Harry and Bid who never mentioned the word 'love' but always showed it; who worked hard to make us what we are today. Thank you so much, from Jet, Jim, Harry and myself.

Acknowledgments

To my sister Jet who helped me through the first stages but in the end had to leave me to my own devices.

My brother Jim and his wife Marian who offered money if it was needed to get the project into book form.

Joanna for her suggestion about the recorder.

Steve for the listening ear he gave me on many a trip to Dublin.

Gerry the schoolteacher from Cellbridge who advised me to give the manuscript to a book club in Limerick for a review.

The Granary Book Club in Limerick that gave me a rating of four out of five along with some useful tips that gave my confidence a huge boost.

Alan for his work on the front and back covers

To Garrett Bonner and Steven Weekes at Original Writing, my sincere thanks for their professionalism and support.

Aidan Corr for his direction and editing

To Margaret and Seán Jackson from Ahane whose eyes were the first to see the manuscript apart from Mary with the ten little fingers who kept me going every day with her enthusiasm and belief.

To Seán Curtin whose photograph of Upper Carey's Road brought back many happy memories of my childhood years.[*]

To Jethro Stokes for his marvellous work with the camera

My daughter Sorcha, her hubby Gar, my son Cory who thought the whole project to be a great idea and wants to wait until it is in book form to see what my childhood was like.

And most of all, the woman who started the whole thing six years ago, my wife Mary. Thanks Love for putting up with all the twists and turns I took to get this completed.

---

[*] Seán Curtin's Picture of Upper Carey's Road circa 1950's features on the front cover of this book.

To THE FOLLOWING BUSINESS COMUNITIES FOR THEIR

GREAT FINANCIAL SUPPORT, MY SINCERE THANKS

The Imperial Three Bridges Bar and Lounge *Upper Carey's Road.*
TMH Solutions *Co .Waterford.*
Bob Sweeney *Car Dismantlers, Castleconnell, Co. Limerick.*
Food Fair *William Street, Limerick.*
Dr. Brian Scanlon *John Square, Limerick.*
Cross's Funeral Undertakers *2 Lower Gerald Griffin Street, Limerick.*
Panda Tool Hire.
Limerick Paints *Pennywell Road, Limerick.*
Prestige Car Rentals *Dublin.*
South's Pub *O'Connell Avenue, Limerick.*
Elm Fireplaces *Delta Business Park, Limerick.*
Tony Connolly Menswear *Patrick Street, Limerick.*
Rooney Auctioneers *O'Connell Street, Limerick.*
Eamon Grimes Wine Shop *Mulgrave Street, Limerick.*
Dan Lehane *Thomas Street, Limerick.*
Mike Gleeson Shoes *William Street, Limerick.*
Noel Martyn *Mungrete Street, Limerick.*
Tile Centre *Upper William Street, Limerick.*
Whelan's Photography *O'Connell Street, Limerick.*
Rene Cusack, Fish Stores *Alphonsus Street, Limerick.*

Author's Note

I used to think the sixties were the most innocent of times.
Later on I changed my mind and thought it was I who was
innocent.
Now I wonder did I have any brains at all.

PJ Taylor
September 14 - 2009.

Introduction

When PJ Taylor asked my advice about writing a book on his childhood memories of Limerick's Carey's Road, I hesitated.

Since the success of Frank McCourt's Angela's Ashes, 'memory lane' has become an over-subscribed market, PJ's limited literary knowledge was a factor that demanded consideration and I was not convinced that genuine enthusiasm would be sufficient to overcome the obstacles.

I have been proven wrong.

The book gives an insight into Limerick life of the 1950s through the eyes of a child that is a mixture of innocent sincerity, humour and often brutal honesty.

Similar to many other areas of the city in the early post Word War II era, living in Carey's Road had its disadvantages. Those who resided in the tiny bungalows at the upper end of a road that stretched from Edward Street to the Roxboro Road, endured limited facilities but in a strange way it bonded families and neighbours together through a similar desire to maximize the positives.

In this book, PJ takes us back in time and into his home. We meet his mother and sympathise with her as she tries to find a balance between the unquestionable love that her husband has for her and the similar love that he shares with Arthur Guinness.

Christmas time is a mixture of childhood excitement and fear of imminent disappointment and sorrow. It's Christmas Eve and PJ and his three siblings peer through the half door, hearts in their mouths, in anticipation of what condition their dad, Harry Taylor, will be in when he arrives home.

PJ shares memories of his years in the lower classes of Sexton Street primary school, the brutal corporal punishment and almost constant fear. He tells of the happy days: camping with the boys scouts, visits to his granny in County Limericand a miscellany of childhood incidents that he recalls with almost uncanny accuracy.

The book is written in a manner that demands the interest of the reader. It is a story that has been seeking release from the writer's inner memory for over five decades and, particularly, for those of us who can relate to that era, it strikes a familiar chord.

Aidan Corr,
Journalist.

PREFACE

Pop never told us he loved us, neither did Mam. They didn't have to. In our house love was shown in other ways. Pop wouldn't show it often, but when he did, it was done with big neon lights. Mam's lights were on every day, every hour, every minute. In this environment Jetta, James and I received all that was good, allowing us to grow into confident and happy people. Harry, our brother, was too young to remember. He was nine years old when Mam died, at the age of 49. Harry relied on the three of us for reassurance of how much he was loved.

It's Christmas Day 2003, I'm at home in Hilltop, staring out the window, my eyes fixed on nothing. There's the sound on the road of kids with the latest Christmas craze: scooters with their petrol engines. There are 11 of them racing around the patch of green in front of my house and it's driving me crazy. There's no Christmas tree, no decorations, no sign of Christmas in my house. There hasn't been for 30 years. The sounds of the scooters fade as I keep staring; I'm falling into a trance, going back, thinking of Pop. I'm doing it a lot lately and wondering why, why after almost 22 years, is he on my mind everyday. Maybe, it's because I never really mourned him or is this what happens heading into your sixties?

BETWEEN THE THREE BRIDGES

CHAPTER I

It's the third week of November 1947; Bridie Taylor has a bad migraine. She gets them regularly, but *Mrs. Cullen's Headache Powder* isn't working today. She's not sleeping and the pressure from her conscience is mounting. Bridie is married to Harry; they have a daughter of 11 months and live at the top of Number 9 Bedford Row, which is in the shadows of the four large stone columns at the entrance to the Franciscan Church at the bottom of Henry Street, Limerick. For a long time now they have been calling her over, and today she is going to answer that call. She asks Angela, her sister-in-law, to look after Jetta for a while, and crosses over the street to the entrance of the church.

Her heart is pounding which increases the pain in her head. She enters, looks around, there's only one confessional with the light on overhead. She looks at the name of the priest on duty hoping that he's someone she knows. She doesn't. Maybe he's new. There's no one waiting, she can go in. The door creaks as it opens. She walks into the darkness and as she falls to her knees she can hear the sound of snoring.

'Oh God', she thinks 'he must be old, if he was young he'd be awake and he's not going to understand'.

She knocks on the shutter gently. He's still snoring. She knocks again, calling 'Father, Father'. He wakes, rubbing his eyes, grunting while shifting his body to a different position.

She starts: 'Bless me Father for I have sinned.'

'Wait a minute, wait a minute woman, I'm not ready.'

She's in trouble now, he's grumpy.

'Go on, go on', he says 'I haven't all day.'

'Bless me Father for I have sinned.' There's silence.

'And?' he says

'And what Father?'

'How long has it been since your last confession woman?'

'Well Father, I can't remember.'

'What do you mean you can't remember? Is it a week, a month, two months?'

'Oh it's much longer than that Father.'

'How long then?,' he asks sharply.

'It's more than a year and a half Father,' she says nervously.

'A year and a half, what in God's name possessed you to leave it go that long? Are you in from the country? Where do you live?'

'Across the road, Father'

'Across the road, you're living across the road and it's been one and a half years since your last confession. I want to know why you have left it so long'.

'Well Father, you see, we can't have any more children.'

'Why not? Is there something wrong with you? You're in the wrong place, I'm not a doctor'.

'We can't afford it, Father. You see my husband and I live in one room, we have one child, and he works here and there, most times he has no work.'

'You can't afford it, so what you're saying is, you and your husband are practicing some sort of avoidance, would that be right now?'

'Oh well, I don't think so Father.'

'Well woman, I know so, do you realise that you are in a constant state of mortal sin. And if you were to die for any reason in that state you'll burn in hell forever? You'll have to go. I cannot give you absolution while you are in that state.'

Later that night a terrified woman conceived a son, yours truly.

My grandmother, several days after my mother died suddenly, related the substance of this story to me. It managed to inflict on an already hurt young man a feeling of deep rage against the men clothed in black, in the guise of a spiritual comforter who terrified the members of their flock, who also had the power to control what people did in the marriage bed.

I was 21 at the time and wished every kind of disease and pain on that man for what he did to my mother. I had no way of discovering whether he was dead or alive not even a name to go on. I thought if he was old then he must be dead by now. And for weeks I hoped he died in pain, surely he's the one who is in hell, and then it dawned on me, sure if it wasn't for him I wouldn't be here at all.

It's four weeks since Mam's death and the absence of her presence is hard to bear. I have so many questions now, questions I should have asked her long ago, but what son thinks his mother will be dead at 49? I decided to visit Nan in Cappamore. Surely she'll be able to help. I want to know about the early years, how Mam met Pop, that small room upstairs in 9 Bedford Row, what was I like as a child? She would be more forthcoming now in her experienced time of mourning.

Nan is constantly bent over, her face old and scarred with too many wrinkles, her body strewn with aches and pains, she hardly ever laughs - how can she? She has given 15 lives to Cappamore, and just buried her eighth. But Nan is tough and knows no other life. Her stare is terrifying. It can send a pit-bull terrier scurrying to its box.

Her front door is slightly ajar. I knock gently saying, 'Hello Nan, it's Paddy.' As I open it, there she is sitting in the corner by the open fire, under the picture of the Sacred Heart, its small lamp glowing underneath. The room is surrounded by pictures of her children living and others long since gone. She's holding a picture of Mam in the one hand and a handkerchief in the other.

'Oh Jesus, Paddy,' she cries, 'why Bid, of all of them, why Bid?,'

She's looking at me for an answer; a woman who has lost so much wants me, a young fellow of 21, who has for the first time in his life a pain like no other. What can I tell her only to give her a hug and stutter the words, 'I wish I knew Nan, I wish I knew.' But I can to some extent feel her pain. Is a mother's loss of a daughter greater than a son of his mother? I don't know. In Mam's death Nan has lost her only daughter left in Limerick. She has four other daughters, two in Northampton, England, one in Australia and one in Cork.

Nan is a regular visitor to Garryowen and it's the only time I see her laugh. But that's all finished now with Pop back on the drink what business has she got in Garryowen? She is the closest bond I have left to Mam, and I want to get closer, but will she let me?

'I'll put the kettle on Nan, there are a few things I'd like you to tell me'

'What kind of things?,' she asks as I fill the kettle.

'Just a minute', Nan let me get the gas going first, 'You can tell me while it's heating.'

There's a similar seat to Nan's on the other side of the open coal fireplace and as I lay my body into it, she's still looking down at Mam's picture.

'Nan, a few weeks ago you told me how I came to exist. Is there anything else you can tell me about that time?'

She raises her head, and there it is that terrifying stare.

'So you'd like to know more would you, how you nearly killed my poor girl?,'

I'm shocked! I can't remember doing anything that nearly killed Mam.

'You and your big bloody head, its well you might look shocked. You were a big whore when you came into the world.

'Your poor mother was screaming for hours before they got your head out. Then there were your big bloody shoulders that took another two hours. Ten pounds seven ounces you weighed.'

'But Nan,' I said in my defence; 'that's not heavy for a baby is it?,'

'What do you mean that's not heavy, Jesus, Mary and holy St. Joseph, listen to him Mr. Experience, Mr. Know It All. Your mother was tiny, 'twas bad her having to carry you around for nine months, Christ! She thought she'd never get you out of her.

'One hour after the Nurse cleaned you up and brought you in for your mother to see you, she said; 'take that bastard out of my sight, I don't ever want to see him again'.

Surely Nan's grief is making her exaggerate.

'The kettle is boiled,' she said sharply, 'make the tea!'

There's silence while I make it. Should I change the subject I wonder as I place the cup in her hand. She holds mine gently and looks at me. The stare is gone, that same wrinkled face has a softness about it now.

She says 'You were the favourite, oh she used to deny it, but you were'.

Wasn't Nan right about my 'big bloody head'?

She looks back at the photograph, 'Oh the light of heaven to you Bid, Oh sweet Jesus, what did I ever do to you to deserve this? Haven't you given me enough crosses to bear? How can you expect me to carry this one, it's too heavy?,'

There's a long silence and it's hard to break it. What can I say? The clock on the wall ticks away, its pendulum swinging, then it chimes six times.

'Is that the time?,' I say.

There's no reply. I want to ask another question. Will I risk it? Can I risk getting that stare again?

'How did they meet Nan?,'

'How did who meet?,' she asks puzzled.

'Mam and Pop.'

'Oh I'll tell you how they met.'

She straightens herself on the chair, there's no sign of the stare. There is a quiver in her voice. I've pressed some kind of a button here.

'Your mother worked in England before the war with your aunts Mary and Nancy. She worked as a parlour maid for a Jewish family in London who were very good to her.'

As she told me this, I remembered seeing at home a small badly worn diary with the year 1939 on the cover. I must look for it when I get home. She continues.

'We all knew here the war was inevitable, so Jack wrote and asked the girls to come home.'

'Who's Jack, Nan?' I asked and jumped with the fright when Nan shouts:

'Jesus, Mary and holy St. Joseph don't you know your own Grandfather's name,' and the stare is back.

'Sorry Nan, I only knew him as Granddad'.

Boy this is hard work. Nan is like a nuclear time bomb. She continues:

'When your mother came home she got a job in the Bedford Hotel in Bedford Row as a housemaid and your father lived next door. He was great friends with Mrs. Dennehy who owned the Bedford Bar. She had two sons Denis and Tadhg which meant he was always in and out of the house.'

Then she grabs my hand and shouts: 'Jesus, but he was an ugly auld yoke your father!

2 Photo of Diary

'I remember the first time we laid eyes on him, after he cycled the sixteen miles from Limerick to Tower Hill, he knocked on the door. It was Jack who answered it.

'Is this where Bridie Coleman lives?,' your father asked.

'It is', said Jack 'and who are you and what do you want of her?'

'My name is Harry Taylor. I have a date with her.'

'Just a minute,' says Jack.

*Nan and Granddad Jack outside their house in
Tower Hill sometime in the early 1950's.*

The big long lanky thing with the ears that my Granddad Jack saw outside his door when Pop called for my mother on their first date. He's the one on the right by the way. The other is his pal and drinking partner Tadhg Dennehy outside the Bedford Bar.

*Picture of Pop's other drinking buddy Dennis Dennehy.
I have no idea who the guy in the middle is.*

Wedding photograph outside The Bedford Bar in Bedford Row, the good looking guy top left, my father, my mother bottom left. Mrs. Dennehy standing in the middle, her daughter Maureen, middle sitting. I have no idea who took this photograph, but cameras were few and far between in those days, and so was their use.

When Jack came back into the kitchen he had a look of confusion on his face. 'What's wrong Jack?,' I asked.

'There's a big long lanky thing outside the door with two big ears and it says it has a date with Bid.'

Then your Mother came down the stairs and said 'was that knock on the door for me Dad?,' It must be Harry.

'Come in Harry and meet my Mam and Dad.'

Your father has to stoop to avoid hitting his head off the top of the door ope.

'Hello Mrs. Coleman', he says, holding his hand out for me to shake it, but I'm stuck to the floor and can hardly move with the shock. My arms are hanging off my shoulders, but he reaches down, puts my hand into his and says, 'Bid has told me loads about you.'

I manage to answer him and say, 'has she now? Well she hasn't told us anything about you, I wonder why?,'

Then he shakes hands with your Granddad, and before we can say another word, Bid says 'we're off down to Tom's for a walk, we won't be long.'

'Will I put your name in the pot,' I ask.

'Yes please Mrs. Coleman,' answers your Dad.

After they left, Jack puts a sign of the cross on his forehead and says:

'Is it a species from another world she's gone off with? What will we do if they get married? How will all the relations react when they see Bid walking up the aisle to that yoke? Is she completely blind Mother?'

'I don't know Jack,' I answered. 'We'll just have to pray that it won't last'.

'Ah, but it didn't take us long to see what your mother saw in your father Harry Taylor'. She's smiling again. 'What he never had in looks was made good in his personality.

'And then we found out that his father owned the well-established tailoring business in Bedford Row.' So we thought Bid would be well looked after.

'When they got married we had a few surprises come our way. Your Grandfather on your Dad's side died years earlier. Harry wanted nothing to do with the tailoring trade. So your mother married a pauper and worst still he was a bloody alcoholic as well.'

I'm now feeling a strong urge to come to Pop's defence. 'OK Nan, he might have been fond of a drink but he never laid a hand on Mam.'

The stare is back only worse than ever.

'Jesus will you listen to him?,' she screams.

I'm starting to shake now and say, 'Well, well, I never saw him do that.'

She's leaning out of the chair as far as she can, 'You did see it,' she shouts and settles herself back into the chair.

'You bloody well did see it, but you were too young to remember, you were in the cot, wide awake, going mad with your teeth. It was when you lived in that small room on the top of the house in Bedford Row, your Mam and Dad were only married three years. Your Dad came home drunk looking for his dinner. It wasn't there because your mother didn't know what time he would be home, and anyway when he would be drinking she'd never do it, saying 'if you can afford to pay for drink, you can afford to pay for your dinner'.

'An argument started and your big six foot two father gave my five foot daughter a thump on the shoulder and put her flying. As drunk and all as he was he said 'Jesus Bid, I'm sorry' and sat down at the corner of the bed. When your mother got up she grabbed a jam jar from the table and let him have it into the side of the head and split him wide open; and your mother says, 'Now you'll have reason to be sorry'. Then Nan starts giggling and said 'one side of his head was red with blood and strawberry jam, I can tell you he never put a hand on her again.'

I had strange feelings at that moment, disillusioned with Pop to think that he would do such a thing and very proud of Mam how she stood up for herself.

'Did he ever tell you about the time the ceiling fell down on you?,' Nan said.

'What ceiling?,' I answered.

'The ceiling in Bedford Row in that small room upstairs.'

'No,' I answered.

'The ceiling in that room was full of cracks, big wide ones, the wind was howling through especially in winter, you were a very sick child always coughing and choking. We used to say if the wind changed direction, you would catch a cold. Your mother couldn't take it any more and made your Dad do something about it. So up the road he goes to Rene Cusack's Grimsby Fish Stores where he was well known. He gets about forty sheets of that fish paper. You know it. It's stiff and nearly see through. He buys paste and a half stone of lime. He pastes all the sheets to the ceiling until there are about five layers of paper and then the next day he gives the whole lot a wallop of whitewash. That put an end to the drafts for about two weeks.'

'Why two weeks?,' I asked.

'Because two weeks later the whole bloody lot came down in one piece, as it was too heavy, and landed right on top of you in the cot. Well you brought the house down with your screams. Your father had to wade into the room to find you in the dark, because it broke the bulb in the ceiling on the way down.'

She was howling with laughter as she finished. I wanted to leave now that Nan was in this frame of mind. My visit was certainly fruitful and gave me lots to think about and I promised not to leave it too long before my next visit.

As I drive home my mind is full of thoughts, especially those early years. I must look for that diary of Mam's. I had seen a new side to Nan, I really wanted to get close to her but in the years to come Nan would want nothing to do with me, even insisting to my two uncles Peadar and Jamie that I was not to attend her funeral.

I'm home under the stairs looking for that diary. There are several shelves there. It's where Mam keeps her latest cleaning gadget, an electric floor polisher. There's the alligator handbag, artificial of course. It's been in the family as long as I can remember. Surely the diary is here. There's a red book with the name 'Cavendish' written on the cover. Inside it shows the weekly payments for various pieces of furniture that Mam would have got over the years since we moved to Garryowen. There will be no arrears in this book. Mam was meticulous about that. There are books from the Royal Liver Insurance Society that will pay for any funerals in the family. That was paid weekly too. There's a book for the Limerick Corporation Housing Department, ten shillings and six pence a week. Again every week paid for in full. A milk book, a book for RTV Rentals, no missing weeks there either. An ESB Book and tucked away in a side pocket of the handbag are three Mass cards, one of her brother Paddy, who died last year, one of her Dad, and a daughter of Pop's sister in Rathbane, Angela named Alma. And there it is, the small diary!

I've had this in my hand before and it was just a book, but now I feel I'm holding a bit of Mam's life. Its cover was originally light pink but it's torn and dirty now. There aren't many entries. I'm trying to figure out how old she was when she bought it. Somebody has written 1942 in heavy pencil just above 1939. Inside the cover page she writes; *Jim Harty sailed for London September 1941,* then there's *Dwyer 30th September.* There's a page with the time for lighting the street lamps, another page has six immovable feasts for 1939. I don't think Mam bought this book in England. Then there's her work and home address - Mr and Mrs Goldstein, 14 Burrstone Road, London, E 8. Other entries are difficult to read as they have faded.

Thursday 19th January, she writes, posted parcel to Mother, one and thruppence.

Wednesday 25th January, bought boots for four and eleven pence ha'penny.

Friday 10th February, Poor Pope Pius XI died today.

She writes her wages, seventeen shillings and six pence a week.

Saturday, 10th June she writes down, five months at the Goldstein's.

There are a lot of empty pages; others have some kind of recipe. I don't think Mam was into having her personal thoughts recorded. What a pity, I could have learned a few things.

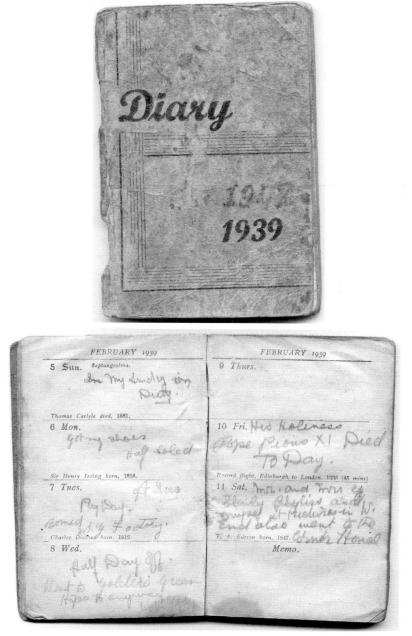

Mam's Diary

On a second visit to Nan one week later I asked her how we came to live in Upper Carey's Road. She said, 'When your mother and father lived in the top back room in Bedford Row, your father's sister Angela lived across the hall in another room. Angela and Bid fell out over your sister Jetta and one of Angela's younger ones. I can't remember the details but the tension was too much for Bid so a house became available in Upper Carey's Road and your father borrowed the five pounds from Mrs. Dennehy to buy the key.'

'How do you mean, buy the key Nan?,' I ask.

'There were no deeds to those houses they were so old, anyone who lived there had squatter's rights. You gave the occupier money, he put the key of that house into your hand after he moved everything out and the house became legally yours. Once you were living in it no one could throw you out'. And there it is the story of how we came to live between the three bridges.

And here I am 35 years later wondering why it is I can't get the early years of that great road out of my head. My wife Mary wants to know why I'm so quiet when I come home, how she has to ask the same question several times before I might give her a grunt in response and can't understand how the biggest mouth in Limerick has gone redundant and won't leave me alone 'til I tell her what the problem is. But it's only a matter of time before I put the poor woman, who thinks I'm gone off her, out of her misery and is relieved to know that my brain is up in Carey's Road all the time and we won't have to go to the Marriage Counsellors or the Divorce Court to end what has been a good partnership.

She says I should write it all down, the whole lot, not to leave anything out. Sure she knows the stories. She's heard them all before. I'm trying to tell her what chance do I have of writing stories of those great years, when my days in school were so bad, how I thought I'd never get out the gate of the Christian Brothers School in Sexton Street every day, and dreaded the thought of going back again the next morning to be thumped and pucked and how my mother would run for the Mrs. Cullen's Powders after ten minutes of trying to help me with the homework everyday. Sure I've never read a book in my life, all I wanted was the comic books with the pictures of Superman, Batman and Spiderman, the Beano, Dandy and Topper, The 64ers telling the great adventures of Buffalo Bill, Kit Carson and Wild Bill Hickock.

I can't spell, if I were to write anything where would the commas, full stops and exclamation marks go? But this wife of mine has planted a seed, I don't realise it, but everyday I'm going to give it plenty of water. Sure I can get someone to type and correct whatever I write. And when I tell Mary I'm going to have a go, she says how pleased my sister Jetta and brothers James and Harry and all the other family members will be to have a record, especially our grandchildren who never met your Mum and Dad.

But this is a difficult road I've taken, a road that will take me five years, of many starts and failures, to have it finally completed with the help of Mary from Ahane with the ten little fingers and Frank McCourt who said a happy childhood is hardly worth your while, who spoke about the likes of me with the quiff and the woolly jumper in the Christian Brothers Schools and how well off we were. He was right! It was you Frank, your first book, the only one I've ever read in my life, and your style of writing that took my brain to a place it never went before and kept it there until the last page. My sincere thanks. I couldn't have done it without you!

CHAPTER 2

Does any child remember any part of its first four years? I don't. That's how long we spent in Bedford Row. We're a family of five when we arrive in Upper Carey's Road, Number 82. My brother James had just arrived weeks before, on the 19th July, 1952.

How we all survived in one room I'll never know, but survive we did. We're living in luxury now. Well, luxury to us. That is compared to what we left behind. Now we have three rooms instead of one. Mam has her own sink; she doesn't have to share it with Angela. OK, it doesn't have a waste pipe taking the dirty water to a gully somewhere. Instead the sink has a galvanized bucket underneath. This bucket is covered by a small curtain. It means though that a careful eye has to be kept on the bucket, making sure it doesn't overflow. When full, its contents of dirty water and tea leaves were thrown onto the street.

When I look back on our time in Carey's Road it had to be the most dangerous place in Limerick City. Jetta, James and I played in a nest of near misses. How we managed to come away from this place alive and free from various plagues or loss of body parts I'll never know. Accidents were many with the odd scar here and there, but in spite of this we and others, in the six years we lived here, would leave this wonderful place with great memories that will last all our lives. Like the large swamp at the end of Lynch's field that ran adjacent to the railway line under the stone bridge that took you to Rathbane and Janesborough, now the grave of hundreds of pups and kittens, drowned in dirty canvas coal bags, by owners who couldn't afford to keep them or even have the room. The two quarries by the Co-op on Roxboro Road that we fished and fell into on many occasions; the half dozen derelict houses with walls full of loose stones, large and small, waiting for the slightest push of a hand or shoulder to fall and kill or seriously injure any of us; or the continuous high limestone walls that we climbed and were used to secure the many engine parts and tools utilized by the hundreds of CIE workers that spewed out the main gate every week-day at one and six o'clock. And worst of all playing on all the railway tracks that surrounded Upper Carey's Road. In spite of us knowing the danger and seeing for ourselves the young lives that were lost and the gruesome way they died, and the terrible dread our mothers had of the odd motor car seldom seen on our roads, sending us to school with the cry of 'keep in by the wall, hold your sister's hand' and if we crossed the road to be sure and not walk in the many lumps of horse manure and ruin the only good pair of shoes we might have.

How most of our great memories were of the things our mothers told us not to do and the things we had their blessings with, like the hoop and stick or the home made trolley; the memory of my mother asking me to go to O'Holloran's shop for the Mrs. Cullen's Powder; and getting a box in the ear because I told her to ask Jetta, 'coz I was playing with Dinny, Fonsey and Noelie. The box came with the words 'I didn't ask Jetta, I asked you. Take your hoop and stick', she says, 'the one that I found under the stone bridge by the railway line that she told me never to go next or near and that I asked Mrs. Meade for the loan of her hatchet to beat the living daylights out of the spokes of the wheel that kept the owner on the frame of the bike it once belonged to.

'You'll be much faster' she says, 'if you take your hoop and stick' and now I'm on my way over the Roxboro Bridge to O'Holloran's shop with the one hand over the red-hot ear that has the ringing in it and the other hand belting the hoop that I'm running alongside with the stick, the two hundred yards to the shop because I didn't want a second red ear. After leaving the hoop against the wall and under the window of the shop, (that wasn't really a shop at all, but a house just like our own, only in much better condition and still standing today). Asking Mrs. O'Holloran for the Mrs. Cullen's Powder and her saying like she always does every time I come here; 'Sure the poor woman is never without a headache'. Coming back out with the powder in my pocket and the left hand still over the ear, to get my simple form of transportation that will get me back to

*The Shop that wasn't really a shop at all and still
standing today. Where I left my hoop and stick.*

Dinny, Fonsey and Noelie quicker than walking only to find it's
not against the wall or under the window anymore. After looking around all sides of Roxboro Road to see if it rolled away
because of the hill, I am bawling my eyes out.

It's not long before every resident is out on the footpath wondering if someone's been killed to find it's only young Taylor
from the other side of the bridge. They're all around asking
'what's wrong love?' They're looking at my face, the back of my
pole, my legs and arms. One of them is saying he doesn't see any
sign of blood at all and wonders what has me so upset. There's
tears streaming down my face running into two big long bogies
hanging from my nose, into froth flowing out of my mouth; I'm
pointing at the place under the window where my hoop and
stick used to be and manage to spurt out the words, 'A dirty,
rotten, filthy louser has stolen my hoop and stick'.

'Oh I see now', says Mrs. O'Holloran, 'that's why he's pointing at the wall.'

'Ah sure God love him,' says a neighbour, 'that's all that's wrong, he's not hurt at all, thanks be to God, it's only his hoop and stick.'

'Oh listen here to me now,' says another neighbour, 'a hoop and stick is a very important piece of transportation to a young man. When I was a young fellow I went nowhere without my hoop and stick and I bet his pals have hoops and sticks don't they young man? Do your pals have a hoop and stick?'

I nod my head in response and increase the volume of the screams.

'He'll be standing around now looking at his friends with their hoops, and he's upset too because his mother has a bad headache, sure the poor woman is never without one, that's why he came into the shop to get his mother a *Mrs. Cullen's Powder*. He probably wants to go home to her to give her the powder,' said Mrs. O'Holloran.

'Sure your father will get you another wheel tomorrow when he finds out your own one was stolen,' said Mrs. O'Holloran trying to console me.

'Come on, there's a good boy now.'

'And then I spurt out the words, 'That's not why I'm crying.'

'Isn't it love? Why are you crying then?' asked Mrs. O'Holloran.

'Because now I'll have to walk home.'

After the dark winter nights comes the homemade trolley season. With the long stretch in the evenings it will be the same as last year with the four of us looking for the scraps of wood and most difficult of all the pram wheels. The ones we made last year will have been well and truly banjaxed from the constant use of too many bodies jumping on because they weren't able to make their own over the spring, summer and autumn months. There will be no teamwork here, it's the 'everyman for himself' attitude. Maybe it was just the timing and the kind of job Pop was working on at the time because after asking him to keep a lookout for any odd pieces of new wood he might have left over at work, here he comes that evening down the hill with several lengths of smashing new wood tied to the frame of his bike. And it looks like I'm going to be the first to get the frame of his trolley started.

'Here', says Pop, handing me a saw, a hammer, a big nut and bolt with a boxful of nails and screws. 'You'll need these if you are going to do it right'. He'll bring a chair out onto the footpath and watch me for hours and won't offer any advice unless I ask him. He's never done this before and it never dawned on me at the time what was going on, how he was looking at the way I used the tools, to see would I have the ability to solve and tackle problems, and I'm loving every minute of it.

This could have been Dinny, Fonsie, Noelie and myself

Mam is calling me in for my supper and I'm telling her 'I'll be in, in a minute.' She keeps calling for the next two hours and I keep answering 'just another minute Ma, just another minute.'

It's getting dark and I'm almost finished. Pop keeps checking to see how I'm doing. And there it is, one brand new homemade trolley, complete with seat and steering only this thing is going nowhere until I get some wheels.

The kitchen floor has enough room to lay my trolley on the ground. Ma lets me eat my supper while sitting in its seat. I can see myself, I'm tearing down the hill at a hundred miles an hour, I have the rope in both hands helping me to steer. I'm passing Lynch's house, I have one leg on each side of the front frame, my head and body are crouched and I can feel the breeze blowing through my hair.

'Your supper's going cold,' shouts Ma.

'OK Ma. Ma, can I bring the trolley to bed with me tonight?'

Ma is looking at me strangely.

'Jesus, Mary and holy St. Joseph, what do you mean can you bring it to bed with you?'

'Ah come on Ma, sure it's new wood, the bed won't get dirty.'

'And where's your sister going to sleep?,' says Mam.

'Well can I lean it up against the wall so, please Ma?'

'What do you want to lean it up against the wall for?'

'So I can be looking at it before I go to sleep.'

Ma is smiling as she says 'OK, just for tonight!'

I'm looking at my trolley and thinking when Fonsey, Dinny and Noelie see it they'll be mad jealous.

In those days we could go where we liked, we just had to be home for meal times. If I tell Mam I'm going to the dump called Corconree on the Dock Road looking for wheels, she'll tell me to keep away from the place, not because of any physical danger but she says it's full of fleas, germs and all kinds of filth. I have to get my wheels and I can hardly sleep thinking of how good my trolley is going to be when I get them.

So I'm off to the dump the following day. It's Saturday. The dump never closes on Saturday. It takes me only fifteen minutes to get there. There's several fires burning the rubber from electric cables, that would be worth a few bob to the young lads waiting around, but there's no sight to be seen anywhere of a pram. If I go home a different way I might spot a banjaxed one lying around somewhere.

I'm back home, frightened, shaking and my mother wants to know why I am looking out the window as it's such a lovely day, I should be out playing. I wandered up and down every road and alley from the dump and there's nothing except a high bockety auld pram that's outside a door in Bowman Street. I thought sure who could own an auld yoke like that? When I went to put my hands on it and started to push it away I heard a baby crying. And when I stood on my toes to see inside the pram, Janie, there's a baby there. I ran like hell all the time looking back to see if somebody called the Guards at the Barracks up the road in Edward Street, and maybe they're on their bikes looking for me. What will Pop do to me if the Guards catch me? I'll be known all over as a baby snatcher.

It's 6 o' clock that evening and I'm still inside our house looking out the window for the Guards and trying to think of a good excuse for Pop when the Guards come so he won't kick the living daylights out of me. And there he is coming down the road with two sets of wheels tied to his bike and they're the big ones too. But I don't notice because of the terror I think that's awaiting me. He is coming in the front door and for the first time in my life I see just how big his hands are. He is looking down at me with a big smile, he is waiting for me to show some sign of excitement about the big wheels. Janie, his hands are awful big! They're like the hands of a gorilla.

'Do you want me to give these to Fonsey Meade or Dinny McGrath or even Noelie Grace?,' he says as he guides me out to the bike that he left against the window and starts to untie the wheels from the frame.

Now I see them and my face lights up. The Guards can do what they like. I have my wheels. The clouds have lifted. The panic has gone.

'Wow Pop, where did you get those?', I ask taking them from his hands, not being really interested in his answer.

I'm over at Fonsey's house. 'Look what I got from my father.'

Fonsey is going mad, I'm off to Dinny's house, then over to Noelie's to show them. Now I'm back home to put on the wheels.

'No, not like that,' says Pop, 'put them on like this.'

'Here, use these there instead.'

And after one hour there it is: one only spanking new trolley. And I'm ready for take off.

So I'm ready to go for my first spin and all the lads on our road want a go. But not before I get mine first.

'Look at Taylor's new trolley,' shouts Eddie Gammell.

I have lots of volunteers wanting to give me a push, hoping I'll give them a spin in return. If I start at the railway bridge at the top of Roxboro Road and turn right, it's all down hill and what a hill!

But I have to be careful, if I go too far into Lower Carey's Road I'll wind up at the bottom of Weston and if the gangs there see my trolley, they'll take it off me. So I'm going to have to jump off after I go under the bridge at the bottom of the hill.

Noelie is the smallest. He gets in front of me between my legs. Fonsey wants to stand up behind me. We don't need a push but I get one anyway. Jetta wants to know why she can't get on and I tell her, 'no girls, no girls.' We're passing Ford's pub gaining speed and Jetta is still shouting 'I want to get on!' There's real commotion all over the street and all the neighbours are looking out over their half doors to see what all the noise is about. There's a big gang of kids running on both sides and behind the trolley. As we pass Lynch's house the road takes a sudden dip and then there's no turning back. Jetta is still roaring;

'Let me on, let me on!'

I'm shouting; 'Will you for God's sake, shut up and go away, I can't concentrate on my steering.'

And now the wind is in our hair. Then someone shouts,

'Look out! here comes a car. There's a black car coming up the wrong side of the road.'

Or am I on the wrong side?

Jetta jumps up on top of Noelie, Dinny McGrath jumps on top of Fonsey, I can't see a bloody thing, I don't know where the black car is, the trolley is going from one side of the road to the other. The poor driver of the car is trying to guess which side of the road he's going to be on when the car hits and kills not one kid but the whole five on the trolley. With the gang running on all sides, everyone is screaming their heads off.

We can't get off because we're going too fast. Then there's a tumble of five bodies sprawling all over the road, with gashes on knees and elbows, and there's my beautiful trolley going straight under the black car, with its lovely new wheels, and smashing new timber, with the two pea tins for headlights that Mam gave me and the number plates that started with TI and four numbers after it, just like the one or two cars that pass our house every day. I close my eyes and sink my head into my shoulders, I can't bear to look, and I know by the noise and crunching sound my lovely trolley is heading for the scrap heap.

There's a mad scatter as the driver gets out from the car shouting,

'Jesus, Mary and Holy St. Joseph are ye trying to get yourselves killed or what, ye little feckers.'

I'm trying hard to hold back the tears after all my hard work, after all the excitement, all I got was one lousy spin on my lovely new trolley.

I heard a story recently about a young lad my own age who also made himself a trolley. He wanted it to look like a fire engine, so when finished, he painted it red, made himself a small ladder, got a little bell from a push bike, painted his wellingtons red, borrowed a red hat from his mother's wardrobe, then a length of strong string, tied the string from his fire engine to the family dog's hydraulics or private parts, to pull him around. A few hundred yards away, an elderly man caught sight of the young man all decked out in his imaginary fire-gear and transportation, smiled to himself as it brought back fond memories of his own childhood. But as he drew closer he could see and hear the poor mutt was in distress as he pulled the apparatus around the street with the young fellow calling out, 'Fire, Fire, here comes the Fire Engine' and continually ringing his bell.

'Now, now', said the elderly man, pointing his finger at the poor dog,

'That's very cruel young man. Don't you know what you're doing to that poor dog is very painful? You should have that string tied around the dog's neck and shoulders.'

Annoyed, the boy replied; 'Sure if I do that I'll have no siren, will I?,'

Like all streets in Limerick city, Upper Carey's Road had its daily horse drawn deliveries. From the Imperial Bakery in Henry Street came Harry Younger, a tall, handsome man, always in good cheer and flirting with all the housewives on Carey's Road and they loving every minute of it. The way he'd leave us put our hands into the bag of oats and feed his horse from the palms of our hands. My mother thinking that Paddy Cotter was the only milkman delivering milk to Upper Carey's Road made an arrangement to purchase one quart of milk every day.

He was an ugly so-and-so, cross looking even when on the rare occasion he smiled. He had four black teeth, one on top and three on the bottom. Then there was the disgusting habit he had of catching his nostrils by the thumb and forefinger of his right hand and flicking a great big slimely snot over one side of the milk cart onto the road to join the constant daily droppings of horse waste that had to wait for a good shower of rain to wash it off the street. He would stop outside Ford's pub, where all his customers came for their milk. He had in his employment a young lad who dispensed the correct amount required by each householder, Cotter would take note, in his little red book, which he always kept in his inside pocket, a separate page for each house and on Friday at 12 o' clock he would collect the money due for the week's supply of milk. After going through Janesborough and Rathbane, Paddy Cotter on his way back would stop at Ford's Pub across from our house, tie the horse and cart to a pole outside the pub while he went in for his two pints of Guinness, and stay there for the bones of one hour, and Mam wants to know why no-one ever told her about the other milk man, the good looking, Dinny Maloney.

'Jesus he's gorgeous', Mam would say. 'Isn't he just like a film star'? She was right. Dinny was good looking, the dark skin, always looking like he'd been back from the sun, and there was the hat, brown in colour, to match his jacket and pants.

Dinny always wore brown, and there was the constant habit of Dinny placing his right hand on the hat, lifting it slightly off his head and putting it back in place, like as if it was too big and had fallen over his eyes and the fag stuck in one corner of the mouth, all added to the overall mystique of Dinny the milkman, and Mam wants her milk from Dinny.

'That milk you gave me yesterday', says Mam to Cotter;

'What about it?,' he answered.

''Twas sour, I had to throw it out and I'm not paying you for it'.

'Well isn't that strange now?,' says Cotter.

'What's strange?,' says Mam.

'Isn't it strange now that all the other people who got theirs from the same milk churn never said a word about their milk being sour, very strange indeed?,'

'Are you calling me a liar?,' says Mam.

'Indeed I am, I have never given any of my customers sour milk', says Cotter.

'Well you can keep your bloody milk. I'll get mine from the good looking fellow from now on'.

Well Cotter was like a lunatic, losing a customer was bad enough, but to the opposition was the worst insult and she was going to pay for it. We were all going to pay for it, in fact the very next day.

Between our house and the Storan's next door stood an ESB light pole. Apart from shedding light on the street of Upper Carey's Road and our house, giving us that extra bit of security in the dark winter evenings, it had another use. To Jetta and the other girls on the road, it was the street swing. Because of its location to our kitchen window, with the rope wrapped around their bottoms, Jetta and the girls could stand on our window sill and take off around the pole several times. But tomorrow a new purpose for our pole was to be found at 12:45.

As we were all at the table eating our dinner, we hadn't noticed that Cotter had his mule parked outside our house, tied to the pole, with its rear end parked in line with our front door. Then right at 1 o' clock it lifts its tail, there's a thunderous long rasp. Mam looks at Pop and says:

'Jesus, Harry will you not be doing that at the table while we're eating our dinner?'

'That wasn't Pop, Mam, that was Cotter's horse,' said Jetta.

Then the smell starts to waft its way in the door and find its way to our table.

'Oh Mother of Divine Jesus!' says Mam, 'that's an awful smell'.

'And that's not all Mam, there's more to come, you better close the door quick Mam,' quips Jetta with her arms folded.

'Like what?,' says Mam.

'Like a flood Mam'.

'How do you mean a flood?'

And then it started. The sound of horse's urine hitting the ground and leaving it again, scattering in every direction but mostly in our front door which is only three feet away.

'Close the bloody door,' shouts Mam, but who's going to go out into the spray and spatters? It lasts and lasts until there's only a dribble. Mam's looking at the state of her floor and walls; she has her hands on her head and says;

'Jesus, Mary and Holy St. Joseph, how am I going to clean this up?'

'He's not finished yet Mam,' says Jetta folding her arms. 'There's more!'

'More what?,' says Mam, 'more pee?,'

'No Mam, the other stuff'.

'What other stuff, oh no! You don't mean sugar do you?'

'Yes Ma,' says Jetta 'and lots of it'.

Up goes the tail again, there's another belt of wind followed by the biggest dump you've ever seen in your life.

Ma is calling Cotter all the dirtiest names followed by curses I've never heard her say before. Cotter must be over the road in Ford's pub looking out the window, laughing his head off.

'Is he finished yet?,' says Pop, trying really hard to hold in the laughter.

'He is,' says Ma, 'and I'm trying to think where to put what he's left outside our door. Jesus, there's wheelbarrows of it'.

'Mam', says Jetta 'there's something else you need to know'.

'What else?,' asks Mam.

'He does that everyday at the same time Mam'.

'How do you know that?,' asks Mam.

'Because since we moved up here last week, he does that at the same time outside Ford's pub every day.'.

'Oh Mother of Divine Sorrows, Harry what are we going to do?,'

'You'll have to make sure the door is closed tomorrow at 1 o'clock' says Pop.

'Is that all you're going to say?,' says Mam.

'Would you not go over there to the pub right now and tell him he's not to put his mutt outside our door again?'

'Ah Jesus, Bid, you can't ask the man to do that'.

'Why not?,' says Mam.

'Because that's a public street, he's entitled to park wherever he likes on a public road, at anytime'.

'Well you're going to have to think of something fast', says Mam.

'Why am I going to have to think of something? I wasn't the one who told him his milk was sour'.

'Jesus Harry you'll have to ring Madigan's Bar for Peadar to come in for his lunch tomorrow'.

'And what good is that going to do?,' asks Pop.

'Because he can park his truck outside our door tomorrow, until I can think of a way out of this problem. If Cotter thinks he has one over on me, he has another thing coming'. Uncle Peadar is one of Mam's younger brothers who drove a truck for a building contractor in Limerick called Madigan's.

'Did you ring Madigan's and leave word for Peadar?,' were the first words that greeted Pop that evening when he came home from work.

'I did Indeed, but they said Peadar was up the country and wouldn't be home until tomorrow night'.

'Oh dear God,' says Mam. 'I'm not going through that again tomorrow, it's as simple as that!'

'Jesus Bid, will you stop tossing and turning? I can't get to sleep,' says Pop.

'I will, as soon as I can think of a way to stop Cotter parking his septic tank outside my front door tomorrow'.

'You're to put your swing around the pole when you come home at lunch time,' Ma says to Jetta at breakfast that morning.

'Why Mam?,' asks Jetta.

'So Cotter won't be able to tie his yoke to our pole today. When you finish school, you're to come home straight away, and put the swing around the pole, and be on it, swinging around, until he arrives and parks that thing of his outside Fords'.

'OK Mam', says Jetta.

It's 12:45 and there's no sign of Jetta. The Presentation School leaves its pupils out for dinner at 12:30. Mam is at the door and there's Cotter's horse clomping down the road. God help Jetta when she gets home, but there's one last chance. Mam thinks if she can stare Cotter down, he'll move over to Ford's with the mule. This should work, because Ma's stare is frightening. The dogs in the street are scared of Mam's stare, Pop's terrified of it and so are we. It's just like Nan's.

But Cotter is staring back while getting off his cart and then ties his yoke to our pole. The stare is now turning into a grin as he walks across to Fords. Ma looks up the road, and there's Jetta running towards our house. Jetta has a terrified look on her face and she knows she's in deep trouble. She also knows what's coming if she doesn't have a good excuse.

'Jesus, Mary and Holy St. Joseph, didn't I ask you to be home and be on your swing before Cotter got here with his horse?,'

'I couldn't help it Mam, our nun kept us all in for an extra twenty minutes'.

'Why the hell did she do that?,' asks Mam.

'Because the spelling was so bad in our homework last night, she was going to make sure that we all got it right before we went home today'.

Jetta had to think fast, she had forgotten all about it until she rounded the corner, by Dinny McGrath's house and saw Cotter's horse outside our front door. She managed to think up that excuse while running the fifty yards from Dinny's house to our front door and Mam swallowed it, hook, line and sinker - provided she didn't meet the nun who never kept her in. Besides, she wouldn't be talking to a nun about a horse going to the toilet outside our door anyway, would she?

Pop had just arrived for his dinner, he's got a grin from ear to ear and he's trying to hide it. Ma looks at the clock while putting the dinner on the table. It's 12:55, she says, 'It can't be true that Cotter's horse does the same thing everyday at the same time, that's just ridiculous, but says she's going to pray to St. Jude the patron saint of lost causes, and St. Francis the patron saint of dumb animals. She closes her eyes and asks if Cotter's horse might be bound and dried up for about one hour today and today only, between 1 and 2 o'clock because Peadar would be sure to be here tomorrow, and Cotter's horse could do whatever he wanted, whenever he wanted tomorrow because he wouldn't be outside her front door. But as she finished her prayer she lifts one of her closed eyelids to the sound of a couple of rasps and a spit.

It was the awful sound again that started the whole bloody episode yesterday. She moves to the small window and looks out at the horse, the tail is pointing skywards and she knows what's coming next.

'Close the bloody door', shouts Mam. Pop is bent over under the table laughing. If she sees him she'll kill him. He's pretending he's lost something and moving his hands all over the floor as if he's looking for it. When Pop really laughs he makes no sound at all, the shoulders just move up and down, which is just as well. So if Pop can keep moving while laughing he can camouflage the motion of his shoulders.

'Jesus, how can an animal that small have so much urine and sugar and manage to empty itself outside my front door and looking heavenward Mam says, 'That will be the last time I ever ask ye two for anything again'.

Pop is under the table and says: 'It's the first time you ever prayed to those saints and who told you that Jude was the patron saint of lost causes, and Francis the saint of dumb animals?'

'Mind your own business,' says Mam. 'Close the bloody door,' she shouts.

Jetta manages to close the door before the cess-pit starts to clear out its intestines.

'What the hell are you looking for under the bloody table?,' shouts Mam.

Pop gets such a fright from the shout that he bangs his head under the table, putting our dinners flying in all directions.

'Mother of Divine God!' says Mam. 'I've got one dumb horse sugaring outside my door and a jackass inside it under the table'.

Pop isn't laughing anymore and says:

'Look I'll ring Madigan's Pub after work today and leave a message for Peadar to be sure and call tomorrow, will I do that Bid?' says Pop.

There's no answer from Mam.

'Right, I'll be off now,' he says.

'You're going nowhere', says Ma.

'Why not?,' answers Pop, confused.

'Because that yoke outside hasn't finished yet, and you'll wait until he's finished. I'm not having any of his waste in my house'.

When Pop arrived home that evening he has good news for Mam. Peadar got the message and will be here tomorrow around half twelve.

'Great,' answers Mam.

'What are you going to do then when he comes with the truck?,' asks Pop.

'If you're here tomorrow for your dinner you'll see'.

'Are you going to get Peadar to park that truck outside the front door?,' asks Pop.

'No, I am not!'

'Well, what are you going to do with it then?' asks Pop.

'I told you, if you're here tomorrow you'll see!'

And Pop says 'Oh I'll be here alright, I don't want to miss this'.

It's 12:40 the following day and Peadar's truck is rolling to a stop in front of our house, but before he has time to turn off the engine Mam is telling him to park his truck outside Ford's pub across the road and to be sure and park it in front of the door and window.

'Right', says Peadar and duly obliges.

Peadar has a full load of timber, plaster board, cement bags, blocks, bricks and every building contraption you can think of, so when he exits the truck outside Ford's we can't see any part of Ford's window and front door. And anyone in Ford's can't see any part of Number 82. Peadar wants to know what all the fuss is about and while Mam is filling him in on the events of the preceding days Pop arrives and asks Mam what Peadar's truck is doing outside Ford's pub.

'You won't have long to wait', says Peadar as he looks out the window.

'Here's Cotter now', says Jetta.

Sure enough Cotter exits the cart and ties the mutt to our pole and walks across to Ford's pub. It is now 12:55 and all eyes are on the mutt's rear end and sure enough as the clock strikes 1 o'clock it is the same routine.

First it's the tail in the air, there's a long spit, followed by a couple of rasps. Then there's the telescopic penis on its way down, and just before the urine starts to flow, Mam grabs two empty buckets and places one of them in the direction of the penis and the other under the tail, runs back into the house and slams shut the front door just in time.

'What the hell are you collecting the horse's urine and sugar for?,' asks Pop, looking puzzled.

'You'll see', answers Mam.

The first bucket is now overflowing while Mam is watching out our very small kitchen window. Then we can hear the thumping sound of horse sugar hitting the second bucket and in a few seconds that's overflowing too. Peadar is looking at Pop with a puzzled look on his face and making gestures that say his sister is crazy while Pop is sinking his head into his shoulders, with the palms of both hands spread out looking back and whispering, 'I think you're right'.

'Right! It's finished', shouts Mam.

'Right, get out there onto Cotter's cart and take the lids off Cotter's two milk churns' says Mam to Jetta.

'Yes Mam', answers Jetta.

'Jesus, Bid, you're not going to do what I think you're going to do are you?,'

'Did I ask you to do it?'

'Well, no', says Pop.

'Well shut up then and watch'.

Mam reaches across under the horses' belly, lifts the bucket of urine, and brings it onto Cotter's cart.

'Stand back', she says to Jetta. After emptying the first bucket into one of the milk churns she puts the lid back. Then Ma tells Jetta to get the other bucket and empty that into the second churn. When Jetta puts the lid on that one, they wash their hands, and we all sit down to eat our dinner and wait until tomorrow. Cotter is not going to notice anything until he goes home to wash out his churns later that evening.

'Just because he never saw you doing it, doesn't mean you didn't do it, sure didn't half the neighbours see you and won't he know it was you'.

'I want him to know it was me!' says Mam.

'Let's see if he parks the yoke outside my door again tomorrow'.

'I doubt it,' says Peter.

The next day at 10.o'clock Mam is at the door, she has her arms folded and there he is coming up the hill, he's got a cross head on him. He doesn't know it yet but he's going to be crosser.

He makes the usual stop for his milk sales outside Fords, but there are no customers with their Billy cans and milk bottles today.

He's puzzled. He lifts his cap, scratches his head and looks around to see where his customers are or why they haven't gathered around as usual. Mam is staring at him, trying to get his attention. She's got a big smile on her face. She stares and wants him to see her, but he won't look over and it suddenly strikes him why his customers won't take anymore milk from him, no matter how well he's washed the churns. Not after what they saw going into them yesterday.

But Ma has to wait till 1.o'clock for the real test. Will Cotter park his horse outside our door today or will it be back at its usual place outside Ford's after he does his rounds? It's a long three hours and Mam is back at the door again. She's got the arms folded again, with the smirk back on her face. Pop is home too, sitting outside on one of the window sills. Here comes Cotter. He's turning left from his deliveries in Rathbane and Janesborough onto our road and there's no sign of him pulling the horse reins to the right to bring the horse to Ford's. Is he going to pull the reins to the left to our house? No he's not. He's passing straight by as he gives one look over at Mam. She has won the battle and the war, but Cotter as he passes Ma, sticks his nose over the cart and with his right hand flicks a big bogey to the ground. Pop looks at Ma, gives her a wink and says 'Good on you Bid!'

I related this story to a friend lately and after a good laugh he said: 'You know you're after reminding me of a story I heard about the time Bill Clinton came to Ireland to help with the peace talks. Before he went home he received an invitation to visit the Queen at Buckingham Palace. When he arrived he met all the dignitaries. After lunch, the Queen asked Bill if he would like a tour of the Palace grounds by horse and carriage.

'I've got two lovely white horses and they would love a little jaunt around the Palace,' the Queen said. 'It's been a while since I had some time with them and I quite like a trot when I get the chance'.

'Why, sure Ma'am,' replied Bill, and around they go on the old, beautiful golden carriage. The Queen is showing Bill this and that and explaining where it came from, who gave it, how long ago etc. Bill is looking at something the Queen is showing when one of the horses lifts his tail and explodes with a horrendous fart. Bill looks at the Queen, she's red faced and says 'Oh Mr. President, I'm frightfully sorry' and Bill says,

'Oh that's alright Ma'am, you shouldn't have said anything, I thought it was the horse'.

By an amazing coincidence Mary with the ten fingers from Ahane took me completely by surprise as she presented me with this picture of Dinny Maloney, pictured far right, on his wedding day, after she typed this story. It turns out that Dinny's wife (Anna) and Mary's mother (Mary) were best friends. Mary's mother took the above photograph on Dinny's wedding day on the 12th April, 1955.

CHAPTER 3

I'm sitting at the table with a face like a poker, it's all because of that lousy dinner Mam gets from Maher's in Parnell Street, breast bones and eye bones. Sure there's hardly any meat on them at all. The dogs won't even give them a smell when they're thrown onto the street after Pop has sucked away any morsel that resembles meat. We get them every Thursday. I hate Thursdays. I'm looking at the eye bone, the socket part is rising out of the brown watery muck that Mam calls soup. It's looking at me and I'm wondering where the eye is, if I put my spoon into the muck and put it to my mouth will the eye be on the spoon? It's bad enough that this stuff tastes lousy, but if I find I have the eye in my mouth, I'm not going to swallow it. So I'm not touching it.

Mam is shouting at me, telling me what's going on, on the other side of the world.

'Look at all the poor children, out there in darkest Africa, who are dying in their thousands every day because they have nothing to eat, nothing at all, do you hear me?,'

'Yes Mam.'

'And look at you turning your nose up at lovely nourishing food. A mortal sin, that's what it is, a mortal sin'.

Pop is busy sucking away on a breast bone; he hasn't a tooth in his head. It's the only way he can get the small bits of meat he thinks are there. He won't wear his glasses because they'll get fogged up from the constant sucking and heavy breathing. He has to suck every bit of the bone on all sides to make sure he gets everything.

His mouth has a ring of brown stain which he keeps wiping away with one hand that also takes the constant watery drop that's always hanging from the end of his nose. As he sucks away Mam gives him a thump that causes a lump of something he's sucking on to leave the bone, and find its way to the back of his throat and stay there. As Mam is saying 'Jesus, Harry will you get him to eat his dinner?,' Pop rises to his feet in an effort to find some air, beating his chest. Mam gives him another thump on the back which releases the said object and Pop is wiping his eyes being glad he wasn't going to end up in Mount Saint Lawrence Graveyard at the top of Mulgrave Street to join his mother, father and two brothers.

Mam shouts: 'Harry will you talk to him?,' If Nan is there, she's giving me the stare and telling me the same story I heard many times before, how when she was my age - that all she got was one meal a day if she was lucky. Some days it was only porridge and other days it might be bread and jam and other days no food at all. How she would go to bed crying with the hunger and the pain in her stomach and I'm wondering how she managed to stay alive at all, with all that hunger, the pain, the starvation and the crying. Well Nan can say all she likes. I'm not eating this stuff.

Sure what do I know about trying to make ends meet with mothers scouring the streets of Limerick looking for nourishment for the home, with hardly any money coming in and if Pop is worried about work, with the demons trying to drag him away from his promise to Mam to stay off the drink. Then I'd be told: 'I'll break your bloody neck if you don't eat that dinner and take that miserable look off your face.' But I'll take the broken neck. It will be easier than having to risk swallowing the eye. When all this fails there's the 'Boodie' Man who lives in the coal room at the end of the kitchen that has no light and is always black with the darkness. I've never been in there. I never want to go in there because he might catch me by the hair of the head and pull me down the hole that Mam says is at the very back. Mam will tell me he will come out when I'm in my bed tonight and take me away if I don't eat my dinner. She's told me that several times before and he never came out because I did what I was told.

But the 'Boodie' Man can come out whenever he likes, he can take away whoever he wants, and I know I won't sleep tonight with the worrying about him, but I don't care. I wish he'd come out now and take Mam, Pop, Nan and this lousy dinner that's gone stone cold, because I'm not eating it. But Santy won't come to my house at Christmas with the broken presents because I won't eat my dinner with the eye and Pop knows it.

He's bent over the fire while sitting on his chair. He has the palm of his right hand over the left side of his mouth. There's a disguised voice for Santy. 'Santy', he says, 'Paddy won't eat his dinner' and Santy wants to know why.

'He doesn't like it,' says Pop.

'Oh that's terrible' says Santy. 'He'll have to eat his dinner or there will be no presents at Christmas'.

'I'll eat it', I'm shouting, 'I'll eat it Santy'.

'Did you hear that Santy?' says Pop. There's no answer.

'Hello Santy,' says Pop, 'are you there?,'

I run over alongside Pop. My elbows are resting on his knees and I'm terrified that Santy might be gone.

'I'll eat it Santy, I'll eat it, look, I'm eating it now, it's nearly all gone. Pop, tell him! tell him!'

'He's gone,' says Pop.

'Janie, where's he gone Pop? Will I get my presents at Christmas Pop, will I? Will I?,'

'Oh we'll have to wait and see'.

Now I'm bawling my eyes out. Pop is gone back to work. I'm shouting up the chimney, 'look Santy, it's all gone, I'll be good from now on, I'll be good every Thursday. Answer me Santy, answer me'.

Pop comes home that evening, Mam tells him that I'm crying all afternoon and will he try to get Santy back, otherwise I'll get sick from the crying. Santy is back again in our house, he's making me promise that I'll eat all my dinner every Thursday and if I keep that promise I'll get my broken presents at Christmas.

When our first Christmas in Carey's Road arrives it's not a good one. Weeks before Mam will be down to Maureen Faye in Bedford Row - she owns the pub now because Mrs. Dennehy (her mother) is gone too old and needs to be sitting down all the time. Sure didn't Maureen and Pop grow up together in the same street, and won't Maureen know why Mam is worried when Pop goes to the pub to play the cards to bring home the turkey and ham. But Maureen has to tell Mam that she can't stop anyone from putting the black stuff to their mouth, especially when all his pals would be egging him on saying,

'Come on now Har, sure it's Christmas, you can always go back on the wagon after it's over, aren't you a great man to give it up for so long, now get that down you.'

Maureen tells Mam that if Pop does break out while playing the cards, can't she keep an eye on him to make sure he doesn't drink too much. Mam has to come home now with an awful headache because of the worry. When Jetta asks Mam why she's so worried, Mam tells her there's nothing wrong that she'll be fine. But Jetta knows, she remembers last Christmas and I don't. 'It will be alright love. Your Dad won't drink this time because he has willpower'.

Jetta asks Mam who is Will Power and why he didn't stop Pop, from putting the drink to his mouth last Christmas. But Will Power must have gone home again and left Pop to throw the drink down his throat. And Maureen Faye, did she forget her promise to Mam and did every jackass in the Bedford Bar buy my Pop a drink that Christmas Eve?

When he dragged the poor old turkey and the lump of ham all the way from Bedford Row, knocked on several doors on the wrong side of Carey's Road before he was dragged by the scruff of the neck into number 82 when the whole house woke to the sound of Mam giving him hell.

'Look at the state of you, making a holy show of me in front of the whole road, you Eejit!'

Pop can't hold his head up straight, no matter how hard he tries.

'I got the ham Bid,' he says 'and look there's the turkey, look at the size of it'.

He's sniffing away trying to get the watery drop at the end of his nose back up his nostrils and no sooner has it gone up, than it's slowly on its way back down again, just hanging away there while he's talking.

'You know what you can do with your bloody turkey and your ham, cook it yourself tomorrow!'

'Ah Jaysus Bid, there's no need to be like that'.

And after a whole year of waiting for the lovely turkey and ham, I have to ask Jetta who's going to eat them now and are we going to get no dinner at all tomorrow.

But there's Mam sticking her hands up the turkey's bum pulling out all kinds of queer stuff from its insides the following morning.

'What's that stuff?,' I ask Mam.

'It's his insides', says Mam.

'Is my insides like that?'

'Will you go out and play love, I have a terrible headache.'

I'm out on the road playing with the broken toys Santy left on my bed, because I ate the lousy dinners every Thursday. Pop is drunk again on Christmas night and all that week. Everything is grand after that because Will Power is back, stopping Pop throwing the drink down his gob. Mam's headaches are gone after another few days, and before we know it, there's another Christmas on the way.

Pop is down again in Bedford Row to win the turkey and the ham. Mam is able to clean the turkeys bum without the headaches and Pop is playing with our broken toys. It's great because I can't remember him doing this before. When the third Christmas comes it's the best of all. Mam says Will Power has helped Pop stay off the drink for nearly two years now and with God's help Will Power will help keep him dry over the Christmas.

There's Pop coming down the hill, on Christmas Eve with a great big cardboard box resting on the frame of his bike. 'Isn't it great, he's home so early on Christmas Eve. Mam', says Jet. She's jumping up and down, shouting: 'He's not drunk Mam, you were right, he's not drunk, Will Power is great Mam isn't he?,'

'Yes love,' says Mam.

I'm helping Pop hold the cardboard box on the bike, while asking him 'what's in it?

But Pop isn't telling. He is just smiling, 'you'll just have to wait and see won't you?,'

Mam is smiling at the door, saying 'You got it Har?,'

'I did,' he answers. He puts the big box on the table, after bringing it in off the bike.

'Ah come on Pop' says Jetta, 'tell us what's in the box?,'

'It's a turkey and a ham', says Mam.

'No it's not the turkey and the ham, sure they're in the oven, didn't Pop bring them home last night?,'

Pop tells us it's a surprise and we'll have to wait until tomorrow, after our dinner.

'Ah come on Pop,' says Jetta, 'give us a clue', as she tries to sneak a peak under the cover of the box.

'There'll be no clues,' says Pop, 'you'll just have to wait until tomorrow, ok?, 'Now go to bed, or there'll be no Santy tonight'.

Jetta says, if we pretend to be asleep when Santy comes we can ask him why our presents are broken every Christmas and could he give us good ones instead. But it's no good, we couldn't stay awake; he's been and gone and there they are again, the broken toys. It's a great big doll for Jetta, it's bigger than last year's, that one had a leg missing, but this one is better even though it has only one eye, and there's a shoe missing. I get a huge tank, it's green. There's a smashing big gun in the middle and it's got lots of batteries. But it will only go round in circles because one of its tracks are missing. James gets a broken rifle and a Butch Cassidy cowboy hat. So we're out on the road showing our presents to all the lads. Jetta is showing her doll to Mary Hayes and Carol Lysaght. She's got one of her fingers stuck in the doll's missing eye and takes the other shoe off, so now the doll looks great.

Fonsey wants to know why my tank will only go round and round. So we ask Pop why Jetta's doll has only one eye, a shoe missing and where the other track of my tank is.

'Ah Santy must have dropped his bag coming down the chimney', he answers.

'Well why is he always dropping his bag coming down our chimney every year Pop, he never drops it coming down Dinny, Fonscy or Noelie's house because their presents are never broken'.

'Ah well, that's because their chimneys are much better than ours, ours is very old and Santy has to take great care when he's coming down our chimney and sometimes he'll let the bag fall'.

So I'm asking Pop if he can fix our chimney for next year, so we can get toys that won't be broken. Pop promises that he will. Then Jetta and I want to know what's in the cardboard box, so Pop agrees to let us see after we've had the dinner. When Mam puts the turkey on the table with the ham for Pop to stick the knife in the turkey's belly, Mam says to Pop in a soft voice, 'What will we do if the luck leaves us next Christmas, with the playing cards and the Christmas raffles?,' Pop says back, 'if that happens it'll have to be the breast and eye bones' and isn't it great to see Mam smiling all the time, with the headaches gone, I'll have to ask Santy for the turkey and ham next Christmas if Pop doesn't win at the cards because I'm getting awfully tired of eating the lousy soup. And I still haven't managed to get an eye in my mouth yet.

So Jetta asks Pop why he didn't bring Will Power for Christmas Dinner, because he's a great help to him. Now Pop wants to know who's Will Power and Mam laughs and says 'I'll tell you later'.

When Pop puts the cardboard box on the table, he says we'll have to close our eyes for a minute, while he takes the surprise out. We have our hands over our faces with the fingers slightly open to see through.

'You'll have to turn around now', he says. 'I can see what you're trying to do. Now go on, turn around!'

It's hard listening to all the sounds that's coming from the box and trying to guess whatever it is that Pop is taking out of it. He says we can turn around now. And there's the surprise on the kitchen table. There's silence from the three of us. We can't believe what's in front of our eyes. It's a film projector, with big spools at each end. We're jumping all over the place, screaming and shouting.

I'm gone out the door like a bullet, over to Fonsey's house, knocking on his door. When he comes out I'm telling him about the film projector over at our house. But he says he can't make any sense of what I'm saying, because I'm talking too fast. And I'll have to slow down, take a deep breath if he's to understand one word of what I'm trying to tell him. But I'm gone up the road to Dinny's house: he can't understand what I'm talking about either. And by the time I get to Noelie's house I can't talk at all. Noelie is standing there at his front door wondering what has me so excited and jumping all over the place, and asks why I bothered to knock on his door. I'm still jumping all over the place, running out onto the road, shouting at the top of my voice, 'we're going to have the pictures in our house'. I'm asking Pop and Mam can Dinny, Fonsey and Noelie come to our house today and watch the pictures. They're smiling away and I'm gone out the door again, not waiting for their answer. I'm over at Fonsey's door a second time, beating it down again. Mrs. Meade answers the door this time, and wonders what has me so excited. She says she'll get Fonsey for me and I can hear her saying to him inside the house that Paddy Taylor is at the front door and can't stand still. He's talking very fast and I think he's going to burst, 'So will you go out to him and see if you can understand what he's saying, because I haven't a clue'. When Fonsey comes out, he says he knows what I'm trying to tell him, as he heard me shouting it all over the road a few minutes ago, and wants to know if he can come and watch whatever it is we're showing. And I'm gone again to Dinny and Noelie's and manage to tell them to be sure and come to our house in the next half hour to watch the pictures. There's a queue outside our door now, because everyone in Upper Carey's Road has heard that the Taylor's have a film projector in their house. There's hardly any room for Pop to use his elbows as the house is full waiting for the pictures to start.

He's trying to get the film from one spool down into the projector and back up again to the other spool. He's got his glasses on with the film under his nose trying to see it. The tongue is out at one side of his mouth. There's a big cheer when Pop shouts, 'Turn out the lights'; and the sheet that Mam has taken from one of the beds lights up on the wall with a blob moving all over it.

'What's that thing?,' shouts Dinny McGrath.

'It's a bit of damaged film,' answers Pop.

But I know what it is. It's the watery drop from Pop's nose that fell on the film when it was under his nose as he tried to get the film into the projector.

'Take off your Hopalong Cassidy hat, James Taylor', shouts Mary Hayes. 'I can't see'.

And on comes Mr. Magoo to cheers and applause, from our packed house that has people stuck in every nook and cranny, with another gang waiting outside.

There's no sound, only the odd frame with the few sentences to let us know what Mr. Magoo thinks he sees. And after five minutes, Pop is shouting for the lights to go on again and everyone wants to know 'what's on next?,'

'Rocky Marciano the great Italian boxer', says Pop. 'He's fighting a guy called Joe Lewis, who's nicknamed the Black-bomber, because when he gives you a dig, it's like been hit by a bomb'.

So on comes the film. There are big words on the screen that say Round Six and everybody shouts: 'Where's the other five rounds gone?' Pop shrugs his shoulder with his hands out and says: 'That's all I got, but we got the best bit'.

'Why is that?' asked Mam.

'Because whoever has the other five rounds won't know how the fight ends will they?,'

So for the next two and a half minutes Rocky has the head down, throwing punches all over the place and lands only the odd one on target. Then he hits Joe Lewis a dig under the chin that puts the black bomber out between the ropes and into the crowd. After a count of ten Rocky Marciano is declared the new world champion. It's time for the lights to go on again to cheers and applause. 'Is there anymore?,' shouts Noelie Grace. Pop says he saved the best for last, Ali Baba and the Forty Thieves. We all know about the forty thieves who were smuggled into the Shah's castle in the forty big jars. Sure we saw it before in the Lyric Cinema and we want to see it again. When that's finished it's time for the next lot who've been waiting outside our front door to see Rocky, Mr. Magoo and the Forty Thieves but James, Jetta and I can stay and see them all again.

When everyone has gone home we want to know if Pop owns the projector. We're very disappointed when he tells us that it's only on loan, but we can show it again tomorrow night before he brings it back the next day. And if we're good we might have it again next year with different films.

A few months later I'm sitting at the table with my miserable face because I won't eat the soup with the eye. So Pop says:

'Are you there Santy, can you hear me Santy, he won't eat his dinner again Santy' and Santy says there won't be any presents if I don't keep the promise I made last year. I said, 'I don't care'. When Pop asked me why I don't care I said, 'because there's no Santy, that's why'.

'Who told you that?,' asked Pop.

'Jetta told me'.

'You better not tell James, because if you do, you'll get a thick ear', but I'm thinking 'why should I tell James, let him find out for himself and I don't have to risk finding an eye in my mouth anymore'.

About fifteen years ago Mary and I were having lunch with some friends at the Glentworth Hotel. It was a luxury we gave ourselves every Sunday. As I found myself in the company of many women and the conversation being on the feminine side of things, I began to look around, hoping I'd find some form of distraction and there it was, an elderly man, sitting on his own, sipping away on a cup of tea, his half finished dinner plate beside the teapot. It was none other than the great Mr. Whelan, the provider of food, clothing, furniture and especially Mr. Magoo, Ali Baba and Rocky Marciano's Round Six. I excused myself from the girls and went over holding out my hand and saying 'Hello, Mr. Whelan'. When he looked up at me he had a confused look on his face, as he reached out to shake my hand.

'It's Paddy, Mr. Whelan, Harry Taylor's son.'

'Ah Jaysus', he says 'Is that you Paddy? Sure I'd have passed you out and never recognised you, how are you at all?,' his Dublin accent still as strong as the day I first met him. 'And poor auld Har, sure there's never been another like him. Sit down. Will you have a cup of tea or something?,' As we shared the remainder of what was left in the pot, he talked and talked about Pop.

'Did you know your father and the Ulster Bank that was across the road from our shop in O'Connell Street, got me and my wife off to a great start in business when we opened up all those years ago?,'

'No, Mr. Whelan, I did not know that. Pop never said anything to us'.

'Ah Jaysus, sure wait till I tell you, we could only get enough money off the bank to buy the old building and a small bit more to get Whelan's Chemist and Camera Shop open. Your father made every shelf and counter in that shop, worked all hours of every day and night, week-ends included, for half nothing because we couldn't afford to pay him the proper wage. He painted everything and anything that didn't move; after that didn't he start on the top floor and over the next two months walloped everything with wallpaper and paint.

'My wife and the two kids moved into the top floor, then we rented the next two floors out to local businesses to make the monthly payments on the loan. I remember saying to your father the day after he finished the shop, when we opened for business, 'the first camera that's sold today Har, the money is going into your pocket' and Jaysus sure weren't the two of us waiting till 5 o'c before someone came in'.

'He just wanted to have a look at some cameras, but between your father and myself we bullied him into buying the bloody thing for £7.00. You know Paddy, not another tradesman was allowed into that building or our house to put a coat of paint, a sheet of wallpaper or a nail on the wall while your father was around. In the forty years he must have painted and papered the bloody thing ten times. He put two extensions out the back, a new roof, new floors. If anything came into the place it was always under his arm'.

'Then of course there was the laughing. We were always laughing when Har was around'.

I interrupted Mr. Whelan: 'You know Mr. Whelan, you were responsible for me, my sister and brother having three of the best Christmases of our lives'. He looked at me confused.

'Do you remember giving Pop the film projector for Christmas?,'

'Ah Jaysus, I do indeed' he said. 'I remember the first year we went into the hiring of those things we had three available. I told Har if there's one of those left over when we close on Christmas Eve you can take it home for yourself and the kids over the holidays'.

When I told him about the crowd in our house, the roaring for the rest of the Rocky Marciano fight, he laughed and then the tears ran down his face as he said; 'isn't life hard all the same, they were good times, they were indeed'.

Mr. Whelan lives in a Nursing Home. At the time this photograph was taken he had celebrated his 90th Birthday.
He didn't remember me as his memory comes and goes, his son Bernard says I got him on a good day. He's laughing because I told him I was Harry Taylor's son.
Before I left he kissed my hand four times and said "there'll never be another Harry Taylor"

I wanted to convey to this man his contribution to our family's welfare, all the contacts and the good customers that came to Pop from him down through the years. But I don't think he fully understood what I was trying to do. We shook hands as we said goodbye and for the rest of the day I couldn't get that man and those Christmases out of my mind.

Recently he took my hand and kissed it four times and said, 'Sure poor auld Har. There was no one like him'.

Then I asked myself a question about the broken presents, where did they come from every year and why were bits always missing? For days this tormented me, a telephone call to Jetta gave me no answers until months later I happened to drive down High Street, off William Street, to call into Barry's hardware shop. As I parked my van, my mind flashed back to the time Mam would bring me down to Hogan's restaurant now replaced by new buildings as most of Limerick is.

When I walked into Joe Barry's shop, his front door would be in the same place as Hogan's entrance was. After I get my goods I'm back in the van and I'm asking myself could that be the source of the broken presents?

Auntie Maura worked for Hogan's Restaurant all her life. She would go to the Bedford Bar and leave a message for Mam to come in for a day's work in the kitchen or waiting on tables. It might be a Holy Day or a farmers' day at the paddocks in Mulgrave Street, which meant more bodies in Hogan's Restaurant. Sometimes if Mam was downtown shopping, she might pop in with me to see if there's any work coming up soon, and when she does Auntie Maura will always give me a cream bun from under the glass counter. If there is work Auntie Maura will always tell her to bring me along as I can play with Kevin, other times she'd ask for Jetta to play with their daughter Mary as they're both the same age.

Mam would always make sure that we had our best clothes on going down to Hogan's. We would be left upstairs in a house of three floors, filled with red plush carpets, no damp patches anywhere, no musty smell. Instead a fragrance like I never smelled before and then best of all a room filled with toys, the

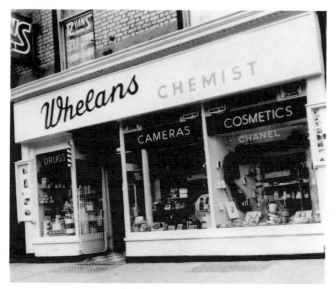

Whelans shop then.....

......and now

best that money can buy. Then the penny dropped. We could be playing with toys in February or July that we would find at the end of our bed that Christmas. Now I have this strange feeling, a feeling that I never felt before, thoughts I never had before, like why I never felt deprived leaving Hogan's house or even hard done by. That beautiful comfortable, warm house with the lovely beef, roast potatoes and gravy they would give me on every visit. And wasn't it great that Mam and Pop could depend on Hogan's Restaurant and Whelan's Chemist every year for a great Christmas especially when Will Power was keeping an eye on Pop?

CHAPTER 4

From the time of my first memory to the day my mother died, I cannot recall her having on her frame anything that she bought new. If a dress, skirt, blouse, cardigan, jumper or shoes didn't come from Pop's sister Eileen in New York it came from Mam's sisters Tess in Australia or Nellie in Northampton, England. Pop's frame was also covered in clothes given by customers who were of similar height and shoe size. Our Uncle Dave in New York, Eileen's husband's parcel would come to the rescue if work was scarce. Or worse still Pop's customers weren't responding to the many hints he would leave every day like, 'Jesus, boys but that's a grand suit you're wearing Sir. I wouldn't be one bit offended if you offered it to me the day you're going to throw it out'. Or 'Would you know of anyone in town who might be able to add an inch or two to a pants from a suit a customer gave me last week as it's too short for my long legs?,' He might be told 'Sure couldn't you do that yourself Har, seeing that you came from a tailoring family?,' But as work became more plentiful Pop's dependence on New York and customers' kindness lessened. Every few years would see a new suit, shirt, tie and good quality leather shoes on Pop's tall, thin frame.

Mam's priority was the table and trying to improve the quality of what went on it, her four kids and Pop. What would she want with new clothes? Sure she never went anywhere to socialise except after we moved to Garryowen when she would accompany Pop to bingo during his longest attempt to stay off the drink. But she took my breath away the night she appeared from the bedroom door in a dress that went all the way down to her shoes and matched the artificial pearl necklace and earrings. I shouted, 'Janey Mam, where are you going, you look smashing!' Then Pop appears dressed in a black suit with shiny stripes down the outside of each leg of his pants. Jet wants to know what that black thing around his neck and under his chin is called. They say they haven't time to tell us what a dickey-bow or a ball is, as they're going to be late if they don't get going. Pop says we have to go to bed now and be good, that our next door neighbour Mrs. Storan is going to keep her ear to the wall or there will be no surprise when we wake up in the morning.

I'm not a hundred per cent sure, but I think Pop was wearing dentures that night, if he was they were borrowed along with the rigouts he and Mam were wearing.

Jet and I have comics to read. After that it's a game of X and Os. I climb off the bed to make a pee in the pot that's under it. I'm standing up firing away when Jet tells me to hurry up, that she wants to go as well. While Jet sits on the pot piddling away I am asking her why boys have a teapot and girls a moneybox. She says she doesn't know and there we are sitting on the bed with our underwear off looking at ourselves scratching our heads trying to figure out why we're so different. Then Jetta shouts, 'I know!' She says 'All babies look the same and the only place they're different is down here', pointing to her groin.

Pop and Mam on their night out at the ball. I'm not sure but I think Pop was wearing dentures that night. If he was they were borrowed, just like his suit, shoes, shirt, dickie bow and Mam's complete outfit.

James is 12 months old and fast asleep in his cot, that's between the two double beds and away from the damp fungus ridden walls. Jet says, 'When people used to come up to Mam in the street to see James after he was born to say 'Congratulations Mrs. Taylor, is it a boy or a girl?' they have to ask because Mam would get very upset if they started fiddling with James' clothes to see if he had a teapot or a moneybox'. I'm five at the time and Jetta is seven. I've asked her 'Where do babies come from?,' She says, 'Birds with big mouths, for the babies to sit into fly all the way from heaven and leave them under a head of cabbage in the night when everyone is asleep.' I'm asking her why Mam and Dad won't tell us when we ask them questions like these, and why do they tell us 'That's the why! Or shut up, go out and play!' She says the best person to ask is Nan.

To give Mam a break, Nan would take Jet, and myself to Tower Hill and James too when he was old enough. A few years later, having spent an entire week out there, Jet, James and myself came back to Carey's Road and on catching sight of Mam at the front door, I made the remark 'Janey Mam, you're after getting awful fat'.

'Am I?,' she says, and laughs with Nan as we make our way into the house.

That evening I told my mother 'Mam, Nan showed us a photograph of you and Aunty Nora and you used to be gorgeous'. Mam laughed and asked 'Am I not gorgeous anymore Paddy?'

'No Mam, you're not', I answered.

The photo Nan showed me of Mam, Jet and Auntie Nora
*(not shown). **When I thought she looked gorgeous.***

After another two weeks we're back in Tower Hill again and Nan says when we go back to Carey's Road later in the week there'll be a big surprise waiting for us. But she won't tell us what it is.

But when we arrive Mam and Pop aren't there. James says, 'Uncle Peadar's truck is coming up the hill'. It's easy to know his truck because it has a Viking's head with big wings on the front. When it gets closer we can see Pop and Mam in the truck alongside Uncle Peadar.

Mam has a bundle of something in her hands, she's all smiles.

'There's your surprise now,' says Nan and when Mam gets out of the truck she's not fat anymore. She brings the bundle over to Jet, James and myself and says,

'You have a new baby brother, his name is Harry'.

Jet wants to hold him so Mam lets her have him for a few minutes and I whisper to Jet, 'how come we didn't see Harry when we were out in Nan's back garden where the cabbage is and shouldn't we have known about the baby before Mam because we were in Nan's house for a whole week while Mam was in Carey's Road?,'

Jet won't answer me because she's talking to Harry, tickling his nose. I'll have to wait until she stops. So when I ask her again, she says, 'Harry must have been put under the cabbage after we left Cappamore. Mam Pop and Peadar had to go and collect him; that's why we got here first'.

Janey! Jet is brilliant all the same. I wish I could be like her and know everything.

A couple of weeks before Harry arrived, Mrs. Mullane buried her third infant and apart from nearly sending the poor woman to an early grave, it managed to scare the living daylights out of me. The sight of those three small white coffins in her front room over three consecutive years, the image of Mrs. Mullane and her haunting cries echoing down the hill of Carey's Road for hours and everybody wondering why God would do such a terrible thing to a woman who could give so much to those children had they lived and leave others to parents to be neglected.

Some will shake their heads and say 'It's a mystery'. Others will speak of how God works in mysterious ways. But no one has an answer. I'll ask Mam and Dad why they died; they'll give us the 'that's the why' to every question. So it's Jet to the rescue again.

She will always call me away and explain things.

'Holy God wanted them back in Heaven', she said.

'Why Jet?,' I asked.

'Because they were too beautiful and Mrs. Mullane had to have them baptised before they went back, otherwise they'll go down to Limbo'.

'Where's that Jet?'

'Limbo is a place God made for babies who don't get baptised. It's completely dark and once they go there that's it'.

'That's what Jet?'

'They can never come out again'.

'But Jet, that's lousy! The poor babies can't walk out of the pram to get baptised'.

'I know that', she says. 'It's up to the mother's to bring them down to the church'.

'But shouldn't it be the mothers that go to Limbo, and not the babies Jet?,'

'It should, but that's the way it is'.

And I'm pulling Mam's coat asking, 'Is Harry baptised Mam'? And she's says 'no'.

'Can we bring him down to the church now Mam?,'

'For what', she asks.

'To get him baptised Mam'.

'We'll be doing it next Sunday', she says.

'But Mam, Harry could be dead by Sunday. Can we bring him down now Mam please?'

'No, we'll do it on Sunday', Mam says again.

'But Mam, Mrs. Mullane's babies were taken off her because they were too beautiful. Harry might have to go back too Mam, so can we bring him down to the church now Mam because he might die tonight and then he'll have to go down to Limbo, and he'll never be able to get out Mam'.

'Harry is a fine healthy baby like all the rest of ye were when we brought ye home. Mrs. Mullane's poor babies were very sick and they were baptised and they are in Heaven now, where they're happy. So stop scourging me about Harry. He'll be baptised on Sunday'.

So I'm asking Jet 'Would it be the same if she and I baptised Harry and if he died tonight would Holy God take him up to Heaven and not throw him into that dirty rotten lousy dark place called Limbo'. But Jet says, 'It has to be a priest who does the baptising'. When I ask her why, she says, 'they have the special Latin words that only God can understand and they have the power as well'.

So I'm up half the night watching Harry in the cot making sure he's alive. If he dies I won't let anyone take him away to that dark lousy place. When Jet gets out of her bed to use the potty later that night, she wants to know why I'm sitting up looking at Harry. When I tell her she says if I say a lot of Hail Mary's, a load of Our Father's and Glory Be's, I'll get loads of plenary indulgences. Now I have to ask her what they are, she says, 'It's like paying Holy God for your sins in advance.

'If you say a Hail Mary to Holy God, He will give you five hundred indulgences, if you can get up to five thousand of them God will buy up a lot of the big sins. He might even take Harry up to Heaven if he dies before Sunday'. Jet's gone back to sleep, I'm saying a load of Hail Mary's trying to keep count at the same time, but when I wake up the following morning Harry is still alive. I can't remember the amount of Hail Mary's I said last night, so I have to ask Jet what's the most important plenary indulgence I can get for the smallest amount of prayers, because I have to get them done fast, in case Harry dies tonight. Jet says 'You'll get ten thousand indulgences if you do the Stations of the Cross in the church'. But I don't know what those things are. When she tells me I'm down at the Dominican Church looking at the pictures of all the terrible things those dirty rotten lousers did to poor Jesus. I have to go around them five times, say five Hail Mary's in front of every picture. I think I'm going to be here for ages. There's people looking at me, smiling.

Family photo before Harry arrived.

They must think I'm a little saint because all the ones that are doing what I'm doing are very old and ready to go off any minute. I think they're hoping that there will be a special place for them in Heaven, if they pray like this. After four hours I'm finished I can go home now, and not worry anymore about Harry. If he's dead in the morning when I wake up, I can tell Mam when she's bawling her eyes out like Mrs. Mullane did, that Harry is OK and in Heaven because I have done the Stations of the Cross for him and she won't have to cry anymore.

'Look at those two dogs Mam, why are they stuck together Mam?,'

Wallop!

'Ouch! Mam, what did you hit me in the ear for?,'

'That's the why', she says.

'But all I said Mam was what are those?

Wallop!

'Ouch! Ah Janey Ma will you stop hitting me for asking you a question?,'

'Shut up and don't be looking at those dirty things'.

'Why Mam?'

'That's the why'. Mam pulls me in by the arm and slams the door shut. 'You shouldn't be looking at those things?'

'Why Mam?,'

'I told you already, that's the why'.

So I have to ask Jet again and see what she tells me. When I asked Pop he told me to go out and play and when I asked him again he said, 'Did you not hear me the first time I told you?,'

Jet says that dogs stuck together are like the Holy Trinity, it's a mystery because nobody knows the reason why.'

And why weren't they stuck together anymore after Mrs. Meade came and threw a bucket of water on top of them Jet?'

She says, 'That's a mystery too'.

Now I know why Mam and Pop say 'that's the why' and why they told me to shut up because they don't know either, and they won't say they don't know.

Everyday at twelve o'clock we have Religious Instruction for thirty minutes. And a couple of days later the Christian Brother who comes to tell us about God is asking the class does anybody know what a mystery is? And I have my hand held high in the air. I'm saying, 'I know brother, I know'. There's no need for me to be in such a state because nobody else has their hand up.

'OK Taylor, it seems you're the only one whose going to tell us what a mystery is'.

And with my chest stuck out and a big smart smile across my face I answer, 'a mystery Brother is the Holy Trinity.

'Well done, Taylor. Good man'.

'I'm not finished Brother'.

'Go on then'.

'And two dogs that are stuck together on the road because nobody knows the reason why'.

There's a long silence. The brother has a strange look on his face and the whole class can't believe that I've got the right answer. I've got the look on my face that says, 'I knew and none of ye Eejits did'. The Brother says, 'come up here' and up I go to the top of the class like a peacock with all the feathers blooming.

'Hold out your right hand', he says.

'What did I say wrong?'

Wallop! Right across the right hand.

'Now the other one,' he says.

After I get the second one, it's under the armpits with the two hands and the tears flowing down my face, partly from embarrassment that I could have been so stupid again. I'm thinking back a few weeks ago when he asked the class what the nine First Friday's was and not a single hand went into the air.

'Alright then, since not one of ye know what they are, I'm going to enlighten ye. If ye go to Mass at eight o'clock on the First Friday of every month for nine continuous months and receive Holy Communion for doing that, God will make sure you have a priest at your side when it's your time to die and leave this earth. Any questions he asks?,'

And my hand is high in the air. 'Brother if you went to Mass and Holy Communion on the First Friday of every month for seven or eight months and missed the last one or the second last one because you were sick, would you still get the priest when it's your time to die?'

'No' says the Brother, 'It has to be every month without a break'.

'So would you have to start all over again Brother?

'Yes', he says.

'Can I ask another question Brother?'

'Go on', he says.

'What's so good about having a priest near you when you're ready to die?,'

'Because he can give you the Last Rites', answers the Brother.

'What are they Brother?'

'The Last Rites is when the priest puts oil on your feet and hands, puts the sign of the cross on your forehead, asks God to forgive you your sins and when that happens you go straight to Heaven, guaranteed, the minute you take your last breath'.

'Can I ask another question Brother?'

'You can'.

'If you were out in the Sahara Desert Brother and were close to dying because you had no water and you had done the nine First Friday's would you get a priest Brother?'

'Absolutely!' he answers.

'How would he get there Brother ?'

'I have no idea'. 'But you can be certain that the Good Lord will make sure that you have a priest before you go, even if you're out in the Sahara Desert'.

'Suppose you never did the nine First Friday's Brother but said three Acts of Contrition before you died would you go to Heaven then Brother?'

'Absolutely!' he answers.

'Brother wouldn't it be easier to say the three Acts of Contrition before you died than having to get up every morning at seven o'clock to get Holy Communion for nine months?'

The Brother says, 'Taylor, you'd be much better off if you concentrated on answering questions instead of asking them'. And look what I got now for answering his question and I don't even know what I said wrong. I wanted to ask him if someone did the nine First Fridays every year for twenty years does that mean they'd have twenty priests at their bed when they're dying. But I won't, in case I get another two wallops.

A couple of years later Dinny McGrath tells me I'm awful stupid, because I thought babies came from under a head of cabbage. So I ask him,

'If they don't come from there where do they come from?'

'From their mother's stomach Stupid', he says.

'How can they come from their mother's stomach?,' I ask.

'I don't know', says Dinny, 'but that's where they come from'.

'Look at that dog over there; do you see how big its stomach is, and all those things sticking out of it? That's where the pups get their milk.'

I'm telling Dinny 'that's stupid' that he's trying to make a fool out of me, and it isn't working. It's Jet to the rescue again. When I tell Jet what Dinny McGrath told me she says, 'he's right'. I'm in total shock.

'But that's disgusting Jet, that can't be right.'

Jetta is trying to explain to me about Mam, when she was very fat a year ago, before Harry arrived, when she came home in Uncle Peadar's truck she wasn't fat anymore. My face is contorted. There are all kinds of disgusting thoughts going through my head.

'But you told me that babies come from under a head of cabbage?'

'I know I did, that's what grown-ups tell us when we're four or five'.

'So that's where you and I came from, Mam's stomach?'

'Yes' she answers.

'Ah Janey, that's lousy Jet. Are you sure?'

'Look you'll get over it in a couple of days.'

'Ah Janey Jet, I'll never get over that.'

For the next few days Mam is asking me why I've gone off my food and why I'm looking at her all the time, especially her stomach. But of course Jet was right, I did get over it. And now there's more questions coming her way. Now I want to know how the babies get out. So she takes me away to a spot where no one can hear.

'You know where a woman's two things are, don't you?'

'Yes' I answer.

'Well from in between those'. Jet is waiting and looking at me for some kind of reaction, but there isn't one because I'm numb with the shock and fright.

Jet thinks she has explained the details very well, in a way that I can understand. She's thirteen now and starting to have airs and graces. She wants to talk like a lady and look like one too. But Mam says she can talk and pretend all she wants, but as regards looking like one, she'll have to wait her turn like the rest of us. But Jet isn't explaining it the way I need to get the clear picture.

She's talking about the bottom half of the female form, but like everything else in my life I get the picture completely assways, because I think she's talking about the top half. And there are all kinds of images flashing across my brain and I don't like any of them. So there's another week of very little food and looking at Mam's top half which isn't very big and is always well covered up, it's just as well. Now that I'm over the shock it's back to Jet again.

'How does the baby know when to come out Jet?'

'It takes about nine months for the baby to grow inside the stomach. When it's ready to come out the woman gets pains in her tummy. And the opening between the two things gets bigger for the baby to come out. Sometimes the woman gets no warning at all and the baby just pops out.'

At this rate I'm going to die of starvation because Mam is taking me to the doctor down at the dispensary. She's telling him that I was always very good to eat even when I was sick. She told a woman outside the doctor's room when we were on the benches how I'm a fussy eater.

'He won't eat this or that, but he'll eat loads of what he does like, the things that are of no bloody use to him at all. I can't get him to eat eggs, parsnips, carrots or anything that's good for him. And bread and butter, Jesus, Mary and holy St. Joseph he'll eat what bread is in the house. But he's gone completely off his food for the last few weeks. And he's constantly moping about the place'.

Then she leans over to the woman on her right and whispers, 'He's giving me a very strange look all the time and if I go near him he'll move away.'

But I can hear her and if she asks me what's wrong I'm not going to tell her. I think she's disgusting and dirty but the other women are looking at me, and saying,

'Ah he must have picked up something in the air. The doctor will give him a bottle or tablets that will give him a bit of a boost.'

I wish Mam would stop talking to the two women because one of them has a big stomach; it's massive, if her baby decides to pop out any minute I'm out of here.

'We'll give him a tonic', says the Doctor, 'that should do the trick.' Now she's shoving half the bottle down my gob, she wants me to make a quick recovery. She's giving out to me because I don't want to be next to her.

'Will you stand still for two minutes?,' she says, ''til I get this down you'.

But I have another question for Jet when she comes home. 'How does the baby get into the woman's stomach Jet?'

This time she puts her arms around me and walks me away to another quiet spot. I know I'm going to get another shock because of what she said the last time we done this.

'You know the father's teapot?'

'Yes'.

'Well he puts that into the opening between the woman's two things'.

Now I have this horrible image of Pop being on top of Mam's chest doing this horrible, disgusting, vulgar act four times for Jet, James, Harry and myself. And isn't it just as well I'm getting all this information by instalments, I might have fallen over and died from the shock if I got the whole lot together. Now I know why Mam is always washing herself and the rest of us so often. A week later Mam has me back at the doctor's again.

She's telling him the tonic isn't working at all, how I'm washing myself four or five times a day, she's wondering if I've got some kind of compulsion. So the Doctor asks me why I wash myself so much, when your mother used to have ask you five or six times a day to wash yourself before. But I'm keeping my mouth shut. The Doctor tells Mam that I'll probably grow out of it. But I'll grow out of nothing for another while because I've got more questions for Jet and she has the hand around me again after I said I thought all that disgusting stuff would be a mortal sin, and 'won't Mam and Pop go down to hell for doing all that dirty stuff?' .

Jet says, 'It's not a sin, it's only for people who are married'.

'You mean Christy with the pigs' sister can't have any babies so?

'Yes', answers Jet.

'God will only give babies to those who are married'.

But it's only a matter of time before I get used to the ideas of babies and how they get here and stop looking at Mam and Pop with disgust, and get those awful images out of my head. Another two years will pass before I realise that it's from the bottom half of the female form that we all make our entrance into this world.

CHAPTER 5

I couldn't have been any older than five at the time. It's January, our first winter in Carey's Road, and I can't remember a colder one. There's crooked gutters full of rusty old holes that are barely held together with loose brackets and the odd piece of wire over our front door and two windows. Looking back I'm wondering why they were there at all as most of the rain that fell on our roof found its way into the many buckets and basins that Mam had waiting under the beds for such occasions? Now the gutters are packed with ice and the thaw when it comes only lasts for an hour or two creating icicles that stretch so far down we can reach and pluck off with our hands and lick to our hearts content. It's on one of these nights that had a bitterly cold breeze tearing down our hill that this story begins.

It brings Pop around the stone wall of Dinny McGrath's house with his two hands on the wall drunk out of his skull, while trying to keep his leather shoes steady on the lumpy ice that's under him. He comes to the six stone steps that take the pedestrian down to the houses of Nellie with the sticks, God love her, whose two feet are facing east and west all the time, Mickey Fitz and Peggy Ryan. Will he be able to descend without slipping and hopping his skull off the corner of one of them? He has another choice though. He can carry on down the road. He won't have to worry about getting a belt from a car or a bus as there are very few of those on the road. No mechanically controlled contraption would negotiate these hills if it was out on a night like this. But as drunk and all as he is, Pop knows if he stays on the road, he could fall over the small wall that separates the road from the houses. So he parks his backside on the first step and slides his way down each one and somehow manages to get back on his pins in an upright position when he gets to the last one, and wonders how he managed to get here from the Bedford Bar and never fall on his ass. The wall that's across from Fitz's, Ryan's and Nellie's house comes to his assistance to help him find the last hundred yards home.

As he passes Nellie the cripple's house, there on the ground and stuck to the bottom of her door is a black and white Jack Russell, looking up at Pop shivering away. Pop makes his way over to Nellie's door and knocks hard, three times. When Nellie answers she says, 'Jesus, Harry are you lost again? Your house is on the other side love'. Pop is shaking his head from side to side, and so is the watery drip that's dangling away while following the motion of his head five tenth's of a second later, hitting each side of his jaw without sticking to either one.

'I'm not lost Nellie. It's your dog, he's freezing God love him, will you let him in out of the cold?,'

'Jesus, Harry, that's not my dog at all. I don't have a dog Harry', says Nellie.

'Well will you take him in out of the cold then Nellie?' asks Pop.

'Oh Harry, I couldn't do that'.

'Why not?,' asks Pop.

'Because I have four cats in the house; sure there'd be blue murder if I left him in.'

So Pop makes three unsuccessful attempts after bending down, to try and take the mutt into his arms, each time falling on his hands and knees. Nellie is apologising each time that she can't help, she has to hold onto her two sticks, otherwise she'll be on the ground as well. Pop's fourth attempt at getting the mutt into his hands and getting on his feet is successful. He says goodnight to Nellie as he negotiates his way across the road, on the black lumpy ice.

He is now trying to find the key of number 82 using one shoulder to lean against the wall and holding the Jack Russell with his right hand. The key is not in any of the pockets in his right side, so it's the other shoulder against the wall while trying to transfer the still shivering mutt with the other hand to his left side. After finding the key, he's now trying to feel for the keyhole in the dark as the old reliable ESB pole with the large bulb has gone out of action tonight. The tongue is stuck out one side of the mouth as usual and the watery drop has extended itself another two inches in the last fifteen minutes and is only centimetres away from the mutt's head when the key eventually finds its way into the slot and opens the door. Pop is now entering a far more dangerous place than the icy road that took him from Maureen Faye's public house in Bedford Row to the damp house we call home.

Before I precede any further with this story I need to tell you that I am happily married to a woman who loves dogs and is convinced that they have a brain just like ours. She is beyond any reasonable discussion as to why they haven't, I'll get back to this later. But this story is one of the reasons why I know that dogs have nothing that thinks or reasons like a human brain.

This poor mutt that Pop has in his arms and is still racking away from the hours it spent in the miserable cold, if he had a brain just like ours, would at the moment Pop lifted him into his arms and feeling the warm alcoholic breath down on top of himself would be thinking, 'Thanks be to God at last someone has taken pity on me' and when he found himself in our house might be thinking to himself, 'Isn't it great to be in out of that awful breeze, and if I keep my paws crossed I might get some grub. If I do some tricks and show myself to be a valuable asset to the house, I might be left stay a while, maybe even get adopted'. But that of course would only happen if the dog had a brain just like ours. But this Eejit of a gobshite having spent the last number of hours in the cold without ever opening its mouth decides now once it's in out of the cold at one o'clock in the morning, to bark his head off. Pop is trying to shut him up putting his hand over the mutt's mouth saying, 'will you shut up for F's sake, you'll wake her up and we'll both be out on the road if she comes out.' But it's no use. Pop can't stop him no matter how hard he holds the eejit's mouth. He's cursing like blazes at the dog saying, 'Is this the thanks I get for bringing you in from the cold you effin eejit of a dog?,' Then the dog and Pop jump out of their skin when a voice shouts, 'what's that piss-smeller doing in my house?,'

'Ah Jesus, is it yourself Bid?,' says Pop.

'Who else do you think would be sleeping in your bed waiting for a drunken Eejit to come home, smelling of Arthur Guinness and would you ever remove that disgusting string of snot off your nose? Are you going to answer my question?'

'What question was that love', asks Pop still with the dog in his arms, and the snot dangling away this time about twelve inches long. He's trying to get it back with the odd sniff but it will only travel half way up before it slides its way down again. The mutt is still barking its head off and Mam and Pop have to shout at one another to be heard.

'The only question I asked you, what's that piss-smeller doing in my house?'

Pop is swaying from side to side and so is the snot. He's trying his level best to stay on his feet and look sober.

'Well you see Bid, I found the poor thing shivering away outside Nellie Davis' house, so I thought I'd bring him home just for the night Bid.'

'Well you can bring him back to Nellie Davis' house,' says Mam.

'Why would I do that Bid?' asks Pop.

'Because he's not staying here, that's why.'

'Ah Jesus Bid, just for the night Bid.'

'Are you deaf as well as stupid?,' asks Mam. 'Get that yoke out now,' she shouts.

With all the barking and shouting going on outside the bedroom door I eventually wake from a very deep sleep, rubbing my eyes.

'Ah Jesus Bid, sure if he gets a bit to eat and a bit of heat into him he'll stop barking and go to sleep just like the rest of us.'

'I'm going to tell you one last time to get that flea -ridden thing out of my house before they all hop off his body into everything I have in this kitchen and everything else here including beds, clothes and body parts.'

I am now making my way to the back of the bedroom door and reaching for the handle to open it, to see what all the commotion is about. And it's at this precise moment that Mam takes charge of the whole situation; she opens the top half of the front door, with the wind howling through carrying the heavy snow that has been falling for the last ten minutes into our tiny hall-cum-kitchen. She grabs hold of the flea-carrier by the scruff of the neck and tail, throws him out and upwards into the night sky with the white flakes. When I open the bedroom door and look to see what's going on, there on its way out the door is the rear end of a dog, one side of his ass is black and the other white. He's looking back. I can still see his face to this day. He's got a look on his face like if he had a brain like ours that says 'Mother of Divine Jesus, what possessed me to do that?,' Then Mam slams the top half of the door shut and says, 'Don't ever bring one of those disease ridden things into my house again!'

'Are we getting a dog Pop?,' I ask.

'Go to bed,' I'm told and I know the sound of Mam's voice when she means business. So I'm gone back to bed to listen to Pop asking Mam if he can have a cardigan or a jumper to bring out to the mutt to keep some of the cold off him.

'Jesus, Mary and holy St. Joseph, I have hardly enough for the children and you want me to take one of their jumpers for that yoke out there; and I'll never see it again,' says Mam.

'Sure I'll get it back in the morning, when he's finished it Bid.'

'The only item of clothing that mutt will get from this house is a leather shoe up its arse if it ever comes near this house again.'

Now Pop is inside by the fire that earlier in the night had the whole room warm. He's got his big hands, with the elbows resting on his knees over the few cinders that are burning away. He's trying to get all of his body parts around the fireplace and the snot that started out as a drip when he left Maureen Faye's is now broken and stuck to one arm of the sleeve of his overcoat. And there's another one on its way down, about two inches in length. Mam is outside at the kitchen sink washing her hands up to the elbows, trying to get anything by way of germs and other things unseen to the human eye along with those that can be seen off her hands from the mutt who must be scurrying its way back to Nellie Davis' front door, and if it had a brain would be saying to itself, 'The next person that takes pity on me and brings me in out of the cold will get me on my best behaviour.' Mam is still giving out hell, while washing her hands a second time. She says 'Jesus, Mary and holy St. Joseph, what does anyone see in those mangy articles at all?

'Everything they look at has to get the wet nose first, they shove it into everything, smelling and sniffing, and what are they looking for? I'll tell you what they're looking for, other dogs' water that's what. And then their owners will say 'Walkies' they imagine their dogs love to go walkies, their mutts don't give a sugar about walking, it's just another chance to go piss smelling. Then they are sitting by the fire in their owner's house, scratching everything, and there are all kinds of living things flying off their coats, into and onto carpets and clothes that's taken all over the house. When the scratching with the paw doesn't work they go into a frenzy with their teeth trying to bite whatever it is that's trying to bite them. Then they're licking their private parts and after that they run to their owners and lick their faces and kissing them. Jesus! It gives me the creeps just thinking about it!'

Mam is shouting all this into Pop in the sitting room, but he's not listening. He can't listen because I can see him through the hole in our bedroom wall. He's still sitting down by the fire; he's fast asleep with his head resting against the mantelpiece.

'Are you listening to me in there?' says Mam but she doesn't wait for an answer and on she goes. 'Then there's the vomit. Jesus! You never know when or where they're going to throw up. And what do they do only eat it. Jesus, Mary and holy St. Joseph, what kind of a creature eats its own vomit? Mother of Jesus, we've only just got rid of Cotter's horse from outside the door and all his waste, and you waltz in here to my house, that I'm working morning, noon and night to keep clean and free from germs, with that thing under your arm.'

There's silence now, and Pop is gone into a deep sleep. His snores can be heard now that Mam has stopped. I have to make a dash for the bed, now that Mam is coming into the bedroom. I'm under the sheets alongside Jetta. She has managed to sleep through all that noise and confusion and Mam is getting into her bed muttering away and I can't understand one word she's saying. And that's it, the one and only time we had a dog in our house.

Years later I would discover that there was always a dog in Mam's house in Tower Hill but I never understood why she hated dogs with a passion. My mother was a very strong religious person. She believed that God created man and woman in his image, the beautiful birds, cats too even though we never had any; the rats, maggots, spiders and snails but the dog, that was something that crawled out of the slime millions of years ago and over a long period of time managed to grow legs, later on a nose and in no way was God responsible for its existence.

It couldn't have been very long after this event when Mam took me off to town one Saturday morning. As we were walking up towards Dinny McGrath's house, his mother is outside the entrance of the stone wall sweeping the footpath. Mam has me by the hand when we and Dinny's mother meet; it's stop for a chat time about how lovely a day it is and half a dozen other things that I have no interest in at all. So I'm there swinging the shoulders from side to side, still holding onto Mam's hand when up the road comes Mush. Mam and all the mothers in Carey's Road says we should never go next, nigh or near Mush and when we ask why, we're told he is very old and cranky. He's in terrible pain because he has arthritis. When I ask Mam who is Arthur Itis, she says 'it's a disease people and dogs get in their bones'. She says Mrs. Mullane told her a couple of days after we moved here that Mush attacked a young boy and nearly bit the hand off him, and that's good enough for me. I've been keeping well away from Mush since I arrived here.

But he's getting awful close to me now and I'm getting scared. I'm trying to tell Mam with the good manners, saying 'Excuse me Mam, Mush is coming over to me,' but Mam isn't listening. She's glued to Mrs. McGrath and whatever she's saying. I'm still holding onto Mam's hand and moving around the back of her legs, now he's lying down between Mam and Dinny's Mam. He's looking up at me, I don't think he's a cross dog at all. So

I move back to where I was before, he's still looking at me. I think I'll give him a rub with my hand and when I do, he seems to like it. I think he likes me, Mam and Dinny's Ma are still at it and haven't seen Mush at all. I'm giving him loads of rubs with my hand, he's loving it. Wait till I tell Dinny, Fonsey and Noelie how much Mush likes me. Mush has never let anyone rub him not even once. I think I'll give him a cuddle. So I put my head down on his back, there's a sudden burst of energy and a snap. There's silence that seems to last for ages. Mush has just taken a bite from under my eye. He's gone like a bullet from a gun and I'm wondering is that the old dog that Mam said could hardly move because of Arthur Itis. Then I see blood on the ground dropping from my head and the silence is broken by my screams.

Dinny's Ma and Mam are gone into a rant. They're both shouting 'Oh sweet Jesus, Mary and holy St. Joseph'. My screams can be heard all over the road. There are neighbours opening the bottom half of their front doors coming out onto the road, running up to see where the screams are coming from.

'Quick Mrs. Taylor, bring him down into the house,' says Mrs. McGrath. As we're walking down the concrete steps to Dinny's house, Mam is starting to cry. She says, 'Jesus, Mrs. McGrath I never knew that bloody dog was between us at all, if I did I'd have hunted him away.'

'Oh I know that, Mrs. Taylor. Sure I didn't see him either,' says Mrs. McGrath.

By the time we get down the steps and over to Mrs. McGrath's front door, Mrs. Mullane and Mrs. Moloney are at the top of the steps wanting to know what all the screaming is about. They have to come down the steps into Dinny's house to find out. Nellie Davis is there as well, but can't come down as she's gasping for breath after climbing up the steps, from the lane that Pop slid down on his backside weeks before. Mrs. McGrath is wiping all the blood of my jaw and Mam is in an awful state. Mrs. Moloney is trying to console her. Mam is saying, 'Why didn't I keep an eye on him, look at the state of his face, is his eye alright? Oh Jesus what'll I do if he looses his eye?,' All the fussing and crying is making me worse.

'Mrs. McGrath was a nurse before she got married,' says Mrs. Mullane, 'so Paddy will be in good hands.' I can hear Mrs. McGrath telling Mam that I'll need a stitch or two. I'm asking Mam what's a stitch or two. But she won't answer me but keeps saying, 'Oh sweet Jesus why didn't I keep an eye on him?'

Mrs. Moloney and Mrs. Mullane and half a dozen other neighbours that have landed into Mrs. McGrath's house after hearing all the screams all say together, 'Sure Mrs. Taylor, you can't be watching them every minute of the day, for God's sake.' There's more trying to console Mam than me. I've got the hiccups now, I'm crying so much. Then I hear the dreaded words, 'he'll have to go down to St. John's for the stitch or two', and I'm still asking Mam what is a stitch or two. But she can't hear me because all the neighbours are telling each other about the time their young one's got hurt or nearly killed and how they felt just like Mam does now. Then Mrs. Moloney says she'll go down to the hospital with me and Mam if Mrs. Mullane looks after her gang while she's gone. Mrs. Mullane says that that won't be any problem at all. Mrs. Hayes says she thinks that I'll have to get an injection, and I'm off again with the screams. Mrs. Storan says, 'why did you have to say that in front of the child?' Mrs. Hayes takes offence and says, 'he'll have to know sooner or later, won't he? What's the point of putting it off now until he gets there to the hospital and finds out then?,' Sure it's a wonder anyone can be heard at all with all the screams from me, the crying from Mam and all the neighbours around her and more around me.

As I look back and think of those wonderful neighbours how one day they might be fighting or not talking because of something stupid like Jetta won't let Mrs. Hayes' daughter Mary play on the swing that's around the pole between our house and Mrs. Storan's, as Jetta owns the rope and Mrs. Hayes will come down and rap on the front door and demand that her daughter Mary gets to go on the swing while Mam tells Mrs. Hayes what to do with herself, politely of course. Or Dinny, Fonsie and Noelie and I might come back from the Lyric Cinema after watching a cowboy film and we want to be just like Audie Murphy or John Wayne and do what they did on the screen that afternoon. When Dinny might pretend to knock me out by hitting me on the head with the butt of his toy gun but instead doesn't get his aim right and gives me a right clout and splits me wide open. Dinny has to go and tell my mother what he did and it's down again to the nun with the funny walk and thick glasses to stop the bleeding. Now Mam and Mrs. McGrath aren't talking.

But if you need a cup of sugar a drop of milk or the odd bob or two you only have to ask. It's like we're like one large family. Mam might say to me, 'Go up to Mrs. Mullane to see if she would have the loan of two bob 'til Friday,' and off I'd go and come back with it because it might be Mrs. Mullane's turn next week if Mr. Mullane doesn't have the work. One person's problem is everyone's problem. When a disaster visits a house they'll all pull together. Maybe one or two of the neighbours that are now in Dinny's house weren't talking before, but they're all talking now.

Mrs. McGrath is telling Mam to hold a piece of cotton wool under my eye as we start the twenty minute walk down to St. John's Hospital. I'm asking all the time if I have to get an injection. Mam promises me that I won't have to get one for a dog bite, so I'm not so bad with the crying now. My jumper and pants has drops of blood all over them. When we get into the Out Patients in St. John's Hospital it's full of children bawling their eyes out, but when they see the sight of me with all the blood they stop and I start, now that I'm in this place. I'm getting awfully scared again and I'm asking Mam what's a stitch or two and is she sure I won't get an injection? She won't answer me because all the mothers in the Out Patients Department are asking her what happened to me. And here we go again with 'it's the all my fault' story, that she was too busy talking to one of the neighbours and never noticed the dog at her heels and she wouldn't mind but she had been telling us everyday to keep away from that dog. He is too old and dangerous. There is a chorus from all the women in unison all saying the same things Mrs. Moloney said earlier. Now Mrs. Moloney is saying, 'That's what I told her, that's exactly what I said. Sure it could be any one of us down here this morning, with ours.' I'm thinking, I wish to God they'd shut up because it's me whose down here. I should have done what Mam said. I'll always do what Mam says from now on.

The small nun with the funny walk and the thick glasses shouts, 'Taylor' and as she comes out to take me in I'm scared stiff. When I'm brought into another room it's full of silver basins, scissors, cotton wool balls, bottles of all shapes and sizes and there are four or five of those awful injection things. But I won't be getting one of those things because Mam said I won't, so they can do what they like to me. There's two nurses and a doctor who want to know what happened and Mam is off again about Mush, and it being all her fault. They take the cotton away from my face and clean me up. I can hear the doctor saying, 'He'll need a stitch or two' and again I'm trying to get Mam's attention to answer, to know would she tell me once and for all what's a stitch or two? But again she's too busy telling the story about Mush. Mostly now how she'll never forgive herself, she says, 'What would I do if he took my son's eye out? Sure I'd never forgive myself?,' She said that about ten times already. So I keep whispering to her to find out what a stitch or two is. I can stop trying to ask her now as the doctor has an injection needle in his hands and he's trying to stick it in my eye and I'm bawling my eyes out again.

Mam is a dirty rotten louser for telling me lies, I still don't know what a stitch or two is. Mam and the small nun with the funny walk and glasses are holding me down and after five minutes of screaming and roaring my head off, now I know what a stitch or two is. It's all over. Mam says I can have whatever I want but I don't want to talk to her because she told me a dirty rotten pack of lies, and I never want to see a dog again as long as I live.

The People's Park at the bottom of Carey's Road is the best bit of grass area apart from the two bits on Lower Carey's Road.

It's where Fonsey, Noelie, Dinny and myself can be found most summer evenings and weekends. It's also where half of Limerick can be found with their kids and dogs. The park didn't have much in the shape of children's pastimes like swings or slides. In fact it had nothing at all except buckets of flowers, the water fountain and acres of grass. There's only one part of the park where we are allowed to play in if there's nobody else using it.

When we play football we want to be like the great names in England and Spain like Puscas, Stephano, Stanley Matthews and others. We are running around the park when a midget of a dog thought it a great idea to run after me barking his brains out. I have no idea what caused him to pick me out of the four of us. I've forgotten all about the ball and the greats in England and Spain. I'm running around in a continuous circle roaring at the lads to get him away from me. But all they're doing is roaring their heads off! It must be twenty circles I've made now and I'm getting awfully tired. When I keep looking back at the lads, the mutt doesn't seem to be tiring at all. Then he decides to jump at my backside. There's a sudden snap at my ass, when he lodges his teeth into the backside of my new pants. It would have been better for me if he had taken a bit out of my backside. Now he's about six inches off the ground, his teeth are stuck to the material of my pants and he's dangling away twisting and turning, trying to get some kind of a grip with his hind legs and nails that are tearing into the flesh on the back of my legs giving me deep scratches.

Dinny, Fonsey and Noelie can't stop laughing, there's a big ripping sound from my pants as the dog finds the ground, runs away with half of the material from my pants in his mouth. When I go home with both hands covering my backside so no one can see my embarrassment, it's back down to St. John's for more injections. The nun with the funny walk and the thick glasses says I'm one of her best customers. After getting a box in the ear from Mam she is giving out yards about it being the only good pants I have and doesn't listen to me when I try to tell her I was minding my own business when the mutt followed me. I'm always getting walloped for things that I didn't do and for nothing at all. Pop says, 'If you done nothing at all what about all the times you did something and never got caught, take it out of that.'

Then there's Babsy Noonan over in the corner. This poor woman's husband left her months ago to fend for herself and look after four kids. Every stray dog on the road or passing through will wind up outside or inside her door. She doesn't have a bike like the other residents on the road. Her only form of transportation is the pram, the type like the American automobile, big frame, big wheels, big springs but she uses it for transporting coal, the dog or dogs that befriend her, not the other way round, and last of all two of her young kids, and Mam will tell us everyday to keep away from her house, kids and dogs and most of all the pram. Apart from Pop's bike and the odd trolley I get to make, it's the only form of transportation available to all the kids on the road. But Mam said that pram carries more than coal, dogs and kids. She says that it has things living in it that haven't been discovered yet. It has never seen a bar of soap in its life, and she doesn't want that ol' yoke or any of the things that's living in it brought into her house on our shoes, hair or clothes. 'Do ye hear me now?'

'Yes Mam,'

But it goes in one ear and out the other. As Babsy lets all the kids have the pram, she isn't worried about the odd scratch or dent the pram will get in its role as our mobile playground or pastime. So James, Fonsey, Noelie, Dinny and I have a contest to see who can shove the most bodies in the pram up the steep hill past Lynch's house. James wants to go first. He thinks because he's the smallest and the youngest, if he gets the four of us up the hill first that we will let him into the gang. So the starting place is across the road from Sheehan's house, where the hill starts to rise. James manages to get the four of us in the pram, half way up the hill. At this point he has the two arms at full stretch. He's grunting and groaning and the four of us in the pram are shouting, 'Come on James, you can do it.' He's on his toes now and has stretched at so far an angle his nose is only twelve inches from the ground. The two back wheels of Babsy's pram are slowly lifting off the ground. James won't give in as he tries to put one leg in front of the other, the back wheels are now more than twelve inches off the ground, we're starting to lean more and more forward until the law of gravity takes over. When James can't take the strain anymore we come forward one on top of the other and land on James' two hands and fingers that are wrapped around the pram handle. He screams in pain taking his hands from under the rusty chrome handlebars and putting one hand under each armpit. Then he goes into a screaming silence. We know he is in terrible pain but we can't stop laughing. He's running around in circles then up the hill to number 82 and I'm the first to stop laughing because I realise that Mam is going to want an ear or two to box for sitting inside Babsy's cesspit, and then for causing poor Jim the awful pain he's in.

Dinny, Fonsie and Noelie have run for cover and are nowhere to be seen. I'm standing halfway up the hill, waiting for Mam to call me up for the box and Babsy's pram is on its way down towards The People's Park. But she won't be worried about anyone stealing it, sure who'd want to steal that yoke. When Mam does come to the door she's worse than I thought. She's got both hands going, telling me to get up here right away. When I get closer she's talking through her teeth in a low voice. Mam never shouts or screams in the street. She waits until I get inside the house. She says it's not ladylike to shout in the street. She won't smoke in the street either for the same reason. When I walk past the front door my eyes are blinking like crazy waiting for the thump on the back of the head which is stuck in my shoulders as far down as I can get it. I have a hand partly held in the air to protect myself and it's a couple of lefts and a couple or rights into the jaw, ears and skull with the usual verbal onslaught of 'Jesus, Mary and holy St. Joseph', all said through the teeth. 'What did I tell you about that dirty, filthy yoke? How many times did I tell you not to go near it? How many?' And when I try to guess how many times by saying 'Twenty Ma,' she'll give me another box and say, 'Don't you dare talk back to me when I'm talking to you!'

James is still holding his hands under his armpits while still screaming his head off and taking them out for a look every few minutes. He's shouting, 'Look Mam, look at my finger nails, they're all black Mam.' I look at Mam and she's like Rocky Marciano with the left and rights again. Dinny, Fonsie and Noelie must be laughing their heads off listening to the wallops and screams of Mam tearing into me. But will I go on Babsy's pram again when Mam isn't looking? Of course I will and more than once too.

That's it. No more dealings with dogs of any kind again except to take that dislike I would inherit from Mam for the rest of my life.

After I got married and had two children, my daughter finds, shivering outside the front door, a dog in the month of January and here we go again. She wants to bring the mutt in and I'm saying 'There's no way that p. smelling article is coming into my house' but Mary and my son Cory gang up on me and I have to say 'OK. But I tell them that the dog has to stay in the garage and 'I don't want her anywhere near food, my food that is.' Sorcha will never let me forget about that dog and the way I treated her. Then Sorcha gets married, buys a house across the road and before she starts a family brings home a little Shiatsu, who I have to say after coming to and fro from each house over a six month period won me over and the poor mutt hasn't a clue who she belongs to. I started a depression five years ago and according to my wife Mary, this little thing is a major cause of getting me through it. I don't know, she could be right and Sorcha and herself can't believe I'm the same person treating this mutt which I nearly forgot to tell you is called Bobbie. But then after four years I notice that Bobbie is getting on my nerves. I don't like her looking for my attention, wanting to sit on my lap for the strokes, and I realise I'm coming out of the depression. I'm getting better and Mary isn't a bit happy. She is saying, 'Don't you dare talk to Bobbie like that.'

'Like what?,' I answer.

'Like she's a dog.'

'But sure she is a dog.'

'I know she's a dog but that's no way to talk to her.'

So I say, 'How do you want me to talk to her, like she's a person?'

'Yes,' says Mary, 'she's got feelings you know.'

'But' I say, 'she doesn't know what I'm saying.'

And Mary says, 'How do you know she doesn't know?'

And I say, 'How do you know she does?'

Mary says, if I don't talk properly to Bobbie, Bobbie will be getting my dinner or the dinner I thought I was getting. Or it might be thrown on the table any old way, with the usual comment, 'It's true what my father said all the same,'

And I'll say, 'What did your father say Mary?'

'He said never trust a man who doesn't like dogs.'

And I'll say, 'Why did he say that Moll?'

'He said they have no feelings, no heart.'

Then Mary says, 'Bobbie was very good to you when you were depressed. When no one else could put up with you, there she was every night by your side. You used to be very kind to her, why can't you be like that now?'

Then she'll turn to Bobbie talking away to her like the mutt can understand every word she's saying. 'Isn't he very bold Bobbie talking to you like that, like an old dumb dog and didn't you look after him so well when he was the one that was like a dog, and now he doesn't want to know you at all. But you know who loves you don't you Bobbie?' And the mutt's tail is going like crazy.

'Look at her,' Mary says. 'Do you see how she knows what I'm saying to her?'

I'm looking at a woman I used to know as a perfectly sane, intelligent, wise, well balanced and caring individual and how lucky I was to get thirty five good sane years out of her and I better get prepared to call the guys with the white coats very soon. Then Mary says, 'Read me a bit of some of your writing love, not too much now, I want to wait until it's finished, then I'll read the whole lot together.'

So for pure devilment and just to wind her up I read to her the part about Pop bringing the Jack Russell home out of the cold. When I finish she says; 'Aw isn't he very good? I never re-alised Pop was so kind to dogs.'

So I have to tell her that Pop was never kind to dogs.

Mary says, 'wasn't he very kind to that Jack Russell?'

'He was drunk Mol. He wasn't like that when he was sober.'

Mary's facial expression changes, when I get to the part about Mam expressing her disgust at dogs, she's in shock. 'Your mother never said that about dogs.'

'She did,' I answer.

Mary says, 'Your mother was a lovely woman, a lady.'

'Yes', I answer. 'My mother was a lovely woman, and she was a lady. She was a lovely woman and a lady who hated the sight of dogs. You only knew her for about twelve months before she died.'

'I can't imagine your mother saying that. Did she really say that about dogs?'

'Yes', I answer.

I can see there's a small bit of a grin at the side of her mouth. 'Are you going to publish that?,' she asks.

'Yes', I answer. 'Because you want to know why I don't like dogs. It's my upbringing, it's part of what I am. And if I told my mother before I met you that I was going to marry a woman who loved dogs, do you know what she would have said to me?,'

'No,' answered Moll.

'Don't ever have anything to do with a woman who loves dogs!'

CHAPTER 6

When Nan calls to Upper Carey's Road I'll have her pestered to take me out to Tower Hill now that Granddad is dead. I never wanted to go before because of that awful long black tooth he had growing out of his bottom gum, the way he'd stick it out over his top lip and frighten the living daylights out of me. I'm glad he's gone and I'm glad all the wailing and crying is finished, from Nan, Mam and Jetta over the last two weeks. She'll say 'for goodness sake, you'll be crying to come home after an hour', that you're bored because you've no one to play with.

She's right! But I can't tell her, I only want to go because I'll get the spin in the car out and back in again, when she's sick of me bawling to come home. But she'll always give into me, believing my promises that I won't be asking her to come back and when I get up the following morning to the sound of Uncle Peadar washing himself outside the house by one of the four barrels of rainwater at each corner, with his white enamel basin on a window sill that has a mirror, shaving brush, soap and razor, while stripped to the waist because there's no running water on tap at Nan's house. That comes from the hand pump at the bottom of the second hill next to Uncle Tom and Auntie Rosie's house. I'll have a pain in my hands from the two white enamel buckets that Nan keeps side by side on the dresser in the kitchen, with the white linen thrown over the tops to keep the flies out. When they're nearly empty, Nan will ask me to go down to the hand pump at the bottom of the hill and fill them up with the water that doesn't taste like water at all. And by the time I come back up the hill to Nan's house with my arms three or four inches longer and the wellington boots that I always wear in the summer full of water and listening to Nan giving out about the two buckets being half full and sending me back down again for more because one bucket will last no time at all and I might as well go back down now and save myself the trouble of going down again tomorrow. I'm asking myself on the way down the hill again, 'what possessed me to want to come out here at all?,' and wished I was back home again playing with Dinny, Fonsey and Noelie. I'll be looking out the kitchen window at the trees across the road blowing in the wind while listening to Radio Éireann and the awful boring music they'll play. There'll be no Buddy Holly or Bill Hailey music on this station, the church won't allow it, because it's not music for the Christian ear. Then Jack the postman will call with a letter or two from the aunt's in England.

He'll lean against the wall, telling Nan all the latest local news, like who's dead, who had a baby, who got a job, the names of those that have gone to America or England because there was no work to be found. Tower Hill and Cappamore is full of Ryan's and Coleman's. And Nan is asking Jack in response 'is that one of the Ryan's or Coleman's that has a son over in England? 'or 'is that the one married to such a man from such a place?,'

Then Jack will say 'Goodbye' and as he throws the leg over the saddle of his bike, Nan will ask him, 'What's the time Jack?'

I'm trying to figure out why Nan is asking him the time, when there's four clocks in the house, and every one of them working in perfect harmony.

He'll tell her the time as he cycles away, then she'll shout back like she does everyday,

'Is that new time or old time Jack?'

And Jack will always say, 'Old time, Missus'.

I'm asking Nan what does she mean by new time and old time. She says the clocks in Limerick go back once in October and forward again in April every year. But in the country they stay as they are. I tell her in all the time I've lived in Carey's Road I never saw any of the clocks that Pop brought home on his bike move anywhere. She laughs, and says, 'the clocks don't move, it's the hands that move. It's 2 o'clock here now but in Limerick it's only 1 o'clock, and I'll need to have your Uncle Peadar's dinner ready by new time, because he works by the time in Limerick. Do you understand?,' she asks.

'I do Nan', I answer. But I haven't got a clue what she's talking about, and I couldn't be bothered trying to figure it out. Sure what good is it, understanding that stuff?

And now the boredom is back again. I'll try to break it by going down to Uncle Tom and Auntie Rosie's. They've got five daughters but I can't stay here too long playing with five girls, because I'll turn into a right Nance. But if Nan wants to kill a pig the boredom is gone. She'll go to the shed by the side of the house, pull one from the batch of ten she'll breed every year, bring it to the kitchen table with its head hanging over one end. She'll ask me to hold its legs while she cuts its throat and lets the blood flow into a white enamel bucket on the floor. She'll do all this while the pig screams its head off with every ounce of energy it has. It seems to know it's time is up, and when the awful screams have gone, its belly is cut from its throat to its private parts and Nan is pulling all kinds of stuff from its insides that's making me sick.

She'll cut and saw it into several pieces and hang them from the ceiling. Its head looking at me every time I come down the stairs. She'll take a piece down every day and cut some slices for the dinner to join the thirty or so potatoes with the two heads of cabbage taken from the half acre of land to the back of the house. Then it's into the big black pot which hangs from the cast iron bar, with all the holes for hooks to take the other black pots of all shapes and sizes, that swings into the kitchen floor from the open turf fire. There'll be too much for the three of us, but that's all part of the daily exercise. The rest will find its way back to the pig shed as slop, as the spuds and cabbage if left in the ground too long will rot away. The next day I'll be crying to come home as there's nothing to do, and Nan will be calling down the holy family again, saying what possessed her to bring me out here at all, that I'll have to "wait another two days because your Uncle Peadar is up the country so you might as well get used to it". When he's home it's not so bad. He might fix a puncture or wash the car; whatever it is, it's worth waiting for him to come home in the summer evenings, because he'll let me give him a hand. If I'm there over a weekend it will be well into the early hours of a Sunday morning when he'll come into his bed that I have to share every time I come here. He'll be all hands and legs thinking I'm the one he was with a few hours earlier, telling me he loves me, kissing and mauling me with the awful smell of porter off his breath. I'll be shouting 'get off me you clown' but it's no use. He's too big and strong. The next morning I'll tell Nan about him and how I nearly suffocated last night and she'll kill herself laughing. When the dark nights come she will tell me stories by the fire about the banshee that appeared to people up the road, right outside the graveyard and were never seen again. And it would be no good saying Masses or doing the rosary for people that the banshee took away, because she'll take them down to hell and there's no coming out of hell once you get there, and that's good enough for me. I'm not stirring outside the door, especially in the dark winter nights, and I'm too young to realise that's why she's telling me the whole pack of lies in the first place.

That might be followed by her taking the long pin with the small ball at the end from the bun of hair at the top of her head, watching it fall all the way down her back and resting on the seat of her chair.

'Why is your hair so long Nan?' I ask.

She says it's for all the baldy men in England, that Uncle Peadar is going to cut it very soon that her hair will be very short and it will take another six or seven years before she can cut it again and send it over to the company in England that makes the wigs for the baldy men. They'll send her over some money very soon and she can buy some chickens as the one's she has are too old, and are hardly laying any eggs at all these days.

The next day Nan is wearing black and while throwing a shawl of the same colour around her head, she's telling me we're going to a wake up the road to a neighbour's house. It's been an hour now and I'm getting awfully tired. I'm learning that 'up the road' in the country is not the same as 'up the road' at home. I keep asking her when are we going to arrive at the neighbour's house because my legs are so heavy, I can hardly lift them off the ground. She's telling me to 'Shut up' and I wish to God Peadar would come and take me out of her sight back home to Limerick. When we do arrive, there are loads of horses with carts and only one or two cars with crowds of men dressed in black standing outside the house. Nan takes me in. There's a coffin between two chairs in the middle of a big room, with women bawling and making an awful racket! There are six big candles placed on brass stands burning away around the coffin. It's the only light in the room, and Nan has left me standing by the coffin while she's telling all the women how sorry she is for their trouble, whatever that means. And when I turn my head sideways there's an ould guy in the coffin. I've never seen a human being that colour before. I'm just high enough above the box to see his nostrils and somebody has shoved cotton wool up there and I'm wondering did he have the watery drip like Pop. He's wearing a white shirt and has a rosary beads wrapped around his clasped hands, there's a smell off him that's making me sick. He must be starting to rot already. Nan takes me out of the smelly room to the farmyard where there's a band playing. And I don't understand why the women inside the house are making such an awful racket with the crying, and men outside in the yard dancing, drinking, smoking and laughing, when there's an ould guy inside the house that needs to be buried soon! Later that day, I'm back with Nan on the road again, heading to Tower Hill. We'll get there quicker this time because we're on a neighbour's horse and cart.

Nan will call to our house every Saturday morning. She likes to be needed. It's no trouble for her to knit a cardigan or a jumper, that she spent the evenings knitting away in Tower Hill for those of her many grandchildren who need them the most. Then there was the large bundle of coloured material she had Peadar bring from the car on one of those Saturday mornings.

'Have a look at this Bid, and tell me what you think of it,' says Nan.

And Jetta wants to know what it is and who it's for?

'It's a patch work quilt' says Nan, 'for your mother and father's bed. Lets put it on the bed Bid and see how it looks', Nan says, while walking into the bedroom.

'You won't be in a hurry to get out of that in the winter mornings Har,' quips Nan.

Mam is delighted and asks Nan how long it took her to make it and did it cost her any money.

'Not a penny', answers Nan. 'As you can see there's a lot of different materials which I had left over from other work'. She says it took her two years because she had to wait until there was enough down saved from the ducks she put to the sword. All agreed how well it looked on the bed. Nan was right about it being warm and cosy in the winter months but when the summer came the sweat would pour out of Mam and Pop in the bed.

Nan was always asking Pop if he could fix this or that, it might be a chair or a radio or God knows what else. She'd have it in the car for him to fix or she might spot something that Pop brought home and say 'what are you doing with that Har? Do you want it? I could use that now under this or on top of that or it would look lovely on top of something else'. 'Lamp' was a word Pop used if someone put their eye on anything they might want for themselves, which was why he used the expression 'hide everything' when she'd walk in the door.

The only time Nan is not visiting Carey's Road is when Pop is on the tear. She won't want to be around when he's home and doing his level best to argue with anyone who will give him the time. The problem for him is nobody will, most of all Nan. The combination of Nan's stare and Pop's determination to tease would be too explosive. It won't however last much longer than one week, two at the most. If he has enough money Pop loves the drink, he's an alcoholic but he also loves Mam. She can't stand it when he's drunk.

There are too many side-effects - apart from his antics or cantankerousness, there's the awful bad manners like the breaking of the wind or as Pop calls it, a good old fart! When Pop goes on the tear it's usually well planned. He won't have touched a drop for a year or two. And if there's a wedding on the horizon Pop is making plans for the said day and Mam knows the signs only too well. He'll work late nights and weekends' making sure that

Mam has her housekeeping money and none will suffer while he's indulging himself and making Arthur Guinness a richer man. He'll be home late every night with the dinner that Mam might have cooked for him, slurping and supping from the plate and the watery drip dropping away into whatever he's shoving into his mouth. It will be the only solid food he's had in two days and he's leaning over to one side letting off every few minutes, breaking wind that doesn't sound like wind at all. And it's get out of the house and open all the windows time.

Pop will never get a good night's sleep during his period of self-intoxication because there's no way he's coming into Mam's clean fresh bed when he is making all kinds of noise and could wind up having a watery accident on her clean sheets. If he manages to eat while drinking he is allowed in, when he doesn't, it's hot tongue and cold shoulder time. He'll be down at the Bedford Bar over in the corner playing his favourite card game, - Forty-Five, and if there's enough lads for a game of rubber, six players, he's there until the needle and cantankerousness sets in. Then the game is abandoned, he'll be banging his big right hand that's holding a card on the table, 'have a look at that you Effer' he'll shout, and the lads will be giving out and wandering why the cards are so wet; saying, 'Jesus lads, somebody is spilling their drink onto the cards, will ye be more careful?,' Sure it's not the drink at all, only Pop shoving the cards close to his eyes, under his nose, because he's half blind and doesn't know where his glasses are and the cards he's holding will be collecting the watery drip all the time. Now Pop wants to know is somebody saying he's sloppy. And one of the lads says, 'I never mentioned any names'. Then he says, 'I know you didn't mention any names, but you were looking at me when you said it, you miserable Effer'. And now there's blue-murder, as Pop rises to his feet, telling the guy who is sitting across from him, who is his playing partner to say it to his face and when the partner asks, 'say what to your face?,' Pop can't remember and is on his feet, shouting.

The other lads are saying, 'Jesus Harry, calm down, it's only a game of cards for crying out loud'. Pop looks at him and asks what it's got to do with him anyway and when he tries to give him a dig, misses and falls over the table, spilling the drink on the floor. Maureen Faye says 'that's enough, go home Harry Taylor' and Pop won't argue with Maureen, drunk or sober.

She is too good to him. If he needs a few pounds until he has a job finished, or maybe no work at all, it's Maureen to the rescue, and home he'll go. He might take the bike and if he does it will be as drunk as he is, when he gets home. Its 'Mr. Thorn I'll get under your skin time'. But Pop loves Mam more than Arthur Guinness. He'll love Arthur Guinness for one or two weeks while Mam has the headaches and won't speak to him. He'll get half-cooked dinners if he's lucky and she knows it won't last too long either but she can't afford to let him off the hook. If she does, it could last much longer. When he does go back to work and stops the gulping, Mam will come around, not too quickly, as she will have her week or two of making him pay.

There's no toilet in our house for the family waste to be disposed of. Our toilet is under the bed in potties and Mam trained each one of us how to use it when we arrived in Upper Carey's Road.

All around us were new Corporation housing estates like Rathbane and Janesborough, Prospect, Weston and Lower Carey's Road. Every one of these dwellings has what Mam and Pop considered to be a luxury; a toilet with its own door light and most importantly a key. Every time I'm on the potty Mam will keep telling me not to pull up my underpants unless my bottom is good and clean. 'What would I do if you got knocked down by a motor car and had to go into hospital to be un-dressed by the nuns down at St. John's and they saw the state of your underpants, if you didn't clean your bottom properly and wind up making a holy show of me? I'd never be able to show my face again'.

I used to lie in bed at night thinking if I got a belt from a car coming down Carey's Road. Dinny, Fonsey and Noelie are looking down at me on the ground. Jet is bawling her eyes out and the ambulance is coming to take me to St. John's Hospital near the big Cathedral, when I get there I've lost consciousness. I'm on the operating table. Nan is there crying her eyes out too. Pop looks very worried and keeps smoking, one fag after the other, he can't stop pacing up and down the corridor. There's a doctor telling Pop, Nan and Mam that it doesn't look good and that I may not see another day and all Mam wants to know is, was my underpants clean?

At the bottom of the hill to the left of the road and just before the bridge that's now gone, stood a small old bungalow, where two elderly people lived called the Sheehan's. They had a grandson who might be a year or two older than me. He lived with his parents in Janesborough, and would come down to visit them regularly; the lads and I would find ourselves in the back-yard of this lovely old house. Mr. Sheehan had every kind of vegetable growing there, and right in the middle of it stood a small galvanized hut. I'm sure I spent many days here, but my memory recalls only one event and it was that small hut. On one of those visits I said to their grandson Jim, 'where can I go to the toilet?' and pointing to the galvanized hut he said, 'in there'.

I have a confused look on my face as I walk over. I put my hand out to catch a piece of rope that I think is a handle and as I open the door a swarm of Bluebottles race into my face. As I'm getting over the shock I see there's a white enamel old rusty bucket under a plank of wood that's nailed to both sides of the galvanized walls. The plank has a hole in it just above the bucket. There's a woeful smell in here and the Bluebottles are starting to make their way back into the hut and down into the white enamel old bucket. There's about twenty or thirty pieces of the Limerick Leader cut into neat squares hanging on a piece of string attached to a nail on one wall close to the bucket. So when I look into the bucket through the hole in the piece of wood there are several deposits of family waste inside the bucket and I think it won't be emptied until the bucket is full.

If we had a back-yard my Pop would have one of these and it would be much better than this one but still this is luxury and I'm going to get a chance to have a go on this contraption.

So when I drop the pants I have to lift myself up onto the plank to get my backside onto the hole, and when I do my feet are several inches off the ground. As I'm doing my business I can feel a good few Bluebottles walking over the cheeks of my backside, but it doesn't bother me. But if Mam knew I was putting my bottom onto a yoke like this there would be hell to pay. So I'll have to keep my mouth shut about why can't we have what Sheehan's have in their back-yard

I'm swinging my legs in and out, I haven't noticed I've kicked the bucket backwards with the heel of one of my shoes. It doesn't make a noise because there is no floor under the bucket, only grass. But it does disturb the Bluebottles who rise from under the plank, they're all over me, hitting my face and one or two have landed on my lips and I can't get the thought out of my head that they've been walking all over the family waste in the bucket for the past few days and am I going to be back in hospital again unconscious only this time I might die. So I'm waving my hands all over the place trying to keep them off me and away from my mouth. I'm trying to spit the germs that were on the legs of the Bluebottles off my mouth. I'm off the plank of wood, still waving my hands, trying to get the flies away. My pants are down around my ankles. I'm getting dizzy from all the waving and turning around. I stumble and fall against the door which opens causing me and all the Bluebottles to exit the hut. There's a terrible bang when the door swings back against the wall which causes all the lads and the elderly Sheehan's to look around in amazement at the sight of me stumbling all over the place, trying to get my balance and my pants up at the same time. It will be many months before I'm seen in Sheehan's house again. Maybe someday we might have a lav. just like theirs.

Pop had his own potty under the bed and Mam was always giving out about it. 'Jesus, Mary and Holy Saint Joseph, Harry Taylor, if I asked you once I asked you a thousand times, to keep that empty. Why do you wait 'til it's almost full to the top before you throw it out?,' Pop and Mam's bed is one of those big old fashioned one's.

There is a lot of open space between their bed and the floor, it is a great place for storing things that only need taking out once in the blue moon, like Christmas decorations. But Mam's problem is she doesn't want Mrs. Mullane, Mrs. Storan or Mrs. Hayes and all the other housewives in Upper Carey's Road looking into her house at the pee-pot under the bed, if the front and bedroom doors are open at the same time.

Our front door is the original one and has all the signs of it like a lot of other doors in Carey's Road. It is the half-door, just like those on the front cover of the book, with Noelie Grace's Dad leaning on the bottom half while looking up at the camera. Ours has layers of different colour paint skins and is riddled with burst bubbles and dribbles from years of good summers. The frame is completely rotten at both ends and has several layers of mortar poured into the bottom of both sides. There is just enough room when the bottom half of the door is closed against it to let the rats out onto the street. No self-respecting rat would want to stay in our house, it's too clean! The top half won't close against the frame unless it gets a good thump. Without the thump the top half will slowly swing its way back against the wall, as it is hung off level. With so little room in our house and three kids running in and out the front and bedroom doors, and leaving them open, Pop's potty is clearly visible to any passer-by who can't resist the temptation to have a good gawk at what's going on inside our house. But it's the contents of Pop's pot that's driving Mam round the bend.

He'll lie in bed every night with one hand behind the head and the other resting on the lovely patchwork quilt that Nan made, while smoking his favourite fags John Player Please, worrying about work or the lack of it, or where he's going to get money for this or that, he'll get through four or five at least, before the eyes close and off to sleep he'll go. Each cigarette will have been sucked to the last and thrown into the pot under the bed; after several nights of peeing and smoking the pot will have a thick scum of disintegrated fag ends on top of all the urine and that's what the neighbours will see if the door is open.

And Mam is always shouting 'close the bloody door' while Pop is getting it in the ear every day and instead of doing what he's told comes home one evening with a large white square bread bin.

'Did you get me a new bread bin Har?,' says Mam all smiles.

'I did not', says Pop and proceeds to walk into the bedroom. When he comes out he has the potty.

'Well I don't believe it,' says Mam 'you're cleaning out your potty and it's only half full'.

'No I'm not', says Pop. 'I'm throwing it out'.

Mam is confused as Pop walks outside throwing the thick scummy liquid into the gutter. Then up goes the potty over the wall of the derelict house next door to ours that has its old door and window opes blocked up. When he comes back in he says to Mam,

'I can pee away now to my heart's content and if Mrs. Hayes or Mrs. Storan want to look inside our house they'll be able to see nothing'.

'And why not?' asks Mam.

'Because it's got a lid, I can put whatever I like into it'. Mam doesn't like it but she'll put up with it.

There's a wedding coming up. It's a daughter of Pop's sister Kathleen, one of two aunts who live in Thomas Street. There's tension in the air and Mam can see the signs that Pop is going to break out. I'm going to the shop every day for the Mrs. Cullen's Powder and when the day arrives it's Saturday with Pop all decked out. There's hardly a word spoken between then when he walks up the hill past Dinny's house. We all know that sometime later that night, he'll be falling around the corner, blotto drunk and looking for an argument with anyone or anything that wants to give it to him. But surprise, surprise, its 8.00pm that evening and there's Pop rounding McGrath's corner as straight as a dye, looking as sober as a judge. We find out the following day, he decided to go on Bulmer's Cider thinking it would have no affect on him at all and it didn't, or so he thought. He's thinking how surprised Mam is going to be when he walks in the door cold sober so early in the evening.

That would have been the case had he not decided to go into Ford's pub across the road to have just one more, which turned out to be four or five.

And that's what Pop's problem is; he just doesn't know when to stop. Mam would have no problem with him having a pint or two before coming home every night, but he just can't do that. So there he is inside Ford's. He's started a sing-song that we can hear across the road, while we're all sitting around the kitchen table wondering how long it will be before he starts an argument with someone and is asked to leave, or worse is thrown out.

It's neither. Here he comes and it's only 9:00pm. As he steps outside the door he looks great, not falling to one side or the other. Off the footpath he steps and stumbles onto the ground on his hands and knees. He looks very confused and doesn't understand why he can't get up onto his feet. He looks around for some assistance but there isn't any. There's nothing to lean against, so he has no choice but to crawl on all fours across the road to number 82 and when he gets there knocks on the bottom half of the front door, with the top half wide open. When Mam looks out in response, she doesn't see anyone, and comes back to the table. When he knocks again, he's saying, 'Bid, are you there Bid?,' When Mam looks out a second time, she's wondering where the voice is coming from and thinks it must be her imagination and again goes back to the table. Mrs. Storan is looking out the top part of her front door and wondering why Harry Taylor is on his hands and knees outside his own front door, calling for Mam. But he keeps knocking saying, 'Bid, Bid will you let me in please?,' and when Mam comes to the door looks down at Pop and says 'Jesus, Mary and Holy Saint Joseph, what are you doing down there on your hands and knees you Eejit, you're drunk aren't you, you dirty Eejit!'

'No Bid, I'm not drunk, I swear to God, I'm not drunk. I just can't get up on my feet that's all'. He's not his usual drunk argumentative self and Mam can't figure out what's going on.

So she opens the bottom half of the front door and says 'get in you Eejit!' And off he goes into the bedroom, onto the bed, like a dog scurrying along, after he falls asleep, wakes up at about 3.00am.

He feels around for his fags and matches, lights up, puts one hand behind the head, takes a few drags of a filter tipped cigarette which is very unusual. He must have run out of money or cigarettes and borrowed some. But the filter cigarette is going to have a large bearing on what happens next.

The Imperial Bar & Lounge.
Known as Fords in my chilhood and right across the road from our house

Pop falls asleep with the fag smouldering away in the hand that's resting on the lovely patchwork quilt filled with all kinds of feathers and down that Nan spent so much time making out in Tower Hill. When the red end of the fag reaches the filter it rolls off along Pop's fingers onto the quilt and slowly burns a large hole right under his nose. After fifteen minutes of this Mam wakes up coughing very heavily. She can smell burn and smoke, she gets out of the bed, calling; 'Harry, Harry, wake up,

I think the house is on fire', but Harry is comatosed from all the cider and his lungs full of whatever kind of fumes that's coming off Nan's patchwork quilt. She turns on the light, it's hard to see anything with all the smoke, when she feels her way along Pop's legs up his body, she can see the cause of the smoke emanating from the large black hole on the top of Pop's chest. She's screaming; 'wake up Har, wake up, Jesus, Mary and Holy Saint Joseph, are you dead Harry?' There's no answer. Then she's shouting, 'water, water!' and suddenly realises there's plenty of it right under her feet and down she bends, knocks the top off the bread bin, lifts it up and throws the whole lot on top of his face and chest; and him lying there with the mouth wide open. Then she gives him a wallop across the face, which brings him 'round. He's got tobacco bits all over his head, face and chest. Nan's lovely patchwork quilt has a big hole in it and Pop promises never to smoke in bed again.

CHAPTER 7

Apart from my first day at school when I thought I'd never see my mother again, I have no other memories. But of the Communion class at the Presentation School for boys and girls, I have plenty and all because of the erratic nun Sister Rachel. She had fiery red piercing eyes that could frighten the living daylights out of any human, animal or even something from the spirit world. The rattle that came when she walked fast from the Rosary beads clinking against the large black Crucifix dangling from her waist, that glaring red face between the white apertures around her head, with the black veil flowing down her back from her head all added to the dread of Sr. Rachel.

Her whole goal in life was to prepare you for the walk up the aisle of St. Joseph's Church during the month of May, for your First Holy Communion.

'First we have to learn how to confess our sins', she says. At the moment we can't sin because we haven't been confirmed, but after that we'd better watch out because if we die with the stain of mortal sin on our soul without being to Confession then we'll burn in hell forever. So we have to learn to make our Confession properly, and get it off by heart. When you go into the confession box you're to say:

'Bless me Father, for I have sinned,' and the priest will say, 'How long has it been since your last Confession?'

She says: 'It should never be more than one week' and when I ask her why, she says: 'you won't be able to remember all the sins you're going to commit if it's two weeks, there'll be too many. And you'll have to make sure all the sins are gone off your soul, that's why you have to be sure to remember everything you did wrong. After you told the priest, he'll give you absolution'.

'What's that Sister?,' asks a young girl.

'It's forgiveness child, he'll give you forgiveness because he's God's representative on earth'.

'What does that mean Sister?,' asks another.

'It means he works for God'.

'How much does he get a week?,' I ask, and then I get a wallop.

'What's your name?,'

'It's Patrick Taylor, Sister'.

'That's what you get for being too smart in my class, young man.'

Then there's tears running down my face, I was only asking a simple question. I'll be keeping my mouth shut from now on. And after several days of practising Confession she'll have us out in the yard every day with the girls from the Communion class outside the old stone building. They'll be over with us lined up on the other side, forty of us, ten across and four rows down. The palms of our hands will be held together in front of our chests to give us all that holy look. From the back row, we have to walk out towards the girls. They have to do the same. We meet in the middle and walk up the centre aisle like we're getting married. The clinking of her rosary beads can be heard while she's tearing up and down and shoving the couples closer together, pulling our clasped hands up, mostly the boys if they're down too far. She'll give them a box in the ear saying 'Keep them up, keep them up'. We're only seven and we all feel like a right bunch of sissies. She'll take us out every morning for an hour the same again in the afternoon, until we're blue in the face from it, and can do it in our sleep.

'When you get your First Holy Communion, you're to stick your tongue out for the priest'.

'Isn't sticking your tongue out rude Sister?'

'Not when you do it to a priest', she answers.

And I'm thinking I'm going to love this, I always thought you would go down to hell for doing that. But I'm keeping my mouth shut.

'You'll have to make sure the Holy Communion doesn't touch your teeth', and when another asks her why, she says 'Because it's the body of the Lord Jesus Christ, that's why.

'If you bit the Holy Communion Jesus will be screaming in agony and he went through enough pain, and we don't want him going through anymore now, do we class?' And we all shout, 'No Sister, we don't'.

My brain is telling me it won't be long now when I'll be able to go and visit all my aunts and the few uncles. I'm asking Mam how many I have. She knows why. I'll have the new suit, shirt, tie, socks and shoes. I'll be all decked out. I don't care about that. I just want to know how much I'm going to make out of all of this. But Mam won't tell me. She says I'll have to wait and see because if she tells me, I might get disappointed. So I have to try and guess. Jet will have to get a small share because she gave me some of her's when she made her Communion. She got one pound two shillings and sixpence two years ago. I'll have to give James some as well, he was only two when Jet made hers she didn't have to give him anything because he was too small, but he'll have to give me some of his when his turn comes around and that won't be long, because he's just started school this year. Mam always makes us share everything.

She has me down at Moran's Men's and Boys' Outfitters in William Street, trying on every suit in the place. She's very fussy and I am getting awfully tired, taking this off, and putting that on all the time.

And then it's the morning of the Big Day and the crazy Nun of ours is a different person. She's falling all over us, telling us not to forget this and not to forget that, 'don't touch Jesus with your teeth', and why is she so nice? It's because all the Mams are there, that's why. We don't have to worry about getting boxed around the place today. We're told to go into the church; the girls are on one side, the lads on the other. All the boys are looking over at the girls wondering what kind of amadán we're to be matched with when we walk up the aisle, and I just want to get out of here and start the collection, and get to the aunties.

'It's all over, it's time to go,' but Mam is talking to other mothers outside the church about how well their daughters or sons are looking. She makes me turn around for them to see. 'Oh sure isn't he lovely?' they'll say and I have to pretend I want to go to the toilet so I can get away from all this talking and get on with the collection. 'Come on so', says Mam 'you can go to the toilet over the road in Auntie Nora's house'.

We're knocking on her door and when she sees us she says: 'Oh come on in Bid and look at you Paddy'. Oh aren't you the fine young man, it wasn't too long ago when I used to clean your back-side for your mother'. She always says that every time she sees me.

I'm there looking all shy and the head is down, my eyes are roaming all over the room to see where her purse or handbag might be. I'll surely get two and sixpence here. 'Turn around 'til I see you, oh isn't he getting very big God bless him Bid'. I can see the purse, it's on the mantelpiece. When is she going to go over and get it? She's talking to Mam about some woman down the road who died last night from some old stupid disease, and now she's forgotten all about me. What will I do if I get nothing?

'Will you have a cup of tea Bid?,' she says 'and Paddy, I have a lovely apple tart for you'. I smile and say, 'thank you Auntie Nora'. Because if I don't say the 'thank you Auntie Nora' bit I'll get the box in the ear followed by, 'aren't you going to say thank you to your Auntie Nora for making you the lovely apple tart?,' And Auntie Nora will say; 'ah sure Bid, don't be hitting him, he's only a child', but Auntie Nora would do the same to her daughter Marie if Marie didn't do the thank you routine to my mother. 'Is that all I'm getting, a lousy ould apple tart, I can't put that in my pocket?'

'Oh I nearly forgot we'll have to give you something on this very special day, your very first Holy Communion Paddy'.

Great, she's making her way over to the mantelpiece; she's opening the purse and takes out a half-crown. I have to be nice and mannerly and say 'No it's ok Auntie Nora' and not put out my hand. But she will say, 'come on now Paddy', and I'll say, 'no, no, it's alright Auntie Nora' but if that two and six doesn't get into my pocket because of all this pretending I'm doing, that's making Mam very proud that I'm such a well behaved young man, I'll kill myself. So I eventually give in and take the half-crown and I stuff the lovely apple tart down my throat. It's the first time I'm not really interested in Auntie Nora's lovely apple pie, the best I've ever tasted. Small slim pastry full of apples, not like Mam's all pastry and hardly any apples at all. I want to get out of here fast to the next call. Mam and Auntie Nora are going to be here all day talking. I have money to collect, so I better think of something to get her out of here fast.

But before I have time to think, Mam stands up and says: 'We better go Nora, I have to take Paddy to a good few relatives and we have lots of walking to do'. Mam says we're off down to Shannon Street to see Aunt Sis, Pop's eldest sister and her husband Uncle Frank. They have a fish shop down there. I don't remember them and this is great because it means an extra few bob. When we go down there there's no sign of Aunt Sis, but there's a man leaning against the front door of the shop, he's wearing a long white coat.

'Hello Frank', says Mam. 'Harry told me to be sure to bring Paddy down to see you and Sis'.

'She's not here at the moment', says Frank.

'Ah Janie, I'm getting nothing here' I'm saying to myself. 'But let me see if I have something to give this fine young man'. He takes out a bunch of coins from his pocket, there's pennies, two bobs, sixpences, thruppence(s), tuppence(s) and a load of half-crowns. I'll surely get one of those, and that will be five bob in the pocket and lots of aunts and uncles still to call on. 'Here now young man', he says, taking a brass thruppenny bit and putting it into the palm of my hand. The dirty old louser! I can hear one of Pop's sayings coming into my head. He'd say 'that you may die of the dry rot, you miserable ould flute' but I have to be the well behaved boy again; otherwise I'll get the box in the ear. So I say 'thank you very much Uncle Frank'. 'I'll tell Sis you called', says Frank, and as we're walking away Mam is talking to herself. I think she's saying 'What the hell did we come down here for at all?,' As we get to the corner of Shannon Street and O'Connell Street, there's a woman calling, 'Bid, wait a minute, Bid. But when we stop and turn around Mam says 'Hello Sis, we were just down at the shop; Harry said I was to be sure and call in to see you'. Sis says she got back to the shop as we were half way up the street. She's out of breath.

She's telling Mam she's very embarrassed at her husband Frank giving the young boy a miserable thruppence. 'God, but isn't he a grand lad, not a bit like Har, more like your side of the family Bid'. And I'm saying a small prayer to God thanking him for not giving me looks like my father. She lifts up her handbag and I'm thinking I'm going to get another lousy thruppence here. But my mouth drops when she puts two half-crowns into my hand. I'm so shocked I forget to do the 'thank you very much' bit. I'm speechless, but I wake up fast when I get the wallop in the ear, with the words, 'are you not going to say thank you to your Aunt Sis who's after giving you a whole five shillings at all?'

I have seven shillings and thruppence in my pocket. My ear is ringing like crazy. I say with a big smile, 'I'm sorry Auntie Sis, thank you very much' and Sis says 'Jesus Bid will you don't be hitting the poor lad, I'm sure he's in shock after what he got from that husband of mine, making a holy show of me like that'. Now they're talking about something else and I have to hang around 'til they're finished, it seems I have to put up with this every time we call on an aunt or an uncle. They're finished now and Mam says it's Pop's two sisters next. They're living on the second floor of a big house in Thomas Street.

Its Auntie Ann and Auntie Kathleen. Mam says I'm not to take too much from them, they are widows. When I ask her what widows are, she says a widow is a woman who has lost her husband. I'm trying to figure out how a woman can loose her husband. Did he go out for a walk, get lost and never come home again. I hadn't time to figure it out as Mam is ringing the bell of the front door. When the door opens, there's a very tall woman behind it. She's very pretty. She's got bright red lipstick, black hair and a big smile. 'Hello Bid', she says, putting her arms around Mam. They must be good friends. Aunt Sis didn't do that to Mam at all. I'll get more money here because of that. 'Who have we here now?,' says Auntie Ann. 'Don't tell me, it has to be Paddy'.

I'm smiling away, trying very hard to be the shy, good man-nered boy with the head down and the shoulders turning from side to side, trying to see if she has any pockets, because there's no sign of a handbag. That must be upstairs. The last time I saw you, sure you were in the pram in Bedford Row. 'Do you remember that Bid?' Mam is nodding the head saying 'I do indeed'. Auntie Ann says to Mam, 'don't they grow up very quick Bid, where have the years gone at all? Come on upstairs, Kathleen will be delighted to see the two of ye'. After climbing the three flights of stairs, we're taken into a huge room with a very high ceiling. 'I'll be out in a minute', answers a voice from another room, after Auntie Ann shouts, 'come on out, Harry's eldest son Paddy has made his First Communion today and Bid has brought him up to see us'.

When she comes out, it's another pretty woman. She's got blue hair and lots of stuff on her face. 'I don't believe it', she says, 'that couldn't be Harry's son. Harry doesn't have a son that big'.

I'm moving the shoulders again from one side to the other, the head is down with the innocent shy smile, the eyes wandering everywhere, scouring the tabletops, shelves, floors for any sign of handbags, or purses, watching the movements of the two aunts and what their hands are doing all the time. 'Are you going to be a painter like my baby brother, when you grow up young man?,' Auntie Kathleen says. I'm confused and don't answer. Mam gives me another box in the ear again, while saying 'Answer your Auntie Kathleen when she's talking to you'.

'Ah don't be doing that Bid', says Auntie Ann. My brain is working overtime. Aunt Kathleen comes over and gives me a hug. If I can shed a tear and say something I might get two half-crowns here. And then I'll have a whole twelve shillings and thruppence in the pocket. So I squeeze out a tear and say, 'I don't know Auntie Kathleen who your baby brother is' and it works perfectly! 'Ah sure God love him Bid, sure it's all my fault for opening my big mouth about my baby brother'. She tells me her baby brother is my Pop, and I never thought of my Pop as a baby before.

Then the two of them are trying to beat each other for the purse, this isn't working out the way I planned at all. 'I'll give it to him', says Aunt Ann. 'No, no I'll give it to him', says Aunt

Kathleen, and I'm thinking 'can't ye both give it to me?,' And Auntie Ann reaches me first. I'm doing the usual performance walking backwards with the hand behind the back, saying, 'no, no, no, it's alright, it's alright,' and then Auntie Kathleen is at me to put out my hand and take it, so when I put out the hand they both put a half-crown into it and yes, I have twelve shillings and thruppence. And it's the 'will you have a cup of tea Bid?,' all over again and I have to listen to the three of them talking about whose dead, who's nearly dead, who's got a baby, who's got a job, who got married, how's Har doing, has he plenty of work, how long is he off the drink, any sign of a new house from the Corporation and when they're finished Mam will take me down to Maureen Dennehy in Bedford Row.

She's too busy to talk to Mam because there are lots of people in the pub. But I get another five bob and wow! I'm in business. Now I have seventeen shillings and thruppence. Then it's down to Clare Street to Auntie Mary.

Mam says: 'Auntie Mary lost her husband too' and I'm wondering why do all my aunts keep loosing their husbands, especially when I need them at home to see me make my First Communion, and get the extra few bob.

When we get down to Aunt Mary's house there's lots of sand, blocks and wood in the garden. The door is open and we can hear banging out the back. Mam is standing in the hallway, she's shouting 'hello Mary, are you home? it's Bid' 'Come on Bid,' comes an answer 'excuse the mess', and out comes a small woman with silver grey hair. Mam says, 'It's Pop's sister'.

'Well who have we here? I know you're Paddy aren't you?,' I'm nodding the head with the big innocent smile again. Someone is cutting wood out the back of the house. 'Are you going to be a builder like your Dad when you grow up?,' asks Auntie Mary. I nod my head and say 'yes'. 'I bet he could do with your help here today', she says. When I look out the window there's Pop putting a long piece of wood on top of the roof. He's building a new room for Aunt Mary. She sticks her head out the window and shouts, 'Are you going to come down and say hello to your wife and son Harry?,' My Dad can build walls and roofs. I want to be like him when I grow up. But I'm forgetting about the collection; Pop comes down from the roof as Aunt Mary tells him 'it's time for a cup of tea'. She gives me a glass of orange juice with a lovely cream bun and I'm hoping that's not all I'm going to get. 'Paddy says he wants to be a builder like you Harry', says Auntie Mary. And Pop says I'll have to be good at school or I won't be able to add or subtract for all the measurements I'll have to do when I go to work with him. 'Oh I'm sure he'll do very well', says Auntie Mary, as she puts the tea on the table and I'm thinking if Mam drinks anymore tea she'll burst. 'Come over here until I give you something for making your First Holy Communion' and I'm off again doing the routine. 'Don't be giving that fellow any money now', says Pop. 'I don't think Auntie Mary was ready to give me any money yet, she was taking out a large packet of sweets for me, but when Pop said that, she changed direction and went over to her handbag, picked it up and took out the purse, and pulled out a pound note. My heart stopped, I said to myself, 'Janey! A whole pound! That will be one pound seventeen shillings and thruppence in the pocket!'

But she only took out the pound note first because it was in the way of her change. She hands me a half crown and now I only have nineteen shillings and nine pence and with the disappointment of not getting the pound note I nearly forget to say thank you. It was just as well I thought of it because I'm standing right along side Pop and if I got the box in the ear from him I'd be unconscious by now. Aunt Mary gives Mam a guided tour around the new extension. It doesn't take long, and while they're talking outside Pop is asking me how much I got from all the aunts so far. When I tell him I ask him how old I'll have to be before I can go working with him. 'Oh we'll have to see,' he says. 'You know it all depends on how good you are at school'. I'm asking did he do all that himself and where did he learn to do that kind of work. He no sooner answers one question when I have another half dozen more. So when we leave it's up to Auntie Maura's in High Street to Hogan's Restaurant. I'm asking Mam did Auntie Maura's husband get lost as well. She says 'Auntie Maura never got married', and when I ask her why she said she didn't know. Auntie Maura is telling me how gorgeous I am. She's giving me a bun from under the glass counter and says she has to go and get her handbag but then changes her mind, takes a half-crown from the till and says she can put it back later. Now I have one pound two shillings and thruppence in the pocket and things are going much better than I planned. Mam says we'll have to get the bus to Rathbane and Janesborough because her legs are killing her. There's more aunts and one uncle out there and by the time we get home I have two pounds ten shillings in my inside pocket. Jet and James are waiting to see how much I have, she'll have to get ten shillings, James five bob, and I can have the rest to myself. I'm rich. Jet says, 'We should put some of our money aside for birthday presents when Pop, Nan and Mam's birthday comes around in November and December' and I agree. We do it every year. Mam tells us in August to put our pennies away to buy a present for Pop in October. Nan is next one month later in November and five weeks after that its Mam's turn. So Mam will look after the money for Pop and Nan while Jet will look after the money for Mam. Every year Pop will get a packet of cigarettes, a scarf or a pair of gloves. Mam will get the same.

Nan gets a rosary beads or a prayer book because we think she might die any day now and must be getting sick and tired of saying the same old prayers. There's hardly any beads left on her rosary. But it gives us a great feeling of unity and doing things together.

Sr. Rachel isn't as bad now that I've made my Communion. About fifteen years ago I passed by the Presentation School and decided to go in and see whatever happened to her. There has been a lot of changes here since my time, there's hardly any nuns at all to be seen, there's an office in the old stone building that used to house all the nuns, and when I asked if anyone knew or could tell me, if Sr. Rachel was alive or dead. I nearly fell on the floor when I was told 'she could be found in the cloakroom in half an hour'.

Surely they were mistaken. She couldn't be alive; it must be another Sr. Rachel. When I went to the cloakroom a half an hour later, there she was, the very same Sr. Rachel. No white starch around the face, no black veil flowing down from the head and no large crucifix with the big beads hanging from the waist. She has her head down pulling at something with her hands. I say the words, 'I can't believe you're still here'. When she raises her head, there they are, the fiery eyes, but they're softer now and so are the blood red cheeks. She's as fresh as the day I can remember her. She smiles as I say, 'I don't suppose you remember me?'

'Well you'll have to tell me your name and we'll see', she answers.

'Taylor' I say. Her smile widens, 'Indeed I do'.

'Really?' I say.

'Absolutely,' she says. 'There weren't many of ye by that name in this school at that time' I change the subject and say, 'There's been a lot of changes since I was here'.

She sighs heavily. 'You're right! I never thought I'd see the day when our church would be turned into a club for the local gárdaí. It's downright disgraceful and I don't think I'll ever get over it'.

She asks me what kind of work I'm doing now, how many kids I have, how old they were, did they come to this school when they were young, would they have been in her class and when we ran out of things to talk about I said goodbye and thought what a lovely person and how glad I was to see her. It would change my view of those early memories of her in First Communion Class.

My next teacher was another nun, Sr. Berkman, a lovely fun person, kind and helpful, nothing to write about in this class until I moved next door to the Christian Brothers Sexton Street. There'll be plenty to write about here.

I will come here every day with the fear factor very much on my mind, punishment will be heavy for not having the right answer to anything and some will administer it more than others. There are four grades, A, B, C and D. And my understanding of those grades were that A was for the super intelligent, B for the very intelligent, C was for the intelligent and D. There was no lower than D. This was for the hopeless cases or those who can't be taught anything. It was to the hopeless cases I was sent to. Half of them shouldn't be here at all, as they were too intelligent and I never understood why they were in the class for Eejits like me.

From the small bungalow type classroom at the end of the school yard comes the short baldy headed dirty article who called himself a teacher; and whose only interest in us was what was in our short pants. 'Come up here', he'd say, pointing at one of us who might be lucky enough to be sitting in the front row and 'read that out loud to the class.' It's my first grade in CBS but it's called second class and I have no idea why. When the winter mornings come, I'll be in the front row praying that he will point to me and call me up. And when he does, I'll run over with a big smile on my face because he'll have his lovely warm hands all over my thighs and sometimes up around my bottom. I'll be between his legs at his desk, while he sits on his chair with his chin on my shoulder, reading aloud as slowly as I can. I won't want him to stop as I'll have goose pimples everywhere. I won't want him to stop in the spring and summer either as it's too nice. He's a pervert and we're too young to know. He never went any further, well, not with me. He has a long wooden stick taken from the back of a chair and whacks us in the palms of our hands for nothing. And the guy that sits next to me with the chilblains in his hands begging him to be careful where he lands the stick, but it's always a waste of time.

Then it's to the other end of the same block for third class, and the Christian Brother who must have hated teaching, because of his temper and antics. Did he come from a large family and told of his vocation by his parents like many that we thought followed the call of Edmund Rice, who if the family were smaller, might have been a doctor, a priest, a solicitor or left the family farm? I think so. Brothers of Christ they liked to be called, but acted like children of Satan. We think he's a man because of his height, but he's only a boy. But not as bad as the school head, the small baldy brother with the gut of a pregnant woman in her final days. A bad egg, if ever there was one, strutting around all day with the hands behind his back and making no effort to pull in the five or six stone he is carrying around on the front of his frame. He'll walk from class to class, turning the knob of each door in slow motion and then swinging it gently open to the sound of its squeaking hinges. He won't come in until the door is fully open and against the wall. Then it's enter the gut and ten minutes later the rest that's stuck to it. He won't say anything, only look around giving everyone a suspicious look, including the teacher. And slowly making his way out in the same manner he came in before he's back again tomorrow or It might be days or weeks before he'll visit again with the same routine. He'll wait at the side of the old four storey stone building every morning for those who are late and give them the leather across the palm of both hands so we won't be late again. He'll ask us why we're late but it won't make any difference what the excuse is, and after my first week in third class I'm late and stuck in a queue. He's smiling away with the leather out flexing it up and down on the palm of his hand, gently of course. His smile turns to disappointment as the queue increases in number. He counts us out one by one and says, 'there's too much of ye to wallop.' And we're to be sure and tell our teachers to do the leathering and we're not to even think about forgetting. There'll be no forgetting with me. I'm telling no one anything. I've seen the leather, it's my first time and I don't like the look of it. There are shoes and legs scattering in all directions accompanied by whispers of 'I'm telling my teacher nothing.' They'll want to know why we're late and now that I'm inside the door with my Christian teacher looking at me waiting for an answer to the question why I am late, the whole class wants to know why I'm late. They'll be wondering what he's going to do to me and so am I. Am I going to be the first in class to experience the pain of the dreaded leather? Surely it's down to what I'll say next. There's a change of plan. If I tell him the truth he'll surely say, 'for being so honest I'll let you off this time, but if it happens again you'll get two of the best', so out it comes.

'I slept it out Brother and the Headmaster caught loads of us. He said there were too many and he'd be exhausted if he walloped the lot of us and we were to report to our teachers for the punishment'. I've said the whole lot with a pleasant smile and a soft confident voice, trying to convey my trust in his good judgement. Boy! Am I in for a surprise! I should have stuttered through the whole lot and shook while delivering the speech.

'Come over here', he says while reaching down into his pocket for the leather. My heart sinks with disappointment. He's going to wallop me, the dirty rotten louser after I told him the truth. That'll be the last time I'll tell the louser anything. And after getting the wallop in each hand with my mouth opening as big as I could get it in anticipation of the wallop my hands are throbbing like crazy. This is much worse than the louser's stick in our last class and with my brain and little intelligence my hands are going to be twice their size in ten months time. I'll have the fear everyday. We'll all have the fear everyday. I don't know where to put my hands the pain is so bad. I can see the glaring red skin moving on each hand to the rhythm of my heartbeats and I think an egg could be fried on them, they're so hot! There's tears streaming down my face, the lads are looking at me. I know they're in dread of this leather. We heard about it from lads in other classes, but this is September and when the cold frosty mornings come, the pain will be twice as bad.

To ease the pain of learning and the making of mistakes our Christian teacher will get a good supply of comics every day; the kind that he found in Lenny Holman's schoolbag. The coloured American Dell comics like Superman, Batman and Spiderman. Sure everyone's bag in CBS Sexton Street has the Dell comics. We can swap them with others at the break each day, but now we'll be swapping to keep him occupied with his head in the drawer. He won't want the Gut to catch him or see the twenty or thirty he has there either. And there it is the slow turning of the knob followed by the squeaking hinge. The sound of the drawer with the comics closing, the teacher's call to finish what we're doing and then watching the black gut with the gown coming through the door frame. It looks at me with my hands between my legs, then under my arms looking for a place, any place to put them that might make the pain go away. He says looking at the teacher, 'Did that fellow tell you he was late this morning?,' and now I'm glad I opened my mouth and told the truth and the lads will think I'm not so stupid after all, because I don't know how I could handle the pain of being walloped twice on each hand. Has he gone 'round to all the other classes to check on the other lads that were late this morning? Sure he's got a memory like an elephant; he'll remember every face that was out there and if they haven't told their teacher I bet they're sorry now.

'Yes he did', says our Christian teacher.

'Very good', he'll say and out he'll go with our teacher's face white as a sheet with the shock of nearly being caught with his head in the drawer. He'll get completely lost when his head is there.

He tells us a bus will arrive at our school today around lunch-time. It will have young boys our own age from a place I never heard of before called Hungary. There will be four of them coming into every class. He says we're to keep away from them and when we ask why he says 'they're communists that's why. They don't believe in God, nobody over there believes in God'. He shows us on the map where Hungary is, how that country and Russia are next door neighbours and how the people in Hungary used to believe in God before the Russians moved in. They'll be moving in here if we're not careful, sure they're trying to take over the whole world, and if they do, there will be no one believing in God at all, so you're to keep well away from them, do you hear me talking to you?'

And we all say together, 'Yes Brother.' But it's easy to keep away from them. Sure nobody understands a word they're saying. They'll sit in class every day bored out of their skulls and meet at the breaks with their fellow countrymen down in a corner of the school yard. It feels like we're their enemy the way they look at us with their cold piercing eyes. We're too young to know or understand the things those eyes might have seen back in their own homeland and our Christian teacher is too stupid to realise it too.

We have religious instruction every day at twelve o'clock and today those lads are going to wish they were back in Hungary and under the terror of the Commies from Russia. Our Christian teacher is telling us how God made the world in six days and on the seventh day he rested and it's a mortal sin to work on the Sabbath which is Sunday. There's laughter in the corner, it's from the Commie boys and our Christian teacher thinks they're laughing at him. There's a roar from his mouth that shakes us all into shock. He runs to the corner dragging one of them by the neck of his corduroy jacket. There's tiny spits flying in all directions from his mouth as he shouts out the words, 'So you think it's funny to believe in God do you?' He's got the leather out waving it in the air. He keeps shouting with the spits, 'answer me when I'm speaking to you'. He strikes the young lad on the legs waiting for an answer but there isn't one. Does the poor chap understand? I don't think so! He keeps shouting while hitting the lad and saying, 'You'll believe in God when I'm finished with you.' The poor lad is in a terrible state and so are his countrymen in the corner. They are shouting out words in a language we have never heard before, but we all know what they're trying to say. Our Christian teacher is out of control now, is red faced and getting hoarse from all the shouting with beads of sweat flying off his head that accompanied the spits. It's all over now. Our Christian teacher is at his desk, his chest heaving in and out trying to give his lungs the air they need with his head in his hands. The whole class is terrified with the poor Commie lad lying on the floor crying his eyes out and black and blue from all the thumps and wallops. He won't be able to go to a home tonight that has parents who could console and comfort him. Maybe they're dead, but he should be consoled and looked after wherever he goes tonight. After all he's in a country full of Christians isn't he? My heart won't stop pounding out the beats in my chest and I'm thinking is this how Jesus instructed his apostles when they went around preaching The Good News?

Next week our Christian teacher will talk to us about kindness, mercy and love, but his words will be very hard to swallow.

And before we know it, the ten months have gone. It's summer time again. I was right. My hands are twice their size, but we've got eight weeks and the fear will be gone until September comes with the terror back in my stomach. My hands will be back to their normal size. It will be a waste of time trying to figure out who our next teacher is. We know we've had it easy with the Christian teacher with his head in the drawer for nearly six of the ten months but here we are in the yard, all by ourselves with no classroom or teacher either, with every class room in the school full except the one on the bottom left of the main stone building. But the Brother with the gut tells us to stop loitering around and get to class.

'Who's our new teacher?,' asks Lenny Holman. 'You'll know soon enough, go on, get on with you'. We're in the old four storey building for the first time. It's the bottom far left room and it's 10.15 and we still have no teacher. But who cares, we've nothing to do and we can do this all day and tomorrow too.

Then there's a sudden burst of a door opening in haste and Janie Mac it's him, the Christian teacher! What the hell is he doing here? We couldn't have him again, could we? He's got a big red head on him, he looks like the time he gave that Hungarian boy an awful beating. He's put the fear of God into us, we're stunned into silence.

He's pacing to and fro across the classroom floor. He's muttering away to himself. He looks at all of us like he hates each and everyone. He shouts an announcement. 'You'll be pleased to know you got me for another twelve months, but you won't be pleased to know that I'm not happy about it. I thought I got rid of you Eejits last July, I was looking forward to getting a class that had pupils with brains, boys with some kind of desire to want to learn, only half of you want to learn and the other half want to keep me fed with comics so you can do what you bloody well like, but no other teacher would take you and I have to do what I'm told.'

So he rants away all day banging this and thumping that, getting out the leather strap for the smallest of reasons and walloping anyone who got in his way. But it's only a matter of time before he's back to the Dell comics and Class 4D will be the very same as last year and the summer holidays have come again and it's goodbye to the fear factor.

When September comes there's no possible way we could have the Christian teacher again. We're back in the yard. Roger Browne says we're getting Spud Murphy for fifth class, the geriatric half-way-down-the-road-to-Alzheimer's pensioner, could it get any better? He's been in the school for years, he should have retired years ago, he won't remember half our names, and he won't remember that he's given us homework either. We'll be able to teach him and best of all it's the class with the school clock on the wall of the main building. There's a small wooden door at the back of the clock to wind it up everyday to keep the time. This is the class with the bell to start and finish school and some days I'll have the power to bring every class in CBS Sexton Street to a finish in the evening, to a start in the morning, or to call for lunch-time. So it's another twelve months doss but Murphy would stay in my brain for one day of that term.

There's a guy in our class. He's like half of us here, he's got some kind of learning disorder, but in those days there was no such thing as a learning disorder. You were either intelligent or stupid. But with Murphy this poor young lad's problem is going to stick out like a sore thumb. This lad cannot tell the difference between the letter 'B' or the letter 'P' and when Murphy realises it he'll see this poor misfortune as completely stupid, and the best way to help him is to humiliate him regularly before the whole class. 'Stand up', Lynchie, he'll say. Now Lynchie is not the name of this guy and for obvious reasons I can't mention his name. Lynchie rises to his feet. He's one foot taller than Murphy. He's one foot taller than all the rest of us. Murphy looks up at him. 'Spell plate'. Lynchie' starts stuttering out the pronouncement, beginning with the 'B' sound. He's watching Murphy's face for a reaction. He'll know by it whether he's right or wrong. And when Murphy does react with a look of disapproval Lynchie will simply stop stuttering and spell the word with a 'P', but Murphy will soon see what Lynchie is doing and will change his reaction to no reaction at all and there's poor Lynchie, struggling away having no idea which letter to use. He'll have to guess, and gets it wrong most of the time. There's the embarrassment, the humiliation of the wallop across the face when he gets it wrong again and again, week in, week out until Lynchie can take no more and explodes. How did he take it this long?

He grabs Murphy by the throat with both hands, drags him across the floor against the blackboard, and hangs Murphy's head repeatedly off the board. Lynchie is screaming at the teacher 'leave me alone; leave me alone, I don't know whether these words begin with a 'P' or a 'B'. You keep asking me and I just don't know, why do you keep hitting me?,' Murphy is gone snow white trying to get Lynchie's hands off his throat but he can't. Lynchie releases his hands and Murphy falls to the floor while Lynchie cries uncontrollably. Murphy stands to his fee and collapses into his chair exhausted and gasping for breath. We're all thinking Lynchie is in big rouble now. But when Mur phy dismisses the class tht day, he never opens his mouth to Lynhie aai.

CHAPTER 8

I seldom buy a newspaper and when I do it's the sport pages I'll turn to. After finding one or two items of interest, it's a quick glance at all the other sections to see if there's anything else, and if there is, that gets a similar fate too. News of what's going on in the world generally comes to my ear by way of any of the three national stations, or if I want to know what's going on locally, then I'll turn my ear to Limerick's Live 95FM. I was surprised after a recent purchase of a national newspaper when an advertisement for a free hearing test fell from between the pages onto the floor, as my hearing is a bit on the dodgy side lately, I decided to contact the free-phone number advertised to make an appointment. I reasoned that after forty years of cutting wood, stone, concrete blocks, walls, etc. that my ears had several tons of leftovers from all these jobs and that all they needed was a good scraping down or some power-hosing.

When I arrived for the appointment at the arranged time, on the appointed day, I only had to wait ten minutes before being called into a very small quiet room. I was with a man of similar size and age to myself. After introducing himself and being asked to take a seat, I was told everybody has six ears, three on one side and three on the other. There's the outer ear, that's the thing that stuck onto either side of my head. It collects the sounds and sends them down to my middle ear which sends them to my inner ear and from there my brain receives a message. Then he asked;

'Do you have problems with your hearing?'

I said ' I do'.

Then he asked me to describe them. I told him if someone is speaking and not facing me, I have to ask them to repeat what they said. Then he asked me would that problem be with a woman's voice or a man's?

'Most definitely a woman's,' I answered.

He then asked if there were other sounds while someone was speaking, would you have difficulty.

'Yes, I said, very much so.'

'Have you any difficulty hearing me?'

I said 'none'.

He said, 'I'm going to do some tests. I want you to turn your back to me. I'm going to say some words in a normal voice and I want you to tell me what you think you heard me say.'

So when I turned my back he started and said;

'Finc' or was it 'wine'? I guessed and said 'fine'. Then he said 'toy' or was it 'boy'? I guessed again and said 'boy'. Then he said 'sack' or was it 'back'? Again I guessed and said 'back'. 'Sure' or 'pure'? 'Sole' or 'whole', 'men' or 'ten', and on and on it went.

'OK that's fine', he said . 'Now I want you to put these headphones on,' which I did, then he handed me an electric cable with a button at the end.

'You will hear very faint beeps at five-second intervals. When you hear them, press the button at the end of the cable you are holding. The sound will get fainter all the time, but only press the button when you hear a sound'.

'OK', he said, 'that's grand! You'll be delighted to know you're not deaf. What you have is a clarity problem'.

'Great!' I said, 'But you must explain what you mean by clarity'.

He told me the base sounds go into my ear but the lighter sounds like that of a woman's voice, which has very little base, doesn't go in at all. Also if we went out into the street now and continued this conversation you wouldn't be able to hear everything I was saying to you because of the traffic. There would be too many base sounds going on and all you hear is a muffle'.

'Correct,' I said.

'Did you ever have mumps when you were very young?'

'I don't know,' I answered.

'You probably had. That's what happens to most people. Anyway it can be corrected. We can fit this tiny hearing aid to your ear, it won't increase the volume, but what it will do is, pick up the lighter sounds. The piece that goes into your ear doesn't fill your ear, it allows the other sounds, the base sounds to go through and it can be modified to pick up the lighter sounds and increase them into your ear, so what you get in your ear is full clarity of all sounds that's going on'.

'Great!' I said, 'How much will that cost?'

'About €2,000.00 per ear, but the Government will pay most of it for you,' he answered.

'Will they, that's very decent of them,' I answered. 'Why would they do that now?,'

'Because of your PRSI,' he said. 'You are employed aren't you?,'

'Oh yes,' I said, 'very much so, but I don't think the Government will be that interested in helping me to have clarity of hearing'.

'Why not'? he asks.

'Because I'm self employed and they reckon I can well afford it'.

'Oh dear', he said, 'that's a pity'.

'Not really', I answered.

'Why is that?,' he asked.

'I'll just keep asking people to repeat themselves. Then they'll be the ones with the problem'.

'Well', he says, 'I suppose that's one way of looking at it'.

'Well, it's the only way I'm going to look at it and thank you very much for your time'.

Another telephone call to Jetta to see whether she knew if I had mumps and after two hours of talk she has no idea. Now I'm wondering could there be any other reason for my hearing difficulties and off go the memory banks in search of anything that might throw some light on this matter. Could my first visit to Barrington's Hospital all those years ago have anything to do with my hearing problem?

'Paddy.'

'Yes Mam'

'Come in off the road, I want to talk to you'.

'Yes Mam'

'Sit down and listen very carefully'.

'Yes Mam'

'Yourself and James have to go to hospital'.

That word hospital has given me some kind of a belt, it feels like my heart has just got a big electric shock and I can't speak.

'We're going to tell James that you have to go to hospital for an operation'.

There it goes again, my heart; wants to jump out of my chest, with those awful words hospital and operation. Mam is telling me that 'James thinks he's going in to mind you, to look after you, so you mustn't let on that he has to have the same operation as well.'

There the heart goes again with that awful 'hospital' word and apart from a cough and a visit to the Doctor in the winter every week since I can remember, there's nothing wrong with me. I want to tell Mam that I'm alright, I'll be fine but the words won't come out. She's telling me how brave I am, how proud of me she is, 'and when Pop comes home tonight he'll be delighted to know how mature you are, how strong his eldest son is, sure you'll only be in there for three days and when you come out I'll have them lovely chocolate cream buns that O'Holloran's shop have on the counter every day.

'Sure it's only a small job, getting your tonsils and adenoids out'.

'My what?,' 'What the hell are they and where are they? And is the Doctor going to cut my belly to get these things out? I'm not staying around here, I'm running away'.

Mam comes over to give me a hug. She's got a big long red scar down the left side of her neck.

Ah Janie that's where those things are, these things have to be cut out of my neck and I'm going to have one of those scars too.

Now I'm in the derelict house, two doors down, stuck in the corner crying. I don't want anyone to see me, especially Mam. I don't want her to think her son is a cry-baby. He is, but she thinks I'm brave. It makes a difference from always being in trouble and I don't want to miss out. When Pop comes home he might have a present for me. I'll wait to get the present first. Then I'll do the crying, it could be months away, and I mightn't have to go at all then as the winter is nearly over and the coughing will be gone soon.

Pop has nothing on his bike for me as he leans it against the wall outside our house. Maybe he'll have something tomorrow as Mam puts the supper on the table. Pop is telling James:

'Your big brother has to go to hospital'.

'Why Pop?' asked James.

'Because he's always coughing and choking; these little things in his throat that make him cough. The nice doctor is going to take them out'.

Oh Jesus! I'm thinking, he's going to rip my neck open, just like Mam's. I was right, and there goes that awful bang again. I'm getting awful nervous.

'Now, you're going to have to go into hospital with Paddy to look after him for us'.

Jim starts to cry and asks 'Why can't you and Mam go in to look after him and I'll stay at home and mind the house?,'

'We can't do that'.

'Why not?,' asked Jim.

'Because the beds are too small, they have no beds for Mams and Dads. Look, here's five bob for you to spend on whatever you want' and poor old Jim swallows the whole pack of lies.

Jim is out on the road showing all the lads his five bob, while Pop puts a ten shilling note into my hand. He says I'm growing up to be a big strong young man, how they'll have no worries about young Jim when the two of us go into hospital tomorrow for the operation. 'Oh sweet Jesus', I'm going in tomorrow. I thought I wasn't going in for another few months'. I'm looking at my cardigan, where I think my heart is. It's jumping all over the place. I think I'm going to die; my head is spinning, making me dizzy. The speech is gone from my mouth again. I'm going to hospital tomorrow to get my throat ripped open. Pop has his big hand on my head, ruffling my hair. He's still telling me how good I am again. I don't want to listen to him. He can take the lousy ten bob back and as for O'Holloran's shop, their chocolate creamy buns can go stale. I've got to get out of here but my legs won't take me. I can hear Mam saying to Pop in a whisper: 'Isn't it great the way he's taking it?,' How she thought there would be blue murder but if I could get the sound to come out of my mouth, if the banging in my chest would only stop and my legs could move, I could arrange the blue murder scene no problem at all. But shock is a strange thing and what it does to a young fellow.

When we go to bed Jim won't shut up talking about the five bob, what he's going to buy with it, how he wants to know where they're going to cut me up and I'm not to worry, because he'll make sure I'll be alright but I can't tell him he's going under the knife too. This is lousy. Why can't Mam and Pop tell us the truth? They're always telling us lies and we believe it every time. They won't explain anything either. It'll be no good me asking Mam why she and Nan have a big rotten ould red scar on their necks? She'll just say, 'that's the why.'

Mam is waking me up, telling me to hurry on and get dressed. We have to be at the hospital for 1.o'clock and Jim is still talking about the five bob. I haven't spoken a word to anyone since I can't remember. I'm not able to. There's the hospital and I think my heart is going to jump out of my chest.

'Come on Paddy, don't be dragging your feet', I can't tell her they're stiff because there's no life in them. The words won't come out to tell her. Mam is waving goodbye. I'm looking at her thinking I thought she loved us. How could she do this? I know I did some stupid bad things, but having me cut open, that's not fair. A Nurse is telling us to take our clothes off, including our underpants. Jim doesn't mind but I do. It's a big ward. There's girls in the ward and the Nurse is shouting, 'come on young man, take your underpants off, we haven't all day'. I can hear a woman's voice out in the corridor. She's shouting,

'I'm looking for Paddy Taylor'.

'He's in here Sister,' shouts the Nurse whose waiting for me to undress.

Oh sweet Jesus, they're going to cut me up now.

'Come on young man, we've a special room for you', and now I'm wondering what have I done to get a special room. What's in there? They're giving me a white dress to wear. It ties up at the back. It's too short for me. The Nurse has me by one hand and I'm trying to hold down this thing they've given me to keep my bits covered with my other hand.

'Look what I have for you now Francey,' says the Nurse. There's a terrible smell in the room that they've taken me to, it has only two beds with a young fellow in the other one. I think the smell is coming from him. His face is badly scarred and there's a big roundy yoke over his legs. Then I hear another Nurse call his full name. Can he be here all that time? It must be two years now, when our last teacher told all the class about a young guy in the same grade as us, who was sitting at home, looking after his young sister late one evening, while his parents were out. He had a blanket thrown over his shoulders to keep himself warm in front of an electric fire. The blanket made contact with the fire and the rest is history. He looks terrible and I have to share a room with that awful smell. We never said a word to each other and then the morning came.

I had never been awake so early before, the suspense of what's going to happen next is unbearable. There are two nurses coming into our room. Oh God no! They've got those silver bowls in their hands. I know what's in those things, its needles and injections. Your man alongside me is starting to cry. He must know what's coming next. He's here long enough to know. A Nurse has already given me the injection. She says: 'Now, now Francis, look at how brave Paddy is, not a word out of him'.

Francis doesn't give a monkey's how brave I am. I'm not brave, Jesus I'm terrified, but the sound has left my mouth again. The whole bloody world thinks I'm brave, and I'm not. I just can't get anything out of my mouth and after that awful sting in my arm I'm feeling very tired. They've gone now and I can hear terrible screams from the big ward.

It's Jimmy. He's in there with all the other guys and girls. They're all crying too. He's shouting at the nurses, 'No, no, you've got the wrong fellow, my name is James, you're looking for my brother Paddy. He's not here. He's out there in another ward. Paddy come in, quick, hurry, they're sticking a big needle in me. Please Paddy tell them, there's a big mistake' there's more screams. Jim is bawling his eyes out and I'm inside in the semi-private room with a pillow over my head trying to blank out the sounds of Jim's pleas. He keeps telling the nurses all the time his name is James, he says he's going to tell his mother and father what they did to him. He's calling me a dirty rotten coward because I won't come out and tell them that he's James. He's calling me a coward because the nurses think I'm Jimmy and I won't have to go to be cut up with the knife and he will. He's asking me all the time to tell them. He's saying it's not fair. 'I only came in here to mind you and look what they're doing to me now. I'll never mind you again, I'll never talk to you again, you dirty rotten louser!'

Now they're taking me down a corridor on a trolley. All I can see are lights on the ceiling and the face of the Nurse who stuck the needle in me, she's nice. She's telling me I'm the only boy in the whole hospital who isn't crying, how I'm the bravest boy in the whole place, in all her time working here. And even if I could cry or open my mouth to make a sound I don't think I would. There's too many thinking, including Mam and Pop that I'm the bravest thing around. Jim is still bawling away. His cries are getting fainter and fainter and now I can't hear him at all because we're in a lift. I can feel the lift going down, then it's into another corridor. There are more lights; we're turning into a room. There's people around me who have masks on their faces. I think I'm going to die; my heart is beating so hard. I better say an Act of Contrition to God because I know I'm going to die. Somebody's grabbed my arm. There's a voice behind a mask, the voice is saying; 'I'm going to count from ten down to one, when I get to four you'll be fast asleep'. There's a pinch in my arm, he starts to count, 10, 9, 8, 7, 6, 5 and I'm gone.

The sun is hurting my eyes. Where am I? I'm back in bed. How did I get here? Where was I? My throat is funny; it's full of sticky stuff. A Nurse is calling me, she's saying 'sure wasn't that no trouble at all now Paddy?,' and then it hits me - the operation! They cut me up. Which side did they cut? I'm feeling my neck with my two hands, on both sides, there's no bandage, there's no cuts. I jump out of the bed. There's a mirror beside it. There's no scars like Mam, why is that? The Nurse hands me a silver bowl. 'Now Paddy,' she says, 'you've to spit all that mucus into this'. I'm trying to ask her what is mucus. She seems to know what I'm trying to say. 'That sticky stuff in your throat, that's where you had your operation.' I'm trying to ask her why there's no scar, she doesn't understand. What did they take out and then I get an almighty fright - they've taken my voice away, I'll never talk again, why didn't they ask me first, I didn't mind all the coughing and choking in the winter. I'm able to cry now and the Nurse is back asking me what's wrong?

'How come the only boy in the whole hospital that wasn't crying before is crying now, when nobody else is?,' I'm pointing to my throat, I can't talk. I'm trying to ask her why did that monster of a doctor take away my voice. She doesn't understand, but says 'Paddy you won't be able to talk for another few days, because the Doctor had to reach down into your throat to get those nasty tonsils and adenoids out that were giving you that awful cough all the time.'

That cheers me up and things are looking better. You're going home tomorrow,' she says and I'll be able to spend my ten bob and Mam will have the chocolate creamy buns as well.

'Did you get the chocolate buns Mam?'

'I did,' she answers, 'they're at home on the table waiting for you'.

'Have you got the ten bob Mam that you were minding for me? I want to buy something in the shop Mam' and Mam says I'll have to forget about the ten bob.

'Your father has no work and I had to use the money to put food on the table.'

Now I'm bawling and saying 'Ah Janie, that's lousy. I've had to lie to Jimmy; he won't talk to me anymore since the operation. I thought I was going to die, then I thought my voice was gone forever. I thought I was going to have a big dirty rotten lousy red scar on my neck, like you and Nan. James still has his five bob and I can't eat the lousy cream buns, over the lousy stuff in my throat, because there's no taste in my mouth, and it's not fair!'

It's that lousy doctor down at the City Dispensary. It's all his fault. He's the one who told Mam I should be in the hospital. Every week she brings me to him with my snotty nose and the awful cough. What's wrong with him anyway? He's supposed to be a Doctor. Why is he always dropping his mouth open and closing it again? Why is his hand always shaking? And his skin colour, it's always snow white? He should go and see a Doctor. We should go and see the Doctor he should go and see. He's a monster. Pop calls him Dr. Jekyll whoever he is. I keep telling Mam I'm going to get sick because of that piece of wood he keeps shoving down my throat, every time we go to see him Everybody shouts in here. There's doctors everywhere, there's rooms everywhere. When it's your turn they don't say, 'OK Mrs. Taylor, you can come in now'. They shout 'Taylor'. What kind of a place is this? There's every kind of germ in here, it's a wonder Mam comes here at all. There's children crying, coughing, choking and gawking, there's people farting and praying that they won't die, or they won't have to go to hospital and go under the knife. The man behind the hole in the wall, is banging bottles and pills on the counter while shouting everybody's names. Mam's doing everything but genuflecting. 'Yes Doctor. Of course Doctor. Whatever you say Doctor.' and if you tell me to go jump in the river I'll do it, of course Doctor. Right away, Doctor. The medical card has to be signed first. Then it's 'come over here.'

His hands are shaking again, they're big and soft. 'Tongue out, tongue out' he says. Then he rams the wooden thing down my throat. I can hardly breathe. 'Wider, wider,' he shouts. He's poking away, what the hell is he looking for anyway? He's lifting me up with his hands by the gob. I'm on my toes. I can feel it coming. I told Mam but she wouldn't listen. He's got a smashing white shirt and a black suit. If he doesn't take that thing out of my throat quick he's going to have my breakfast and yesterday's dinner all over it; but he won't. And out it comes. The biggest technicolour yawn I've ever had in my life, right into the fly of his pants. Off goes Mam with the apologies. 'Oh Doctor, Doctor, I'm so sorry'. I'm trying to tell Mam I told you so but she gives me a wallop in the ear, and says, 'Wait till I get you home making a holy show of me, I'll never be able to show my face in here again'. As we walk home up Tanyard Lane she's giving me the odd clout in the ear and calling down the Holy Family.

The following winter would see the same cough return, the same sniffles. It would be as bad as ever, and I'm asking Mam why that louser of a doctor took those yokes out of my throat at all. Sure wasn't I supposed to have no coughs or colds after all she put me through, James is the same but not as bad. She says she doesn't know, but doctors do, that's why they're doctors. So I ask her when I'm sick again can I go to another doctor because I don't want anymore things taken out. 'You'll do as you're told!' she says. We go back again every week but he's keeping well away from me with the wooden yoke. He just gives Mam the prescription for the bottle from the man who shouts 'Taylor' and bangs it on the counter.

And so the search goes on in my head. Did I get the mumps? I don't think that hospital experience had anything to do with my hearing problem, but is there something else I've forgotten? I'll just have to see if I can jog the memory some way. Maybe go back and visit Upper Carey's Road to see if I can trigger the memory cells. But it doesn't. I'm here - maybe four times a week driving my van to and from work, from the bottom of the hill where the bridge was, now gone, the long wall to the left, its height of fourteen feet gets slowly smaller as I reach Dermot Lynch's house. He and Christy Davis are the only living residents of the old Carey's Road still residing here in the new houses. Ford's Pub now the Imperial Bar, the building still intact has small changes. There's the wall with the entrance to Dinny McGrath's house, long since blocked up. Across the road, another stone wall from one bridge to another that housed CIE workers. I turn to drive back down again and as much as I try there's nothing. Maybe I should get out and walk around and when I do, I'm standing in the middle of what used to be Nix's field, now a small green across from Dermot Lynch's house. There's a memory alright.

It's Fonsey Meade. He has a hurley in his hand. He lifts it to hit the sliotar and as he throws the hurley back, I'm standing right behind him and get a wallop into the right side of the gob. My teeth, all of them, seem to move several times with the box he gives me. I'm sure my teeth are going to fall out but they don't. That's it, not another memory. I'll take a look at that photograph at home, the one that has Jetta running up the road, with Noelie Graces' father looking up at the camera. That's sure to get the memory juices flowing. But when I do come home and take it out, it doesn't stir anything at all. So I just have to accept the fact that I got the mumps when I was a kid.

Weeks later there's a telephone call from Jimmy; I just happened to mention Carey's Road, the broken presents, and the stories. He tells me things he remembers and I tell him about my visit to the ear specialist, the results and also how it could be the mumps. He knows I started writing some years ago and how those things are on my mind constantly, like a lot of other things that won't leave me alone. Maybe the concentration levels have been affected with all the wallops I got at school and from Mam. Did that affect my hearing? I'll have to try and concentrate on the other stories, maybe as I'm writing it might trigger something, but I have to wait a long time, a year maybe and a simple comment from Jetta, that's it. It has to be.

Jetta said, 'You were an awful man for taking things apart'.
'He still is,' says Mary.
'Oh he'd play with something for an hour or two; then he'd be borrowing Pop's tools to pull things apart and then try to put them back together again'.

Jetta said I took apart the best doll she ever got just to see what made the doll cry, and he couldn't put it back together again. It would take a while, but later that day there's a memory, one I'd forgotten. Could this be the cause of my bad hearing? How could I have forgotten this one and what it led to? it wasn't too long after my hospital experience.

I wanted to know how far down my throat the tonsils were and how that monster of a doctor got them out and what kind of tools did he use? Why was there no blood? I want to be a doctor when I grow up. I want to make people better. I want to see and understand how things in the body work. And today Jimmy is going to help me.

He's asking why I want him to go into the derelict house two doors down. I have to find out how something works. I want to see what happens when you do a number two. Now he wants to know what I want him for. 'Because you are going to help me' I answer. Jimmy is scratching his head and asking how he's going to help me. I'm telling him by pulling down your pants. But he won't pull down his pants unless I give him a penny. I tell him I don't have a penny but I promise to give him my penny from Christy Davis across the road tomorrow when it's my turn to bring over the potato skins for the pigs after our dinner. Jimmy says he'll have to clear a level space on the ground of the derelict house, as it's full of broken slates, rotten timber, rusty nails, red bricks, loads of old mortar and bits of broken china. He doesn't want to fall over and cut his ass. He won't take his pants down and when I ask why, he says he's afraid some one might see through where the old window and door used to be. So I look out and tell him there's no chance of anyone seeing him because there's no one on the road. Now he tells me he doesn't need to go to the toilet that I'll have to wait until tomorrow. So I tell him he'll get another penny from Christy Davis when it's my turn again to take the skins over the second time. So down goes the pants and I tell him to bend over.

'Go on', I'm shouting, 'You'll have to push!'

'I'm trying to,' he's shouting back.

'Well try harder then,' I'm shouting.

I'm looking up his bum trying to balance my feet on all the broken slates.

'Is there anything coming?,' shouts Jim.

'No, nothing at all, you're getting no money unless you go'.

'Ah that's lousy' Jimmy answers. 'That's not fair', as he pulls his short pants up around his waist, 'well I'm going home so!'

'OK, OK, I'll give you the two pennies,' so Jimmy drops the pants, bends over and starts pushing again.

'Come on, come on, you can do it, you can do it,' I'm shouting.

'Mrs. Taylor, Mrs. Taylor, come out quick Mrs. Taylor'.

It's Mrs. Storan our next door neighbour. She's heard all the commotion from the derelict house, which is right next door to hers.

'What's wrong Mrs. Storan?,' asks Mam.

'Oh Mrs. Taylor, its Paddy and James'.

'What's wrong Mrs. Storan? Have they been knocked down by a motor car?,'

'Oh no Mrs. Taylor, it's much worse than that! You will have to come and see for yourself' and Mam can hear me shouting, 'go on keep going, go on, go on, wow! Look at that!

'Can you see, can you see?' says Jimmy.

'Yeah, yeah I can' and then I get a box into the side of the ear that puts my flying against the wall. I'm cut and tore from slates, nails and glass. There's a ringing in my ear the part that's sticking out is throbbing away. After Mam gives me the box, she lifts her leg up, giving Jim's ass a kick and sending him flying into what was once the fireplace and full of soot.

'Jesus, Mary and Holy St. Joseph, what am I rearing at all? Ye dirty filthy articles! Get into the house now'.

Jimmy and I are ducking Mam's hands and feet. They're flying in all directions, trying to hit us, but we don't want another one of those thumps.

'Wait till your father comes home today, you'll get it.'

'Ah Mam, I only wanted to find out what happened when you go to the toilet, that's all Mam.'

I don't know how she managed to do it, but she must have flown across the rubble like a bird. She wasn't hitting us because of our inquisitiveness, it was because Mrs. Storan would have surely told the whole road by the end of the day about Mrs. Taylor's two sons and the things they were doing in a derelict house and how she'd never be able to show her face outside the door of 82 Upper Carey's Road again.

'You are to go down to Confession right away and tell the priest what you were doing and get that mortal sin removed off your soul. Otherwise you will burn in hell forever.'

And I'm wondering how mothers are the only ones who know who goes to hell, because if you ask a priest they can't tell you. Now I have to worry about Pop's big hands, hopping off my head, and going to hell if I don't get to a priest fast.

The Dominican Church across from The Peoples' Park has no priests in any box at all. There must be very few people sinning in this part of the parish and further down there's the Augustinians, or the 'Auga' as we used to call it. There are no priests there either. Now it's down to the Franciscans, there's a priest here with a queue of about ten waiting to see him. I'm the only young fellow here, they're all old, wrinkled and banjaxed looking like they're going to drop any minute. They probably told the same old sins to the priest yesterday, and the day before. They're all on their knees, mumbling away with their rosary beads, crossing themselves and thumping their chests, but they haven't got anything to tell the priest like I have. He's probably bored out of his mind with this lot. I bet they weren't looking up anyone's backsides like me and now that I'm recalling this event back then, I'm wondering did I at that time go into the same confession box my Mam went into nearly ten years previous. Could it be the same priest? I'll never know. But it is an interesting thought all the same.

'Bless me Father for I have sinned'.

'Go on,' said the priest.

'Father, my mother says I'll go down to hell when I die. She says it's the size of the whole of Ireland, that it's full of dirty rotten lousers and has a massive coal fire that never goes out!'

'What did you do, asked the priest, to deserve that?,'

'Well I don't think it was a sin at all but my mother said it was Father'.

'Tell me what you've done,' said the priest.

'Sure I only wanted to find out something Father, that's all. Can it be a sin only trying to find out something Father?'

'Are you going to tell me what the sin is, and why your mother said you'll go down to hell?,'

'My brother Jimmy Father, he was in it too'.

Priest: 'In what?'

'In the sin Father'.

Priest: 'How long have I to wait before you decide to tell me what this terrible sin is?,'

'Yes Father, I was looking up Jimmy's bum Father, and my mother gave me a terrible box in the ear, when she saw me Father. It still hurts and my ear is ringing all the time. Father don't you think that's punishment enough?'

'And why were you looking up there at your brother's bottom?'

'I want to be a doctor when I grow up Father.'

'And what has that got to do with your looking up your brother's bottom?,'

'I wanted to see how it worked, Father'.

Priest: 'How what works?'

'His bottom Father, everybody's bottom Father'.

'Look, I don't understand,' says the priest.

'Neither do I Father, that's why I was looking up his bottom Father.'

Priest: 'Are you trying to waste my time?,'

'No Father.'

'Then for the last time, why were you looking up your brother's bottom?'

'To see what happens when you go to the toilet Father. Is she right Father?,'

'Is who right?' said the priest.

'My mother, Father.'

'Is she right about what?'

'About going down to hell Father?'

'Yes, she's right, if you keep doing it.'

'But Father, don't doctors have to do that?'

Priest: 'Yes'.

'Will they be going to hell Father?'

Priest: 'No, they won't.'

'Why not Father?'

'Because they're doctors, that's why'.

'Well when they're learning to be doctors, will they be going down to hell then Father?'

Priest: 'Come here to me now and listen carefully'.

'Yes Father.'

'Do you have any impure thoughts?'

'What are they Father?'

'Thoughts that are wrong and unclean, do you under-stand?,'

'No Father'.

Priest: 'I want you to pay close attention to what I'm going to ask you next.

'Yes Father'.

'I want to talk to you about Masturbation'

'Who's he Father?'

Priest: 'Who's who?'

'That teacher fellow, Father.'

Priest: 'What teacher fellow?'

'Master Bation Father. He doesn't teach in my school. I don't know anything about him Father.'

Priest: 'God give me patience! How old are you anyway?'

'I'm nine Father.'

'Oh for God's sake, you're too young to be talking about that. You sound much older to me, are you sure, you're only nine?'

'It's my head Father'

Priest: 'What do you mean it's your head?'

'My Nan says my head is too big and that I talk like an old man, and that I haven't an ounce of sense.'

Priest: 'I think your Nan was right! You're not to be looking up your brother's bottom anymore now, do you hear me?'

'Yes, Father.'

'Right, you're to say three Our Father's, three Hail Mary's and three Glory Be's'

He says the Act of Contrition or something like that, he makes a sign of the cross and when I come out the light is hurt-ing my eyes. There's more people waiting to have their confes-sion heard and they're looking at me and I know they're asking themselves what kind of horrible sin did I commit to be in there so long? So I take my place to say my prayers for my penance, before heading back to Carey's Road, and now that my soul is clean I know Mam won't tell Pop. I won't get a close up of his fist tonight, and my ear is still ringing and is much bigger than the other one.

'Well what did he say?,' asked Mam.

'What did who say?'

'The priest, what did he say when you told him what you did?'

'Oh he asked me a load of questions'.

'What kind of questions?' says Mam?

'Why did I look up James' bum and he asked me did I have any impure thoughts?,'

'What?,' shouts Mam?

'Are you telling me the priest in the Holy Confession box asked you that?'

'Yes Mam,' he did.

'Did he say that actual word, that very word? That word 'impure'?

'Yes Mam.'

'Sweet Jesus, what else did he say?'

'He asked me if I knew a school teacher.'

'What the hell are you talking about? Why did he ask you if you knew a school teacher?'

'I don't know Mam; he wanted to talk to me about a master.'

'What the hell did he want to talk to you about a teacher for?'

'I don't know Mam; he just said he wanted to talk to me about a Master bation.'

'WHAT?,' she screams and I get another box into the other ear.

I'm sent sprawling across the kitchen floor. Now I've got ringing in both ears. Mam's jumping all over the place.

'Jesus, Mary and Holy St. Joseph, what filth is coming out of your mouth and where are you getting it only from a priest in the Confession box, get into bed and wait till your Father gets home! He won't be long sorting you out once and for all. I've a good mind to go down and see that priest teaching you words like that'.

And I'm telling Mam it's not fair, I was only doing what I was told and now I'm going to get murdered by my Father for something I did, and I don't even know what it is I did wrong.

'You told me to go down to the priest, I did that and now I'm going to get killed. You told me not to tell James about the operation, I didn't, you took back the lousy ten bob that Pop gave me, Jamesy got to keep his, the chocolate buns tasted lousy in the shop. I'm sick of being in trouble'.

'Shut up and go to bed like you're told.'

I'm in bed thinking I don't care what Pop does to me, he can kill me if he wants. Later I hear his voice coming in the kitchen, now I care very much, my heart won't stop beating, I'm getting sick and tired of this heart of mine pounding out of my chest all the time. I think it's going to stop any day now. I can hear Mom telling Pop. I can see through the crack in the wall. Pop's shoulders are at it again and now I know he's not going to kill me. I know he's laughing. Mam is telling him it's not funny. She's saying 'isn't it awful, you send your son down to the priest for guidance and he comes back with filth. What is the world coming to at all?'

It's the following morning.

'Your father wants to talk to you before you go to school.'

'Yes Pop'.

'Come over here to me, I want to talk to you.'

Pop has to look and sound cross and I'm going to have to look scared too.

'Your mother tells me you've been in the derelict house, is that right?'

'Yes Pop'.

'And you had James' trousers down around his ankles, and you were looking up his bottom?,'

'Yes Pop'.

Pop's voice is changing. I think he's going to start laughing, because he gets up, goes outside the front door, clears his throat, and comes back in, looking all serious.

'If I every hear you doing that again, I'll...'

He's gone out again. Mam's getting very cross, she's banging things on the table. Pop's back in grunting, 'I'll break your neck, do you hear me now?'

'Yes Pop'.

'Now, get off to school with you'.

'Yes Pop'.

Years later Tom O'Donnell, the local Limerick comedian, told a story on the radio about a guy who went to confession. The light was on in the confessional, there was no one outside and when he opened the door, went in and knelt down, the small door on his side of the confessional box was half open. He could see the outline of the priest's face and on the other side of the box he could partly see the outline of the person telling his sins to the priest. He could hear every sin that the man had committed and tried very hard to distract himself by trying to think of other things, but was unsuccessful. In the meantime, an accident occurred outside the church door, somebody was very badly injured and a call went out to get a priest, so somebody ran into the church, looking around for a priest, saw that there was a light on in the confessional, went over, opened the priest's door, grabbed him by the hand, pulled him out and there's your man on the other side of the Confessional box telling all his sins. He stops and waits for the priest to give him absolution. When he doesn't hear anything, he looks up, stares into the cage, sees a half a face on the other side of the confessional box and says: 'Where's the priest gone?,' And the guy that was looking on and heard every sin said: 'Well, if he heard all I heard, he's gone away for the guards!'

Chapter 9

Everything we have is rich people's rubbish and found its way to our front door in instalments on Pop's bike over the six years we lived here. That bike was also made of bits and scraps and put together over a couple of months of late evenings and hours of patience. Other items might have to wait for the winter months of no work to keep Pop occupied and away from the drink. Like the three clocks, two of which hung on the walls of the kitchen and bedroom; the other a beautiful black marble Roman type with pillars, murals and brass inlays. No tick or tock would be heard from this masterpiece, as its days of keeping time are long gone, its only purpose now is to give a very old bockety mantelpiece a bit of class. And according to Mam will be one of the few items to find its way to our new Corporation house whenever that will be.

The cuckoo clock that kept the time to the nearest second looked good on the wall and extended its arm every hour on the hour, had no cuckoo sound or cuckoo either, and that's why we had it. Instead Pop decided one evening to put one of my lead toy soldiers in its place and called it the 'soldier's clock'. Then there was the big old mahogany clock with the large white face and Roman numerals with its swinging pendulum and the loud ticking sound that came from its hollow insides, and was nearly deafening when Pop got it working, until it's ticking fades into the background after one or two nights in our beds. Pop says, 'That will be coming with us too'.

The very old Pye radio, its life of many stations and languages nearing its end and only capable of bringing us our one national Radio Éireann, sits on the dresser of too many coats of paint which used to have two glass doors on top to show off the delph it once had with two drawers in the middle and another two doors below. The whole thing rests on two legs to its left and a lump of 4 x 2 wooden piece to its right put there by Pop, now the home for different colour, shapes and sizes of cutlery, plates, mugs, saucers and battered pots and pans.

The stained picture of the Sacred Heart hanging high on the wall watches over us every day and under it the small glowing red lamp with the cross inside, hardly ever shines in the winter months, because its source of power is joined to the wire of the radio and attached to a two way adapter that holds a sixty watt bulb. In those months Mam will look at the picture, she'll talk to Jesus and says she hopes he'll understand how difficult things are in the winter, with no money coming in, how the only time his lamp can be on is when Pop wants to hear the news at one o'clock or when we need the light on in the evenings, so we can find the table and see what we're eating, as the bulb, radio and his lamp come on together with the flick of a switch. And if He could see his way to finding work for Pop she'd promise to have His lamp on all the time.

The table, when it came on Uncle Peadar's truck from a house in Mungret, had extendable ends that would never see the light of day in our house, because we didn't have the room and can only be used on three sides as it's shoved against a wall. The chairs which are all different in colour, shape and size, and only a couple of years away from being antiques, if it wasn't for the damage they all had. Pop says none of this stuff will be left into any new house as it's full of tiny holes, he calls woodworm. He says if they were brought into a new corporation dwelling, the house would fall down around us in no time at all. Then there was the day that would change my life forever!

The day that Pop brought home that canvas bag on the carrier of his bike and the yoke that was in it. Mam will be calling down the Holy Family every hour while running for the Mrs. Cullen's Powder and for James and Jett, their homework from school will take a sudden nosedive. They won't want to be in the house either. There are strange sounds' coming from the bag, as Pop takes it from the bike and lays it on the kitchen floor. Mam says, if there's cats in that bag, he'd better get them down to the quarry at the back of Lynch's field, as they're not staying in her house.

Pop laughs and says, 'there will be no going down to the quarry with what's in this bag',

as he pulls it out carefully with both hands. It wails and cries like a gang of cats and I'm asking Pop 'Is it an accordion like Uncle Jamie has out in Cappamore?,'

Pops says, 'it's like it, but this is called a melodeon, it's very old and the woodworm has started into it, and will have to be handled with great care'.

He puts it on one of his knees. There are four fancy timber knobs on top of one end, he's pulling the other end in and out with his left hand, and I'm asking him what's inside the folding part of the melodeon. 'Nothing', he says.

'But Pop, there must be something inside because you're not pressing any buttons are you, so what's making the racket'.

Then Mam asks Pop where he got it; he tells her he was doing a job in O'Connell Avenue and found it in the attic while he was fixing the roof.

'Sure that's a load of ol' rubbish Har, it's full of holes, you'll never get any tunes out of it while it's like that'.

'I know,' answers Pop; 'I'll have to patch it up'.

Then he places the melodeon on the chair, gets his tins of tools, nails, screws, tape and all sorts of bits and bobs. He's working away for the bones of an hour. He's got the glasses on and the tongue stuck out one side of the mouth and the watery drip dropping away onto everything under his nose. He'll give the drip a swipe of his hand and then wipe it onto his pants. So when he's done all he can, the yoke is back on his knee, out goes the tongue again, the head goes to one side, with the left ear facing down towards the melodeon, and off he starts with *On Top of Old Smokey* but it sounds like cats are howling like crazy inside the yoke and what Pop is playing sounds awful.

'What are you playing?' asks Mam; and when he tells her *'On Top of Old Smokey'* I say, 'I know *On Top of Old Smokey* and it doesn't sound like that at all'. I have to shout in order to be heard, but he can't hear me with all the racket. He has to hit seven or eight buttons before he gets the right note, he's at it for nearly an hour and Mam is rubbing her head. She'll be asking me to go down to O'Holloran's shop any minute now for the Cullen's Powder.

She won't ask Pop to stop, because the headache is easier than putting up with him if he's home drunk and looking for an argument. He's playing away thinking he's doing great and the watery drip is flowing away on all the buttons and every time he presses one a flat pedal pops out on the bottom of one end and it's great to watch but painful to listen to. And after one and a half hours Pop has had enough and so have the rest of us.

'Can I have a go?' I ask.

'Oh Jesus, Mary and Holy Saint Joseph' snaps Mam, 'isn't ninety minutes enough from you father for any normal reasonable person to endure, without having to listen to more?,'

'Ah Janie Ma, I'll go into the bedroom.'

'Go on then', she says 'and close the door behind you.'

'Thanks Mam.' I have never tried up to this moment or wanted to try and play anything that would produce a noise of any description from any kind of a contraption in my life before. There's no chair in the bedroom, so I have to pull the old leather straps with the rusty clasps around my shoulder as the bloomin' thing is down around my knees. And by the time I get the straps free of the rusty clasps that have been in the same place for centuries and start to play, Mam tells me to put it away, that it's time for bed because her head is killing her. She just can't put up with the dying cats and missed notes, 'not for another second'.

So I'll have to wait until tomorrow, which is Saturday; I can play for the whole morning, because Mam will be down in the market buying the vegetables for the Sunday dinner when she's finished she'll be into Aunty Maura's at Hogan's Restaurant in High Street just up the road from the market. By the time I arise from the bed the next morning Mam is gone and so is Pop. Jet and James are also gone with Mam. They didn't want to go at all until they heard Mam say she was calling into Auntie Maura. They'll be looking for the creamy buns and hoping for a penny or two as well. So the cats can scream all they like now. I have the tongue out just like Pop. This is hard stuff trying to remember to press the right key while pulling the left hand in and out. It's just as well they're all out of the house for the next few hours. I don't think they'd put up with what's coming out of this thing for much longer. But after an hour I can nearly play '*On Top of Old Smokey.*'

I am concentrating so hard on getting the right button pressed at the right time, while pulling the left hand in and out, I haven't noticed Nan's and Uncle Jaime's shadows through the glass on the bedroom door, standing in the small kitchen-cum-hallway, wondering where everybody is gone, and where that awful moaning noise is coming from? Nan opens the bedroom door and takes the living senses out of me when she says 'Jesus, Mary and Holy Saint Joseph, is that supposed to be music you're playing? Where's everybody?' When I tell her why I'm the only one left in the house she looks out at Uncle Jim laughing saying: 'Jesus, is it any wonder they're gone. I'll be gone too if you don't put that yoke down. What is it anyway?'

Before I can answer, Uncle Jaime says 'that's a melodeon, where did you get it?,' When I told him Pop brought it home last night after finding it in a house, he takes it off my shoulders, loosens the straps, puts it on his shoulders and starts to make a noise that I didn't think was possible to come out of this thing. The cats are still screaming but it's like they're all screaming in harmony. He's great! It's the best thing that could ever have happened today. He has given me so much encouragement just watching him play. I'm taking it all in: his left hand moving in and out at incredible speed playing the required buttons in perfect rhythm on the left side and the fingers on the right flying in all directions. I want to play just like him. He tells me to take my time, slow the tune down, as I get used to moving my hands and fingers that I should increase the tempo. 'Only use your fingers on the right hand first, when you got the right hand working with the right notes then work the same tune with your left hand, on the bass buttons'.

Nan tells me they'll be back in the afternoon and be sure to mention it to Mam.

So I'm off again trying to put into practice everything Uncle Jaime has told me. He was a good man, always smiling and would have been twenty five years old at the time. Looking at some of his photographs he was a handsome man in his day. When I look at photographs of Mam's other family members, they're all good looking too and I'm thinking wasn't it just as well Mam's side of the family had good looks, otherwise I might be afraid to go outside the door.

By the time Mam is home with Jet and James, whose mouths are stained from the creamy buns with the strawberry centre, Pop is back from work. I can play 'On Top of Old Smokey' without missing a note, just using the right hand. They're all surprised and now it's time to get the left hand working with the fingers on two of the eight bass buttons, but they won't leave me out of the bedroom, not with the melodeon blaring away. By the end of the day, I won't leave it out of my hands until both hands are working together and they're all shouting out at me from the kitchen to shut up playing 'On Top of Old Smokey'. If they hear it one more time someone is going to get murdered and Mrs. Storan from next door is trying to beat our front door down above all the noise. She's asking Mam, can whoever is making that awful racket stop so her two young children can get some sleep and hope's Mam hasn't been offended by her asking.

For the next two weeks there's no peace to be found in Number 82 Upper Carey's Road for anyone. I won't want to do my homework. It's throwing the schoolbag on the ground and on with the squeeze box. When I come home from school Jet and James can't get their homework done. They're not stupid like me. Their teachers have them in good grades. They're shining examples to the others in their classes, but for the next few months Jet and James' homework is going to go down-hill because they can't concentrate over the cats and 'On Top Of Old Smokey'. They're out on the road playing all the time and when the rain comes, Mam is calling them in off the road, but they won't come 'til Mam tells me to put away the yoke. Otherwise I'll get a box around the ear and James is the one doing all the running down to O'Holloran's shop to get the Mrs. Cullen's Powder. She won't tell me to stop when there's no rain. She wants me to play just like her baby brother - Uncle Jamie. But she's worried how agitated Pop is. He's smoking twice as much since he's brought the box home; he's wandering from the house up and down the road every night as soon as he comes home.

He'll come in from the walking saying; 'Mother of Jesus, what possessed me to bring that shagging box home at all? Is he ever going to stop playing the bloody thing?,' Mam thinks I might drive him back to the drink and wouldn't that be an awful pity seeing as he's off it now a couple of months short of three years.

I've added a few more tunes to my repertoire. Tom Dunphy's, *Come Down From The Mountain Katie Daly* and peace has returned to number 82, but that doesn't last long either as they'll all be pounding on the bedroom wall shouting 'play something else for God's sake please'. But all the holes that Pop fixed are coming undone, and there's twice as many cats screaming in the box now and it's very hard to tell whether I'm playing the right note or not. I'm playing away when Pop opens the door of the bedroom shouting 'give me that bloody thing!' He's taking it off my shoulders. 'Ah Pop, you're not going to throw it out are you?' 'No I'm not, but if I don't fix those bloody holes in that yoke fast, I will throw it out and you with it'.

So he's got it on the table again with the tools, but this time he's got a special tape and different glue, he's taking much longer this time to fix it than he did before. The tongue is out again, he just can't get the brain to work without the tongue out to the left side of the mouth and the watery drip is off again. It's twelve midnight when Pop is finished. Jet and James are in bed. Mam is by the fire sewing away. The headaches are gone, Pop takes the box, puts it on his knees and starts to play and Janie Mac, what a difference! The cats are all gone, it's great!

'Let me have a go Pop'. He answers 'no'. I ask 'Why Pop?'

'Because it's half past twelve and you'll wake half the road if you start playing now and we don't want Mrs. Storan knocking on the door again giving out that her kids are up and can't get to sleep'. I can't stop thinking how '*Come Down From The Mountain Katie Daly*' is going to sound tomorrow morning when I get it into my hands and before I know it, it's time to get up and it's on with the straps over the pyjamas. I'm lost in the tune, with both hands and all fingers going; it sounds smashing. I'll try '*On Top of Old Smokey*' too but only get the first bit out when they're all shouting at me to 'shut up and play something else'. But I have to go to school now and leave it until I get back.

Next week is going to ruin everything because I have to get up every morning, to go to the Redemptorists with Fonsie, Noelie and Dinny for the Arch Confraternity Retreat. Then we have to go to school and when we get home in the evening, we have to go back there again for another half an hour.

When we go there, the missionary priests with their long black soutans and the white circled badges on the left side of their chests, that has some kind of a cross on it, they'll be telling great stories about the Communists in the Soviet Union, how no one over there believes in God at all, those Communists are wicked people, never to be trusted. They tell us how Jesus is locked away inside the Tabernacle, and God help anyone who goes near it, if they're not a priest. There's the story of the Communist soldier who went inside a church, pointed his rifle at Jesus in the Tabernacle and fired a shot. When the bullet hit the Tabernacle door, it ricocheted back and hit the soldier right through the heart, and didn't he fall down dead on the floor of the church and all the lads are saying afterwards, 'isn't it great that we have the true faith, while the other churches don't because nothing like that ever happens to them'. But I'm thinking, isn't Jesus after getting very violent all of a sudden, sure he wouldn't hurt a fly. He could have killed the soldiers that hung him on the cross, so why is he killing soldiers now, when he didn't kill them then?

Another priest might tell us of the miracles the priests perform out there in those Communist countries. When the Commie soldiers see the miracles they all want to become Catholics and we swallow the whole story, hook, line and sinker. Sometimes those missionary priests would call around to all the houses and give us the Pope's Blessing with the message from the Virgin Mary to the three girls in Fatima that if enough rosaries were said around the world by all the Catholics, Russia and the Soviet Union would be converted. And Mam wants to do the whole conversion on her own.

She'll have us all on our knees every night, there'll be the five Sorrowful Mysteries to be said, first The Agony In The Garden, followed by the Hail Mary's which Mam says, first. Then we'll have the second Mystery 'The Scourging at the Pillar', Pop says the next ten Hail Mary's and then it's 'The Crowning of Thorns', now it's my turn to say the ten hail Mary's, then Mam says 'The Carrying of the Cross' and James' turn comes, before Jet says the final Sorrowful Mystery of 'The Crucifixion'.

Jet, James and I will spend most of our time laughing, looking at Pop's watery drip hanging away there all on its own. Sometimes it won't fall off his nose, it just gets longer and every time he moves his head, it's swinging all over the place and refuses to drop. He'll give us the odd thump and tell us to 'be quiet' he's trying not to laugh as well, even though he hasn't a clue what we're laughing at. I don't think he believes in God at all, he'll only do this because Mam says it's to be done. And she doesn't hear the laughing at all. I think her mind is over in Russia wondering how many Russians we saved tonight after the Rosary is finished.

Pop goes to Mass every Sunday morning. Mam will tell him to take one of us along to keep him out of Maureen Fay's. He'll stand against the frame of the front door for ten minutes after Mass starts. The right leg is two inches inside the church and the left leg is three feet in O'Connell Street. Because he's in the Augustinian Church there's a great crowd of 'men only' in the lobby at the back. The priest will get in the pulpit and start giving out about all the men who come to church every Sunday for Mass and hang around the lobby and how they should be ashamed to call themselves Catholics and he wonders why they come at all, when all they're really interested in is what time the pubs will be open. There's a big shuffle of male bodies coming in from the lobby with their heads hanging low in shame and there's Pop still in the same place all on his own because he never heard a word the priest said because his ears are in O'Connell Street and it doesn't matter anyway because he'll be gone ten minutes before the Mass will end. And all this religious stuff is ruining my musical ambitions.

I can't play in the mornings before I go to school and there's little time after school when the supper is gone and it's off to church again for the retreat.

I always go to the Redemptorist Church the same way: it's through the People's Park, down Barrington Street, up O'Connell Avenue and turn right by the Tech. School and there it is. I must have been day-dreaming one evening because I missed the turn to Barrington Street as I wandered down The Crescent past the Jesuit Church and ended up in Mallow Street instead. There's a couple of small shops as I turn the corner on the right hand side, there's a light on the window of Peter Dempsey's Music shop. He's a tall curly haired man who can play a good few instruments. He's a music teacher also, who teaches most days after school and if you're getting married he'll play at your wedding.

Sometimes he'll have a set of drums, maybe a flute or a trumpet, a violin, even a saxophone for sale in the window. They might be new or second-hand. So when I get to the window my heart misses a beat. There all by itself is a lovely pearly red button accordion, just like Uncle Jimmy's only bigger. It's got four rows of white buttons on the right side and there are six big buttons to change the tone in the middle of the front panel. On the left side there are six rows of bass buttons and the price is fifty five pounds.

I have my elbows resting on the window sill. I'm in heaven. I can see myself entertaining thousands of people. They're saying: 'Look at that smart young man with that lovely pearly red accordion, isn't he wonderful?' Then the shop lights go off and I'm back down to reality.

I'm running up Mallow Street, then through the People's Park with my mouth wide open, shouting with excitement, when a big dirty bluebottle flew into my mouth and stuck in the back of my throat. I fall on my hands and knees, hawking all over the place. There's people coming over asking me if I'm alright. They think I'm going to get sick. I wish I could because I think he's stuck in the holes where my tonsils were. But I can't get him out, no matter how hard I hawk. I think he's gone down into my stomach now and tomorrow I might be dead and never get my lovely pearly accordion, but I have to get home quick. I hope Pop is there, and when I do get home, I'm panting and puffing. Pop and Mam are looking at me wondering why I'm in such a state.

'What happened to you?,' asks Mam.

'There's a smashing, beautiful, pearly red accordion in the window of Peter Dempsey's Music shop, will you buy it for me Pop? Please Pop?,'

His face changes from curiosity to surprise. 'Will you Pop? Will you?,'

Now there's a bit of a grin there as he asks. 'How much would this smashing, pearly red accordion, down there in Peter Dempsey's shop cost me if I was to go down there tomorrow and buy it?'

I'm stuck to the ground in shock. I can't get the words out of my mouth. He's actually going to go down there tomorrow and buy it for me. I didn't think he could just walk in there and buy it like that. Mam is at the belfast sink washing the dishes.

'Well are you going to tell me how much this yoke is or do I have to go down there myself and find out?'

'Only fifty five pounds Pop,' I answer.

There's a crash to the floor of a plate Mam was holding. Then there's silence. Pop's shoulders are starting to go up and down. He's saying 'only fifty five pounds, did you hear that Bid? It's only fifty five pounds.' Now his shoulders are leaping all over the place. He's trying to get a word out of his mouth, but he can't. Now he's coughing uncontrollably. He's on his feet thumping his chest. I think he's going to die on me and if he does I'll never get my lovely pearly red accordion, with all those rows of buttons. Pop has gone red in the face. Now Mam is thumping him on the back trying to stop him coughing.

'There's loads of white buttons on the left side Pop and there's six buttons to change the tone'.

'Jesus, Mary and Holy Saint Joseph, can't you see your father is at death's door and you're standing there talking about a bloody accordion.'

But I've only got one thing on my mind and I haven't heard a word she said.

'Are you really going to go down there tomorrow morning and buy the lovely pearly red accordion Pop?'

'He is in his arse,' shouts Mam.

Pop stops coughing, but his shoulders are off again.

Mam says, 'Your father had only three days work two weeks ago, none at all last week, I'm wondering where the next dinner is coming from and you think he can go down there to Peter Dempsey's music shop and give him fifty five pounds'

Peter Dempsey's Shop -
The shop as it is today and no different from the 50's
except the colour.

'Does that mean I won't be getting it Mam?' I'm trying to be all nice and mannerly and Mam puts her hand on her head and shouts, 'Jesus, Mary and Holy St. Joseph, of course you won't you silly Eejit'.

If I don't get this pearly red accordion my life won't be worth living.

'What the hell possessed you to go down by Peter Dempsey's music shop in the first place? Why didn't you come home the usual way?,' Mam asks.

'But if you can't buy it tomorrow will you buy it in a couple of weeks Pop' and up he rises to his feet laughing and coughing again and Mam is screaming at me to go to bed which I do.

I never took my clothes off because I've cried myself to sleep thinking what will I do if somebody walks past Peter Dempsey's shop when the light is on at night or even in the day time and sees my lovely pearly red accordion, they might buy it and my whole life would be ruined.

But I'll go down to his shop every day after school; I'll put my elbows on the window sill and stare at the lovely pearly red accordion. I'll be gone again into another world, where I'm on the stage entertaining and one day Mr. Dempsey comes out and says:

'Would I be right in saying that you'd love to own that red accordion young man?,'

'Yes Sir, I would Sir,' I answer.

'Would you like to put it on and try it out?,' he says.

And I'm thinking is this really happening to me? I'm going to get to play it. So he brings me in, takes it from the window, puts it on my shoulders and just manages to stop me keeling over from the size and weight of it. Boys! But I never realised it was so big and heavy. 'It takes a bit of getting used to', he says as he adjusts the straps, because it's down around my shins.

'Sit down there now young man and take the weight off your feet, give yourself a few minutes before you start to play. Where are you from at all?,' he asks.

'82 Upper Carey's Road Sir.'

'And what's your name?'

'Paddy, Sir.'

'And your second name?'

'Taylor, Sir.'

'You must be one of the Taylors from Bedford Row, sure there's only the one family in the whole of Limerick by that name in this town. Taylor by name, tailor by trade and lived in Taylor's Street, would that be right now? 'Yes sir'. And would your father be Harry the painter on Monday the plumber on Tuesday, the carpenter on Wednesday and the plasterer on Thursday?'

'He would, Sir.'

'Ah Jaysus, sure I know Harry very well.'

I'm after getting a great idea, seeing that he knows my father very well, he might give me the loan of the accordion for a few weeks and it will be out of the window as well, and if it's not in the window, no one can buy it. But I'll wait a few minutes before I ask him.

'Off you go now, are you able to play anything?'

So I tell him about the melodeon Pop found in the attic of a house he was working in and how I can play two tunes on it.

'Well let's see if you can play one of them on that', but I don't know which button to press, there's so many of them. I have only one row on the other yoke at home. He can see I'm confused and why. So he points to the outside row and says: 'Just imagine that's the same as the melodeon at home' and when I press the first button there's the sweetest sound I ever heard in my life. I have goose pimples running all over my back and neck on Katie Daly, she's floating down the mountain now like never before on this thing, the tune sounds so different, compared to the way it sounds on the yoke at home. I have to close my eyes to really appreciate the sound, when I open them again there's people passing the shop, looking in and smiling at me and my dream is coming through. I have an audience.

'How long are you playing the melodeon,' asks Mr. Dempsey?

'Five weeks Sir,' I answer.

'My goodness, you're a fast learner alright. Is there anyone in the family able to play one of those things?,' he asks. 'Because I know Harry Taylor couldn't play a gramophone'.

'My uncle Jaime from Cappamore, he's very good and plays in the Cappamore band'.

'Ah sure don't I know him very well, that's where you get it from. You'll probably play that by ear for the rest of your life, like your Uncle Jaime.'

I don't know what he's talking about, how can you play an accordion with your ear? Uncle Jaime plays with his hands. But I'm not going to sound stupid and ask what does that mean, when I ask him if I can borrow it for a couple of weeks he looks very cross. 'Sure you can hardly stand up, with it around your shoulders, and if you could carry it, the bould young fellows above in Weston, they'll take it off you on your way home, and we'd all be in right trouble then wouldn't we?

'Oh I couldn't do that, no Sir. I have to go to the Ennis Road now to give some lessons to a young lad, so you'll have to go before I close the shop. But you can call in anytime you want to have another go'.

'Thank you very much Mr. Dempsey', and it's hard to go back home to the old melodeon and that awful sound it makes. So I try another tune. It's not great, but it helps. And I'm down again the following day at Peter Dempsey's shop. He's not there. It doesn't matter because my pearly red accordion is still in the window. I can put my elbows up and dream away again. The following week he's there and takes it out of the window for me to play again. I tell him I'm saving every week to buy it.

'That's great,' he says. 'And how much are you saving every week?'

'A shilling Sir.'

'Good God, a whole shilling every week. Let's see now how long it will take to get the money together'. He has a pen stuck in his ear. Now he's looking for a bit of paper to write, he's muttering away under his breath. He looks at me and says:

'It will take you twenty weeks to save a pound and after one year you'll have a whole two pounds and twelve shillings, that means you'll only have to wait twenty five years before you can come down here and get it. Sure you'll hardly find the time passing at all.'

I'm in a deep depression. I thought it was a great idea that I'd have the pearly accordion in no time at all. Now I don't want to come down here anymore because I'll never own it and it's making me miserable.

When I go home I put the other yoke on. The months pass, I can play twenty tunes now. Mam is tapping her feet or singing along and if Pop is at home he might ask me to play a tune. If I don't know it he'll hum it for a few minutes. Then I'll have it off by heart. I've forgotten all about the lovely pearly red accordion because I know I'll never be able to have it. I don't even dream about it anymore or the hundreds of people looking at me playing on the stage. But today, my life is going to change forever. I've come home from school and Pop's bike is outside the window and that's unusual because I'm always home twenty minutes before him every day.

'Hi Pop,' I say when I come in. I'm sitting at the table waiting for my dinner. Then James and Jet arrive home. And Pop asks me to go into the bedroom and get his slippers.

I must be day-dreaming again because I never heard him. I'm always day-dreaming, it's one of the reasons why I learn nothing at school.

'Do you hear me talking to you?,' shouts Pop.

'Sorry Pop, what did you say?'

'I said go into the bedroom and get me my slippers.'

'Yes Pop'. Now if I was playing close attention to what Pop was saying I'd know he doesn't have any slippers. He never had any slippers in his life, I should be saying, 'sure you don't have any slippers at all Pop'. But in I go to the bedroom. I'm only half looking at the floor and under the three beds, there's no sign of any slippers. I even look at the top of Pop and Mam's bed and all that's there is a smashing pearly red accordion. When I come back out Pop, Mam, James and Jet are all looking at me as if they're waiting for something.

'I can't find your slippers anywhere Pop.'

Pop is surprised and asks: 'Where did you look?'

'I looked under all the beds and all around the floor'.
'Did you try and look on the quilt on our bed?,' he asks.
'I did,' I answer.
'And what did you see?'
'I saw a smashing pearly...'
Then there's a sudden burst of energy. I'm tearing back into the bedroom. I'm thinking surely I must have imagined it. I nearly take the door off its hinges and there it is, my lovely pearly red accordion. My mind is full of questions; I want to put it on. But no, I have to run out and thank Pop and Mam or should I thank Mam and Pop? Who do I go to first? There's a silence in the house that seems to last for ages. It's broken by my burst of shouts, my lovely pearly red accordion and as I run out Mam is first in my path. I don't know what to say. I've never seen her smile like this before. I give her a big hug. I don't remember doing that before either, now I have to thank Pop. He's surprised when I jump on his chest, I put my arms around him and I'm kissing him on the neck saying 'thank you Pop'. I want to go to the bedroom to put it on and play, but I don't think I've thanked them enough so I'm still at the 'thank you's'.

Pop says: 'Are you going to give us a tune on the most expensive thing in the house at all?,' and that's my cue to go and get it and off I go. I only have another twenty minutes before I go back to school, so I'm trying to play as many tunes as I can, and when I go to school I'm asking Mam to be sure and lock the front door, so nobody can come and steal my lovely pearly red accordion.

When I look back and think of the many Sundays Jet, James and I waited at the top of Carey's Road for Pop to come home on his bike to ask him for the money for the pictures, after he's been to Bedford Row playing the cards and the times he might say no. Was he saying no because he and Mam were putting away the few bob every week for Peter Dempsey? And we'd have to play on the road ourselves until all the other kids came home from the pictures. I'll never know. What I do know is it was one of those rare occasions when Pop told me that he loved me in big neon lights!

CHAPTER 10

When Pop is off the drink he has one big distraction, fishing, mostly from the quays near Bedford Row. He'll be home for the supper, in the spring, summer and autumn evenings, it's out with the rod and off on the bike. When the weekends come Mam will ask him to take Jetta or myself. It might have been my first time, but I only remember it for one reason.

After telling me to be sure and keep my legs out from the spokes of the back wheel, because he says if they get caught I could wind up again in St. John's Hospital to the nun with the thick glasses and the funny walk. He keeps shouting back to me, to keep them out, and I shout back that I am. When we get to Punches Cross I have to tell him that I can't keep them out any longer because they're getting awful heavy. 'You'll have to', he shouts back. 'We're nearly at the Groody River'. Then the bike comes to a sudden halt, and I'm screaming my head off. My foot is stuck between the spokes of the wheel and the bicy cle frame. When Pop looks around, his face is snow white. I'm slowly falling off the bike, bringing it down on top of me. Pop is saying, 'Are you alright love, are you OK?,' My screams have gone silent now. I'm terrified. When I look at my foot, it seems to be out of line with my leg, and the pain is killing me.

People have come to our assistance. After five minutes of struggling, my leg is free and the pain isn't so bad. My foot is back in its right position again and I'm still bawling my eyes out. 'Ah sure he's grand', says one of the twenty or so that have gathered 'round us. 'He's only got a few scratches; sure he'll be grand in no time at all!' As Pop wipes the tears from my face with a borrowed handkerchief I'm asking him will I have to go down again to St. John's to the nun with the funny walk. But before Pop can answer, one of the onlookers says, 'There'll be no need to go to any hospital', that I'll only be black and blue for a few days. He puts a shilling in my hand and I think I'll start the crying again, because the crying could be worth a few more bob. I think grown ups don't like to see children crying so I keep the hand out with my eyes closed forcing out the tears. I can feel and hear the clinking sound of another coin hitting the bob that's in my hand and when I partly open one of my eyes to see was it a penny or another bob, there's more on their way into the hand. So I increase the volume which increases the flow. And when I open the other eye I can see there's enough in my hand for Jet and myself to go to the City Theatre on Sunday after the dinner.

Pop's face is still white as he brings me back up the hill of Carey's Road. Mam is at the front door, looking surprised and wonders what has us back so early. As we approach the house, I manage to squeeze out another few dry tears. Mam is giving hell to Pop over the state of my foot, asking him how could he have been so careless, and could he not have put me on the bar of his bike like every other father in Carey's Road.

I'm showing Jet the fistful of money I got and whisper the words, 'We're going to the pictures tomorrow'. Mam has me sitting into the Belfast sink washing my foot with some Dettol. She's muttering away under her breath, 'Jesus, Mary and Holy St. Joseph, my heart is broken with you Paddy. You're always in trouble, it's a wonder you've any blood left in your body at all'. Then she rubs my face and gives me a kiss. I'm totally confused, and don't know whether she's loving me or cross with me. That was the first and last time I went fishing with Pop for another few years.

I'm much older now and have my own fishing rod, it's a bamboo stick, about nine feet long. I bought it from Kevin Hartigan at the top of William Street. Dinny, Fonsey and Noel have one too. We started our fishing years ago at the back of the Co-op on the Roxboro Road. There are two big ponds in there but only one has fish and all we need to catch them is a straight pin that can bend into a hook. We get the pins any Saturday down town from people selling small paper flags for charity, then it's a stick, a piece of thread and a slice of bread, which when we wet it makes some dough and best of all it hasn't cost us a penny. I can fish anywhere now. I can catch anything now, but not when I'm with Pop. He's lucky at everything, even fishing.

There could be forty or fifty men fishing every night at Arthur's Quay and all the big trout will want to go to Pop's worm. I'll be right beside him, maybe four feet away. I can see them but they won't even look at my maggot. I keep changing it and there's Pop with the same one all limp and dead. I'm looking at mine fresh and wriggling all over the place but they won't go near it. Look at them, they're queuing up to his to get hooked. Why the hell is that? It's the same every bloody night. I'm getting sick and tired of it, when I ask him why, he just winks at me as if to say it's a secret and I'll never tell you. But my day will come, I know it, but first I'll have to join the Scouts.

Dinny, Fonsey and Noelie are all in the Scouts and I can't get in because there's a waiting list. It's always the same. I'm always last in the gang. Dinny is the eldest, then there's Fonsey, Noelie and myself are the same age. They're all smarter than me, they know everything, they know the names of all the good guys in the English First Division Soccer League. They're in the best classes in school not like me - the class that's half-full of Eejits. They're always asking me questions they know I can't answer. They're great at playing soccer, hurling, handball and I'm useless at everything. I can't even say 'rugby' properly. They make me feel stupid, but I've no one else to hang around with and I can't join the Scouts. I wish I was like them, clever and intelligent.

We play football on the road in the long summer evenings with Dermot Lynch, Hugh and Teddy McGrath, Christy Davis as well. Mr. Fitz, Mr. Storan and Pop will have a go too but it's only a matter of time before the fathers who smoke are on their knees gasping for air and where am I? Only sitting on the wall at the corner across from Denny's house and told to keep an eye out for Guard Dennehy who might be coming over the stone bridge any minute and catch the whole lot of them. He'll want all their names and house numbers as he knows they all live on the road. He'll be coming back from his wanderings, all over Janesborough and Rathbane looking for anyone who might have broken the law. It could be days or weeks since anyone put a foot wrong in Limerick and to justify his existence he'll want to bring to justice anyone he finds playing football on the road. But if there's no look-out at the corner at the top of the road. Guard Dennehy will be well into the melee of bodies running onto the street trying to wallop the ball up the road. But I'll forget all about Guard Dennehy on his bike after five minutes sitting on the wall, pussing and sulking because they told me I'm useless and only get in the way. I'll start walking on the wall, the high part that many fell off and broke their necks. Guard Dennehy will come over the bridge and pass me out. I won't see him because my eyes are on the wall because I won't want a broken neck either. There he is putting the same names into his book as he did last week. When he's gone away with the ball, and telling them they'll be in real trouble if he catches them a third time, they'll be calling me names while trying to catch me. But I'm on my way over the iron bridge, down past O'Holloran's shop running as fast as I can, listening to their shouts of what they're going to do to me when they

Pat Kearney pictured top second left, now the proprietor of Rooney Auctioneers was nineteen and served in Limerick at the time this photo was taken. He handed me this photograph and asked if I recognised anyone in it? And there at the bottom left was a face I'll never forget. How could I? It was the hardest face that ever stood on top of a garda uniform. The one and only Guard Dennehy. I told Pat he used to frighten the living daylights out of every young fella in Limerick.

Pat surprised me when he said "Behind that cross face was a kind and understanding human being" he said if Guard Denneby caught anyone mitching from school he'd take their name and address, go to court on their behalf and pay the fine of 5 bob and they and their parents would never know a thing about it because he had a monthly quota of prosecutions to meet. Or he might catch a fellow stealing, if he was over sixteen he'd say "Right young man you have two choices, six months in jail or be on your way to the soldiers barracks to join the Army" and up the young lad would go to see the Sergeant and the Sergeant would ask "Have you any references?". "Ring Guard Denneby" would be the answer. "Do you know a young fella by such a name?" the Sergeant would ask. "I do indeed" Guard Denneby would reply. "He wants to join the Army, can you recommend him and was in ever in any trouble?" "Oh a grand young lad" would come the reply, "and comes from good stock too"

catch me, but they'll ask me again tomorrow when they want to wallop another ball around the road. I'll promise them I won't take my eyes off the bridge when I'm on the look out again but it's very hard to concentrate. It's not my fault, it's my brain. It won't stay on the one track. It wants to wander all over the place, day-dreaming and imagining all kinds of wonderful and strange things. Christy Davis says, 'My brain is on the moon' and wonders if I can be trusted to do anything at all.

As I'm writing this I'm wondering why as a child I craved and sometimes wanted to be the centre of attention; how I wanted to be included, to be part of anything that was going on around me. The way I'd raise my voice, do something stupid to get noticed and never really understand why it is. Is it because of those younger days in Upper Carey's Road and my days in CBS Sexton Street, being in the worst class every year, leaving school with a bad record, wanting to look intelligent and inside feeling like a fool? The lads are in the scouts and I'm not, but if I don't get in it will only make me feel worse.

My Auntie Nora, who lives behind the Scout Hall in James' Street, tells me to go and see Tommy Deegan. 'Go down and tell him I sent you.' He tells me he'll have to squeeze me into the Tenth Troop. I want to go to the Fifth where Dinny, Fonsey and Noelie are but Tommy tells me there's no room. Why is this always happening to me? Why can't I be first in something, anything? Why can't they want to be in something because I'm in it? Wouldn't it be great if I could tell them just once that they'll have to wait to join anything that I'm in or knowing something that they don't? It looks like that's never going to happen, and I'll have to settle for the Tenth. I'm glad I did. There are four Patrols. The Beaver, The Panther, The Wolfhound, and the one I'm assigned to, The Eagle. There's a Patrol Leader, his name is Seán Carey. Before we are invested, which means to be official Scouts, we have to pass an exam. That takes about six months and I think I haven't a hope of passing as I'm too stupid and never passed anything in my life. I'll only last the half year before I'm thrown out. Well I'm amazed when after the six months, I pass with flying colours. Now I've got to get a uniform, there's a guy in Marian Avenue, Janesborough, by the name of Pat Frost. He's left the Scouts and he might be the same height as me. If he still has his uniform and it fits me, I'll save myself a good £4.00. It does fit, I'm ready to be invested at St. Joseph's Church and I think I look great in my Scout uniform.

The following week sees me in my first St. Patrick's Day Parade. It's cold and wet; we have to stand around in Sarsfield Barracks for an hour freezing to death in our short sleeved shirts and pants. But there's going to be loads of people lining the streets to see us. Pop will be there too. Mr. Cusack, the man who owns the Grimsby Fish Store in Bedford Row, will always ask Pop to make up a float on the back of his fish truck. Every year it's something different. He won't tell us what it is this year. But the Scouts and all the other associations will finish the Parade before all the business floats come down O'Connell Street and I'll be able to go back and see what he's doing this year.

Auntie Nora

She's 90 and as fit as a fiddle, every night at 9:00pm when I'm thinking of going to bed because I'm tired she's going out to play cards and won't be home till all hours! When George Burns the American comedian was on NBC Television celebrating his ninetieth year on the planet, he was asked: 'Well George, how does it feel to be ninety?' George replied: 'No different to the time I was seventy or eighty'. 'You're known to smoke a cigar or two' asked the interviewer. 'I do', replied George, 'twelve a day'. "But George', asked the interviewer, 'they're Cuban Havana cigars, they're twelve inches long George. Are you telling the whole nation that at the age of 90 you put away twelve cigars every day, come on now George. Surely you're fibbing'. 'No I'm not', replied George. 'And what about a drink?,' asked the interviewer. 'Oh yes', says George, 'I love a Burbon'. 'And how many Burbons would you have a day George?' asked the interviewer. 'Oh, I have to have a Burbon with every cigar,' replied George. 'Oh come on now George,' asked the interviewer. 'Surely at the age of ninety you couldn't be able to smoke twelve cigars and drink twelve Burbons every day. I mean what does your Doctor say?,' 'He's dead,' replied George.

I'm running up O'Connell Street, there's people shouting at a truck. They're saying, 'Good man Harry, throw us a kiss'. Then there are cheers and laughter which carries on up the street. As the truck passes me, there's my Dad dressed up as a mermaid. He's got a big fish's tail he's sitting into, with a long blonde wig that he keeps stroking with a brush. He's holding a woman's mirror in his other hand. Then he lets the brush down and throws the crowd lots of kisses. They're loving it. They all know him. I'm telling the lads, 'That's my Dad'. I'm calling out to him but he can't hear. He looks like a 100 year old mermaid with no teeth. He's got make-up and lipstick on and I'm very proud of my Dad because everybody knows him. When he comes home he'll tell us that The Grimsby Fish Stores got First Prize for the best float and how Mr. Cusack gave him an extra £20.00 for making it happen.

Mr. Cusack

I was surprised to find that like Mr. Whelan, Mr. Cusack is still with us. He was surprised that I was Harry Taylor's son. 'Look', he says, pointing to a large plastered concrete wall, 'Your father built that sixty years ago for thirteen pounds, can you believe that?'

He's the same age as Mr. Whelan, just past the ninety. I tell him I'm writing a book about my father, Bedford Row and Carey's Road, he says he could write one too. 'Did you ever hear of Dot, Dash and Carry?,' 'No', I answer. 'Ah for goodness sake' he says, 'I thought you were writing a book about Bedford Row. Dot. Dash and Carry were three sisters and spinsters all their lives, were never separated from one another. They lived around the corner from the Bedford Bar and across the road from the Franciscan Church. Every day of their lives they would only go across the road to Mass and up the road to Mullany's shop for their groceries'.

We talked for ages about St. Patrick's Day Parades and the floats; 'How your father Har was game for anything' and had me gobsmacked when he told me of the time they dressed Pop up as Mahatma Ghandi; had him walk around the town on another Patrick's Day. I'm laughing because I can see him so clearly in my mind, with no teeth, false tan, sandals, the white sheet, and half a jar of Brylcreem to stick the hair to his head to give him the baldy look; and like the mermaid everybody knowing who he was.

'Your father and I were great pals; and God love the poor man, sure he loved his pints. Wasn't it an awful pity he couldn't enjoy the one or two and not wanting to drink the Bedford Bar dry?' He told me how the fish shop started over a hundred years ago and the name of the company he'd buy his fish from in Grimsby Town, England. Their name was Mudd and the company slogan was 'If you stick with Mudd, Mudd will stick with you'.

It's Tuesday night and we're all sitting around on our timber seats at our Patrols corners. There's eight in a Patrol but mine has nine because of Tommy Deegan squeezing me in.

Old shop in Bedford Row

New shop in St. Alphonsus Street

A stranger has just walked into the room. He's in scout uniform and looks very cross.

'Who's that?,' asks one of the lads.

'It's our new Scout Master, Willie Loughlin'.

'What happened to the other guy?,' asks another.

'He got thrown out,' says one of the lads.

'Why did he get thrown out?,' asks Patsy Moore.

Seán Carey says in a whisper, 'Because he's a Queer'.

There's silence. I'm not going to ask what a Queer is. I'm stupid enough as it is. Let somebody else ask and I have to have a look on my face that doesn't show I don't know what a Queer is.

'What's a Queer?,' whispers Patsy Moore.

Great! I was hoping he'd ask that question. He's been stuck to me ever since I joined the Scouts. I like him hanging around me all the time because he's more stupid than me. He's always asking me questions and believes my answers no matter what I tell him. Now I have to change the expression on my face to a look that shows I know what a Queer is and you're stupid because you don't and were thick enough to ask the question in the first place. The kind of look that has one corner of the top lip curved up and a stare to go with it.

'A Queer is a fellow who doesn't like girls,' says Seán Carey again in a low whisper.

Now I have to change the look on my face again that says 'Sure everyone knows that'. My heart is sinking because I've just found out I'm a Queer. I don't like girls either. I'll have to keep my mouth shut or I'll get kicked out of the Scouts like the other fellow. Then Seán Carey says again in a low whisper. 'He's a homosexual'.

I'm looking at Moore hoping he'll ask the question and when he does, Seán Carey says

'A homosexual is a fellow who prefers fellas'.

Again I have to have that know-it-all look on my face, and my heart sinks again, now I'm a homeless sexual too, because I like fellows as well. Why didn't Mam and Pop tell me I'm a Queer and a homeless sexual?

So when I go home, I burst out the question, 'Mam, Pop why didn't you tell me I'm a Queer and a homeless sexual, I could have been kicked out of the Scouts'.

Mam puts the sign of the cross on her forehead, followed by the usual verbal onslaught of 'Jesus, Mary and Holy St. Joseph', and wallops me into the ear. 'Where did you hear that kind of talk?'

Pop is on the chair shuffling his legs about, grunting and coughing. I know he's trying very hard not to laugh, but I'm getting sick and tired of this all the time. I'm holding my ear, that's hot and ringing from the wallop.

'Have I to stand here all day and wait for you to tell me where you heard that kind of filth?,' says Mam. If I tell her I heard it in the Scouts she'll stop me from going there altogether. So I have to tell her I heard it from two guys walking in front of me coming home that night.

'You're not a Queer or a Homosexual either, do you hear me?'

'But I don't like girls Ma and Queers don't like them either.'

'Oh, you'll like them soon enough, I can promise you that,' she says.

'Yeah, but the homothings prefer fellows and so do I so I must be one of them too!'

'You're not!'

'Why Mam?'

'Because that's the why!'

Mam and Pop are always telling me, 'that's the why' when I ask them questions. They tell me the teachers are the ones with all the answers. Pop is still coughing and choking with the shoulders going up and down. But I don't believe Mam. I'm a Queer and a homeless sexual. I'll keep my mouth shut because I love the Scouts.

At the next Scout meeting, Mr. O'Loughlin or Loughy if you're talking behind his back, is making something downstairs in the main hall. He has wood everywhere. Seán Carey says it's for the Christmas plays. And after two months Loughy has made a collapsible stage. It can be taken down every year and put away upstairs with all the tents and other things in the store room.

Loughy says that anyone who can play a musical instrument should bring it to the next meeting as the crowds will need to be entertained between the plays, and I'm saying to myself, is the dream of playing my lover pearly red accordion in front of a big crowd going to happen? So down I go on the bar of Pop's bike to the next meeting with the pearly box in its case tied carefully to the back carrier of his bike because he says, I'm going nowhere on my own with the instrument that nearly has him broke; that if it got stolen from the bould fellas in Weston while I was walking through The People's Park, I'd better find a new home to sleep in, because there's no way I'd be allowed back into No. 82. After dropping me and the box off at the Scout Hall he says I'm to be sure and wait for him when the meeting is over, that he has to do a small job in Henry Street, and I'm not to even think about going back home on my own with the pearly box. There's another fellow here already with a case that holds an accordion just like mine. Janey Mac! He can't have another pearly red accordion too. Sure Peter Dempsey had only the one on his window and didn't Pop buy that!

Then Loughy says as there's only two young fellows who can play an instrument between the troops we can share the entertaining. But he wants to hear us first to make sure we don't make a holy show of the good name of St. Joseph's Scouts. So he calls the other fellow first, and asks him to play a few tunes. His name is Billy Madigan. When he opens the case, there inside is a lovely pearly red accordion with piano keys instead of buttons like mine. I wonder is he any good. His accordion looks new just like mine. Maybe it's only his first few weeks; I might be able to give him a few tips later on when I get to know him. After he gets the straps around his shoulders and fixes the box comfortably on his chest, he runs the fingers of his right hand down the keys, they're floating away like a ballerina's feet. My jaw is resting on my knees, Janey he's brilliant, and he hasn't played anything yet! He's just warming up! After five minutes he's finished and Loughy is calling my name. I can hear his voice in the distance because I'm in shock. He has to touch me on the shoulder to get my attention. 'Come on young Taylor, you're next', he says. But I can hardly stand up after listening to that. Janey I wish I had gone first! I'm shaking as I put the straps around my shoulders and somehow manage to play three tunes. I know I'm not as good as Billy and there I was thinking I could help him. It's going to be the other way round. We become good friends. Billy will always take the time and trouble to pass on anything he learns. And between us manage to entertain the crowds every Christmas when the plays are on.

Each patrol is given a short play that lasts for twenty to thirty minutes. Our troop would have four plays which will be heard on a Saturday night. The other four plays which will be done by the fifth could be heard on a Sunday night. There will be an adjudicator for each night. He will tell everybody how each patrol performed, and how some actors did. There will be Mums and Dads, brothers and sisters there to see their sons and daughters and so on who took part.

There's great competition between the two Troops. I've been asked to play a grumpy old man with gout in his right foot. I can remember my first lines as the curtain opens. I'm sitting at the table with a huge bandage around my right foot. I bang the table with my right hand saying:

'Confound the old woman my doctor says'. Niall Carey is the idiot butler and John Moloney the idiot parlour maid. They are always falling over or dropping things on my foot. There's great fun and laughter and I really enjoyed those days when I thought I could act.

But we don't win first prize, it goes on Sunday night to Fonsey Meade's Patrol for 'The Monkey's Paw' in the Fifth Troop. And here we go again - last - the same old story. But it was worth every minute, being home every night, going over my lines, trying to make sure that I wouldn't forget or my brain would go blank on the night. And if it did there was always someone behind the curtain shouting a whisper over to any brain that went blank, and more often heard first by someone's brother or sister who might be sitting closer to the stage in the front row and nearer to the whisper, they'll shout across the stage to the head with the dead brain what he's supposed to say. And the whole place ignites in uproar, and the four or five lads on the stage are killing themselves trying not to laugh as it's a very serious play, and points could be lost if they did. To see other lads dressed up as old women and trying to talk like them too, their brothers and sisters, mothers and fathers in the audience trying hard not to laugh. It's hard to forget! But who'd want to forget?

Other troops like St. Michael's just around the corner, St. John's down by the Cathedral, St. Mary's and St. Patrick's are wondering why they don't have plays every Christmas like us. They're told they don't have Loughy, that's why.

Willie O'Loughlin representing St. Joseph's Scout Troop on their 60th Anniversary. With Pat Ring left

He worked as a sawyer for James McMahon on the Dock Road and on one occasion came to the Scout meeting with two or three fingers in heavy bandage. The story going around the patrol corners might be that they were cut off and the Doctors stuck them back together again. Loughy was a man for rules and regulations and doing everything by the book, a strict disciplinarian. If Pop happened to take me down to McMahon's for timber on a Saturday morning I'd see him working away at the saw; if he looked over and saw me he'd give me the Scout salute, the left hand with the small finger held down by the thumb over the left side of the head. He'd smile and if I was close enough he'd give me the Scout handshake. The same hand with the small fingers interlocked. This man loved scouting, it was his life. He was tailor-made for it. It seemed he had a bottomless pit of knowledge and loved sharing it with anyone who had an appetite for learning. All we had to do was ask. If you wanted to do a Scout test for a merit badge his face would light up with enthusiasm. I only ever did the one test and when Patsy Moore heard me, he asked to do the same. I knew I was going to be pestered with questions, while trying to do my own. We were out in Cappanty Woods, it's about four miles from the Scout Hall, or it might be Monroe Valley. We might do two hikes a month. A hike starts at about 10 o'c on a Sunday morning giving everyone an hour before to get Mass over at the Dominican Church. There's always a great turn out, nearly a full troop. Nobody minds the four mile walk. We have the haversack with the enamel plate, knife, fork and spoon, the cup hanging out of the side of the haversack. Some lads might take a frying pan. Mam would always be sure to give me a few sausages or rashers, maybe a small tin of peas or beans. And of course if there is no Spotted Dick or sultana cake my whole day would be ruined. There's always a sing song on the way out and back.

Spotted Dick is a recipe handed down from Nan's Grandmother. Mam will bake one every Saturday or Sunday. James and Jetta will tire of it and when they do I'll get more fond of it and she'll bake two every week. I'll always have five or six slices stuck together with butter that melts in the warm sunshine. I might give a slice to Pat Morris to make sure he stays beside me to make me look and sound intelligent. It would take us about an hour and a half to get to Monroe Valley or Cappanty Woods. There might be another troop from Limerick there before us; if there is, we'll have to find a good spot to set up the patrol fire.

Some will be asked to go and find rotten wood, there's plenty of that. No good Scout will cut wood from a tree just to burn.

Others are asked to go down by the river for three good sized rocks for the fire. Those who are asked to cut wood have to make sure there's a fork in it. We need two of them. Each patrol will have its own fire, so two wooden forks are required to hold a Billy-can on a stick between them. When I think back to all the sounds and smells it's wonderful. The aroma of wood burning and the smoke in the summer sun, the echoes of lads in the wooded area from the four different patrols looking for the rotten wood, the strong aroma of tea, sausages, eggs and rashers on the frying pans and best of all the freedom to roam the country and farmers giving us permission to go where we liked. And if one did have an accident which was rare, he went to hospital to have it fixed and never a thought of suing anyone.

I met a former scout in the city centre recently. He is still very involved in scouting at the age of sixty something. We talked of those great days how they'll never be seen again. I asked if he still went on hikes to Cappanty Moore or Monroe Valley. He looked at me as if I was after asking one of those stupid questions again of years gone by.

'Are you joking? he answered, 'they won't walk down the road to the Scout Hall now. They wouldn't even know how to spell 'hike' either. Scouting is nothing like it used to be'.

I'm thinking how lucky I was to have experienced that life, how better off we all were without the telly, the phone, the car and all the other gadgets that have made life easier but more complicated. What we had can never be replaced. The less we had fuelled the imagination. Nowadays there's plenty of reality this or reality that and Mr. Imagination is getting more and more redundant. The days of turning the kitchen table upside down on rainy days pretending it was a boat, a train or a car, taking the sheet off one of the beds and putting it between the chairs, getting hours of pleasure, cutting bits of wood into guns, climbing the trees in Nix's field to make bows and arrows to play Cowboys and Indians and everyone shouting at one another saying

'I shot you first' and

'No you didn't'

'I did' and

'You're not playing with us anymore, that's the fourth time I shot you, you won't admit it, you're always the same'.

Imaginary horses running around, making the horse sounds, and hitting ourselves on the thigh, saw us use the house for eating and sleeping only. The road was our oyster.

But it's back to Loughy and the tests for the two merit badges; one for cooking and one for fire lighting. Mam has given me eight small pieces of meat, an OXO cube, four potatoes and carrots. She says I'm to quarter fill the billycan, bring it to the boil, put the meat in, then add the OXO cube. Twenty minutes later check the meat, when that's nearly done throw the carrots and spuds in and leave until the veg. are soft. Then serve.

She makes me repeat it four times, to make sure I understand. Then tells me to be sure and 'eat it right away because that's your dinner I'm giving you'. Loughy takes Morris and myself away to another side of the hike site to make sure none of the lads can distract us from what we're doing.

First, is the fire lighting.

He says: 'I want you each to light a fire here and over there', pointing to a spot where he wants each of us to light our fires. 'I'll be back in twenty minutes to see how you're getting on'. He's no sooner gone when Morris starts,

'Taylor, what will I do first? What will I do?'

Let's go down to the river and get three good sized rocks each. But the idiot is just looking at me. 'Look for rocks just like these while I bring them up for my fire', you do the same'. When I come back there he is standing in the middle of the shallow river that has stones of all shapes and sizes with his hands in his pockets, looking at me again, and up to his ankles in water.

'What are you doing?,' I ask.

'I didn't find any'.

'Did you look?'

'Well, not really'.

'No', I said, 'you waited till I came back to do it for you! What's that and that and that over there?'

'Oh yeah,' he says, 'I never saw them, what will I do now?,' he says.

'What do you mean what will I do now you Eejit, bring them up and make three sides for your fire'.

'How will I do that?,' he asks.

'Like we did this morning, when we got here with the Troop,' I shout.

'I didn't do that, I had to collect rotten wood for the fire'.

'OK, ok,' I said, 'I'll show you'. So when I've shown him he says:

'What'll I do now?'

'Go and get more rotten wood. You'll need small bits first, then bigger pieces' and

when I come back with my rotten wood he's still in the same place looking at me with his hands in his pocket.

'Where's your wood?'

'I don't know where to get it', he answers.

'Why didn't you go to the same place you went to this morning when you went looking for the wood for our Patrol?'

'I can't remember how to get there', he says. 'Will you help me?'

So I tell him: 'Here, use mine, I'll get some more. Get your fire going while I get some more wood for my own. Don't forget we only have two matches each, and haven't much time left, Loughy will be back soon.'

When I come back there's no sign of his fire lighting.

'Why haven't you lit your fire?,' I ask.

'The two matches I had blew out in the wind.'

'You idiot, now we've only two matches left between us.'

And after lighting the first match, the wind catches it and blows it out.

'Flip you anyway Morris, now we've only the one match left between the two fires and it's all your fault.'

But when I strike the last match it sets fire to the small bit of sun burnt cluster of grass and within minutes Morris' fire is looking good.

Now I've got to get mine going quickly. It's all ready to go and I've got a small stick in Morris' fire and when it catches light, I'm about to bring it over to my own and there's Loughy coming down looking at me shaking his head in disapproval.

'That's cheating', he says . 'We take a very poor view of that kind of carry on. You could be thrown out on your ear over that'.

I'm looking at Morris, as Loughy rubs him on the head and says: 'Well done, that's a grand fire. You've passed. You've got your first merit badge. I'll have to talk to the other Scout Masters about you Taylor, whether you'll be let stay or not. OK, now its time for your next test, cooking. You might as well get a light from Morris' fire Taylor to start your own, I'll be back in another thirty five minutes'.

When he's gone I'm roaring at Morris asking him why the hell he didn't tell Loughy that I helped him.

'Because he might throw me out as well,' says Morris.

'Well you can do your own bloody cooking, don't ask me anything, because I'm not telling you - understand?'

After I get the fire started I'm trying to remember what Mam told me. Morris is looking at me trying to copy my every move and I'm trying hard not to let him see.

'Ah go on Taylor, tell us how to do it. What do I do? What do I put in first and how long do I leave it in for?'

'I don't think I've done it right and there's only ten minutes before Loughy comes back'.

He won't leave me alone and of course his total and complete dependence on me sucks me in again. I can't resist it.

'What did you put in first you Eejit,' I'm saying. 'You put the spuds in before the meat you clown'

As I'm trying to take his potatoes out of the boiling water, Morris is looking in at my stew. He's poking the meat with a fork. He says:

'Yours looks great Taylor,' and there's Loughy walking down to the two of us again and while Morris is poking away at my stew, I'm trying to get the potatoes out of his can. Loughy looks at Morris and says: 'I see you've swapped fires, let's see how you're doing with your stew Morris,' as he takes the fork from Morris' hand and puts a piece of meat to his mouth.

'Excellent, very good. Now let's see how the potatoes are doing, and the carrots, ah yes, great. And the juice tastes lovely. Well done Morris, that's another merit badge for you. And now

Taylor let's see how you're doing after your miserable attempt to start a fire by cheating.'

I'm standing there speechless, wondering how the hell can this be happening to me? Loughy is trying to sink the fork into a piece of Morris' meat, but it won't go. He manages to drag a piece up the side of the billycan into his hand and after putting it into his mouth, is making all kinds of funny faces as he tries to chew it, after spitting it out onto the ground he spurts: 'That meat isn't half cooked, let's see what the potatoes are like'. The fork won't go into them either.

'They're too hard, what the hell have you been doing for the last half an hour at all?' and stupid me is waiting again for Morris to open up and get me out of this mess again but there's no sign of that happening.

'Why can't you be more like Morris here, and apply yourself for goodness sake. It's not rocket science you know'.

I have to wait a whole two weeks before I'm told I can have a second chance and if I'm ever caught cheating again there will be no need for a meeting. I'll be shown the door. Morris isn't hanging around me anymore. I'm back feeling stupid again. When he gets the two merit badges, he's parading them around on one side of the sleeve of his scout shirt, all the lads are wondering how the hell Morris ever got to pass anything, especially when he just about passed the test to be invested.

It's seven months to Summer Camp 1961. We're going to Dunmore East, Co. Waterford and for the first time Pop is able to afford to give me the money. There's a savings club in the troop and anyone who joins gets a thrift book to save for the summer camp. If I bring two shillings a week to every meeting starting in January, I'll have enough to pay the two pounds, ten shillings for the trip by July and pocket money as well. Most of the other lads have been on camp before and they're telling me what it's like. I'm so excited my appetite is well and truly whetted. Nan gives me five shillings towards pocket money, Auntie Nora gives me two and six and there's a whole pound left over in the thrift book after the money for the holiday is paid. Pop gives me enough to have a whole two pounds ten shillings. I'm rich, so it's off to the CIE bus. It's a special one booked for the Fifth and Tenth Troops.

Noelie and myself at Limerick bus station waiting for the bus to Dunmore East.

It's parked outside the bus station. There's great excitement. Mam has told me to be sure and wash behind my ears and brush my teeth every day and not make a holy show of her. I think she's going to start crying. I know that look and the sound of her voice, when she's going to start I want to get out of here before she does. She might decide not to let me go at all. It'll be the first time I've ever been away from home for two weeks. I've been away before to Tower Hill but that was only for a weekend or a few days. But she's all over me, wanting to kiss and cuddle me, it's driving me mad. I've a holiday to go to, a bus to catch, money to spend and this woman is holding me up.

We're on our way singing every kind of song. *'It's a Long Way to Tipperary'* 'without your mother' shouts Gerry Buckley. *'Heads, Shoulders, Knees and Toes'*, the rugby song *'There Is An Isle'* and many more all shorten the journey to our camp in Dunmore East.

It's 6 o'clock and there's a buzz of excitement everywhere. Everyone wants to get involved in getting the large bell tents up. They had to be taken down from the top of the bus and erected, wood has to be collected, a campfire has to be started, food needs to be prepared and before we know it the bus has gone. It's completely dark. We're all sitting around the campfire. There's another sing-song. Sparks are flying into the night sky. I'm going to sleep in a tent for the first time and I'm thinking 'things can't get any better' but they will. It's time to throw our ground sheet on the grass in the tent but finding a level piece of ground is difficult in the dark. It is also important not to park ourselves in the middle of a pile of cow dung. We're talking most of the night - the stories of other summer camps are recalled and before we know it we're awake to the sounds of birds chirping away.

I'm scratching and itching everywhere. There's all kinds of things crawling all over me, but it's worth it. It's time for the breakfast. It's our patrol's turn to get the breakfast ready. Bread has to be buttered, a fire needs to be started, water collected, porridge to be made, sausages, rashers and cornflakes. If you don't like cornflakes you can have porridge. There's a special tent called the food-store, some call it the kitchen. It's out of bounds if it's not your turn to work there. The troop is called to gather together. We're told the rest of the day is set aside to set up the camp site properly, fit it out. A party is sent to the woods to cut some trees to make tripods for outside every tent to hold the wash basin, racks for towels and Loughy is in the middle of it all showing older lads how to make this and that. And by the end of the first day the campsite looks the business and now it's time to go to the village of Dunmore East.

It's a fifteen minute walk from camp. I want to get my presents for everyone at home sorted out the first night, as whatever money that's left over will be mine. There's just one shop in the place. It's one of those country shops, a Post Office, a Butcher Shop, a Grocery Store-cum-Funeral Undertaker, Betting Office and anything else you need. It's got a bit of a glass counter with souvenirs under it. There's a jar containing long pink sticks of rock, two will do nicely for Jetta and James. Then there's a saucer with the words, 'Good Luck from Dunmore East'. Nan will love that. She'll hang it on her wall in Tower Hill and tell everyone her grandson in Limerick brought it back from Waterford. There's a small glass ball with little figurines inside, when shaken or turned upside down, it snows. That will do nicely for Mam. She won't care what I get her, just as long as I get her something. With her, it's the thought. Now for the big problem - what am I going to get Pop? A packet of cigarettes will do the trick, but I'm in Scout uniform and I'm not old enough to be buying cigarettes. A guy called Pat Jones, he's with me. We don't want to give St. Joseph's Tenth or Fifth Troop a bad name, so we have to leave. Pat asks me what am I going to do, as it's the only shop in the whole place in Dunmore East that presents can be bought in and it's getting to me. I wanted to get the presents tonight and carefully stretch whatever is left over the next two weeks. I have two pounds five shillings left.

We can hear music playing in the distance. It's coming from the harbour area. There's other scouts' heading in that direction too. As we get closer to the pier the music is easy to identify. It's Ricky Nelson's great hit '*Hello Mary Lou*'. There's a canteen in the middle of the long concrete pier. That's where the music is coming from.

We will spend every night of the Summer Camp here. Ricky Nelson will sing his throat dry, by the time we go home the canteen owner's business will have reached new heights on Ricky, glasses of Fanta, Coke and chips. Our steps to the canteen take a sudden stop, when a massive fish comes up from below the pier. It has flopped itself on the ground and lies there motionless. Pat and I look at one another in shock and before we take another step or utter a word, up comes another and lands with a wallop right beside the first one.

Each fish must be the bones of two and a half foot long. We want to investigate and lean over the edge. The tide is out. There's a guy in a small boat ten feet below us. He must have about forty of those fish in the boat and they're all the same size.

'What kind of fish are they Sir?,' I shout down.

'B - - - - -ks,' he shouts back. I'm looking at Pat, wondering why this guy is using such bad language at me; sure I only asked him a civilised question. There's no need for that kind of talk.

'They're Pollack's,' he shouts again.

'Do you want one?,' he asks.

'Yes, please', I answer,

'Take as many as you like,' he shouts and boy am I excited. Pat wants to know what I want with a big ugly looking yoke like that, so I tell him about all the years I spent fishing with my Dad, how I can never catch a fish when I'm with him, that he goes home every time with four or five trout in his bag with a big grin on his face, but I'm going to have the last laugh now.

'Why is that?,' asks Pat.

'Because I'm going to bring it home as a present. I'll tell him I caught it down here, he'll be hopping mad.'

There's a couple of pages of newspaper stuck between two fishing crates. I'm able to wrap the Pollack in it, but its big ugly head and tail are sticking out both ends. And it's off down to the canteen. There's a lovely smell of chips wafting around the entrance while Ricky sings away.

There's four local girls hanging around, throwing the shapes: Pat and I are at the first stage of the sexual process and so are they. It's only a matter of time before some of the lads are jumping all over them, pulling their hair, getting them in the head lock, thumping them in the back, they're screaming their heads off, like they're in awful pain. They're calling the lads terrible names; how they'll get their fathers or big brothers if we don't leave them alone. But they'll be back every night looking for more and loving every minute of it. And I can't get involved tonight because of the big fish with the ugly head that's going to ruin Pop's life. And I'm not letting go of it, no matter how good looking these girls are.

The girls have gone home. They think all their birthdays have come together. There's forty more lads from Limerick who want to follow them every night. They'll be black and blue and minus half their hair over the next two weeks. They'll want to know are there any more Scouts coming down from Limerick this year and will we be coming back again the same time next year. Then it's back to the camp site.

When we get there, I'll take everything out of my haversack; put this beauty that's under my arm into it, wrap it in the few clean shirts that Mam gave me. I'll sleep on it for the next 13 nights and can't wait to see Pop's face when I get home. I'll dream about it every night and the face that Pop will have when he sees it. I still have the two pounds five shillings left; I can spend it all on myself. The sing-song and entertainment around the campfire has started which we'll have every night.

Niall Carey will be telling the same old jokes he told last year and the year before, and one or two new ones. He'll do the commentary on The Grand National with the same old horse names like 'Whitewash', 'Banana', 'Loose Button', 'Invisible', 'Dizzy', 'Strike It Rich', 'Bungalow', 'Dynamite' and 'Right Way'. Then he'll start by saying:

'They're under starter's orders and they're off.' Then he'll raise his voice in an excited manner. 'Right Way has made an instant distance from himself and the rest, because Right Way has gone the wrong way.' His voice is calmer now. We're all laughing our heads off. He's holding a piece of stick in his right hand, pretending it's a microphone. He continues: 'It's Whitewash out in front, followed by Banana, behind him there's...,' then he shouts, 'Banana has slipped, I repeat Banana has slipped'. He carries on: 'It's Whitewash followed by Dizzy, then there's Strike It Rich'. He's holding a pair of binoculars in his other hand, looking out into the distance. He continues, 'Then Dynamite, he's in fourth place followed by Invisible and he's followed by Loose Button, we're coming round the first bend now, and its still Whitewash, he's on the fence followed by Dizzy, Strike It Rich is still in third place and a length behind, 'Invisible' has moved in front of Dynamite. Then he'll raise his voice, and shout 'Loose Button has fallen out, I repeat, 'Loose Button' has fallen out. Then he shouts again, I'm looking for 'Bungalow', he's no where to be seen, he must have gone home. Now it's a five horse race. Then he raises his voice again and shouts 'Strike it Rich' has gone for broke and gone out into the lead. 'Dizzy is going round in circles and is going nowhere. Invisible is nowhere to be seen'. Then Niall gets even more excited and shouts, 'Dynamite has exploded into the lead'. It's down to Dynamite followed by Strike It Rich, behind him is Whitewash. It's a three horse race. They're racing towards the finish line. Then Niall shouts 'Whitewash' is stuck to the fence and it's a two horse race now and only a hundred yards to go. It's between these two now. Then Niall gets into a frenzy and we're all shouting 'Come on Dynamite' others want Strike It Rich to win. Last time he performed this gig Dynamite won and when he's finally finished he decides Strike It Rich is the winner to a huge round of applause and cheers.

Then it's a sing -song, like 'The Pub With No Beer', everyone knows the words of that. 'The Black Velvet Band', 'The Leaving of Liverpool', then Seán Carey will come and do a sketch. It lasts five minutes.

He'll be talking to himself. He'll tell everyone that he's gambled all the housekeeping money, and he is afraid to go home. And unless he can find a way of getting some cash quickly he'll be in big trouble. His voice isn't as loud as his brother Niall so he has to make a huge effort to be heard above the crackling wood burning away on the large fire that sends sparks large and small into the night sky. He asked Pat Jones, Gerry Buckley and myself to take part. How could I refuse? I'm going to be the centre of attention for about two minutes. Pat Jones and Gerry Buckley are quieter. They have to be talked into it and most importantly we have cash, we have two pounds each in our pockets and Seán needs them for the sketch. Seán is pretending to be slightly drunk. I'm supposed to be passing by on the street minding my own business. He'll hold out his hand stopping me saying: 'Excuse me Sir, would you like to make a handy two pounds?,' Now two pounds in those days represented a quarter of a week's wages. So I have to act delighted and say 'yes'.

'OK,' he says. 'I'm going to bet you £2.00 that I'm not here'.

I have my hand on my head scratching it, looking puzzled. Then I have to say:

'Let me get this clear now, you're after putting £2.00 down there on the ground, and you're telling me you're going to prove that you're not here. Have I that right now?,'

'That's right,' says Seán playing the drunk very well.

And I have to say 'Right, I'll have some of that' while taking the £2.00 from my pocket and putting it down very carefully on the ground making sure it's well away from the campfire. If anything happens to my £2.00 I'm in right trouble for the next thirteen nights. Without it I'm going to have a miserable time. So Seán says:

'Right, am I in Dublin?'

I have to say 'No'.

Then he says 'Am I in Cork?'

And again I have to say 'No'.

'Am I in Limerick?,' he asks.

Again, it's the same answer, 'No'.

'Well', he says 'if I'm not in Dublin, Cork or Limerick, I have to be someplace else, right?'

I say 'Right!'

Then Seán says 'If I'm someplace else, I can't be here, right, bends down and takes up my two pounds along with his own.

Now I have to look puzzled as I walk away scratching my head as Seán walks off with my two pounds stuck in his pocket. Then Seán starts talking to himself again, shouting out the words, 'If I can find another two Eejits, like that one, I'll be able to go home in no time at all to the wife with the full week's wages and she'll be delighted.'

And then along comes Pat Jones, it's the same routine, and now Seán has six pounds. Then it's Gerry's turn and when Seán gets to the part where he says: 'If I'm someplace else, I couldn't be here, right?' Gerry bends down grabs the four pounds from the ground and shouts; 'If you're not here how can you take the money on the ground?' and everyone shouts and cheers in approval.

The songs, sketches and commentary of the Grand National will be done again before we go home and at other gatherings every year. But no matter how often we see and hear them, they'll always be a huge part of the scouting way. But Seán has the two pounds belonging to Pat, Gerry and myself and there's no sign of it coming back. I have only three shillings left and I'll surely spend two bob of that tomorrow night on Mary Lou, Fanta and chips at the canteen on the pier. So when I ask Seán for my two pounds he tells me he gave it to the Scout Master and Loughy has an angry look on his face when I ask him for the two pound notes Seán Carey gave him to mind.

'I know nothing about your two pounds, who told you I had it?,' asks Loughy.

'Seán Carey told me, he gave it to the Scout Master, Sir. So I thought that was you Sir'.

'He must have meant the Assistant Scout Master, Tommy Deegan'.

He doesn't know what I'm talking about either, and all of a sudden I'm in a panic, will I ever see my two pounds again? What am I going to do for the next twelve days without any money? When I tell Seán that neither Loughy nor Tommy don't know anything about the two pounds he scratches his head and says 'I was sure I gave it to one of them, it was so dark at the time, maybe I gave it to the Fifth Troop Scout Master Dick Penny, or his Assistant Hugh McGrath. Ask them'. But I'm wondering why I have to go and ask these people where my money is, when it was Sean's responsibility.

Dick Penny and Hugh McGrath tell me they know nothing about my money either.

'Who told you we had your money?'

'Seán Carey,' I answer.

'Well let's go and see Seán Carey and ask him why he told you we had your money'. They're hopping mad and now I'm in big trouble with my Patrol Leader Seán.

'Paddy Taylor has just told us you gave his two pound notes to us to mind, why did you tell him that?,' asks Dick Penny.

'I never told him that at all,' answers Seán.

'Well, what the hell is he talking about so?,' asks Hugh McGrath.

Now the five of them are looking at me. They're very cross. They're going to run me out of the Scouts because I'm a liar and I've no witnesses, how the hell am I going to walk home with my fish all the way back to Limerick on my own with only three bob in my pocket? I don't even know how to get there and there's a sudden burst of laughter that lifts me out of my nightmare. Seán, Dick and Hugh are laughing their heads off.

'You should see your face,' says Seán handing me back the two pounds. It's a wind-up, what a relief! I'm still in the Scouts and the holidays are looking good again. I'll get my own back on Seán but I'll have to wait until Christmas comes again and the next series of Scout plays.

The rest of the first week has Loughy showing us great new things. He'll start something and it's the same procedure every time, never telling us what he's going to do. We have to watch and guess. He digs a hole in the ground. It's the shape of a banana, getting deeper in the middle.

He places a large Jacobs' biscuit tin on its side into the deeper part. He has three iron bars holding the tin six inches above the middle. He covers the top part of the tin with earth mixed with water making a dampish mud. Everyone is watching and there's no suggestions from anyone as to what he's doing. Then he reaches down into the hole placing wood under the biscuit tin and eventually puts a match to it. Then he asks everyone 'who likes doughnuts?,' and everybody but me shouts, 'we do!'

'Well in the next hour, you're all going to have two doughnuts for supper tonight'. There's another big cheer. Then we all want to know what the yoke in the ground is for.

'It's my oven,' says Loughy 'and as soon as it heats up, I'll show you how it works'.

'I've got everything ready in the kitchen tent,' he says, so after checking the Jacob's biscuit tin he removes the part which is on its side in the hole, he has two steel shelves already in the tin to keep and bake the doughnuts and as promised, there's enough doughnuts to give every Scout two for the supper that night. They were the only doughnuts I've ever eaten in my life, and I have never tasted anything like them since!

It's the end of my first week in Dunmore East, anyone passing the entrance of our tent, or has any reason to come in, complain about a bad smell and wonder where it's coming from. Those of us, who sleep here, have no idea what they're talking about. I don't want this holiday to end, but I'll still lie in bed at night thinking of my massive Pollack under my head in my haversack. I wish I was at home now, putting it into Pop's hands and him going mad because I caught a bigger fish than he ever did. But there's another week to go and the complaints about the smell are increasing and nobody wants to come into our tent. There'll be great activity for the second and last week down here, swimming at the beach, football, rugby. We'll be making bridges from trees we cut in the woods close by.

There'll be more sing-songs at night and we're half way into the second week and I'm not allowed into another tent. The four girls down at the canteen are keeping well away from me, I think it's because I'm not their type. It's Friday night, we're going home tomorrow and I've only two bob left for the night. I've spent £2/3/s over the last two weeks on Fanta orange, fries, and Ricky's Mary Lou. I'll never have this much money again. It's been the best two weeks of my life and I can't sleep tonight because of the excitement of the Pollack I'm bringing home tomorrow.

The bus has arrived. Tins, pots and pans go on top and everybody wants to know what that awful smell is and where it's coming from. I'm told to sit at the back of the bus on the way home. Some of the lads are shouting back: 'Taylor, how long has it been since you washed yourself?' Another will say, 'Do you know what a bath looks like Taylor?' And another will say, 'Taylor has a bath once a year whether he needs it or not'. I have no idea what all the fuss is about. The wise cracks are flying all the way home, I'm the centre of attention again; it lasts for hours and I'm loving it.

I'm running all the way home. It's six o'clock on a Saturday evening. Pop will be sure to be home for me to give him the fish. There's Mam at the door waiting. She knows the time I'm due home. I better not let her see I never changed the shirt she gave me, that I used it to wrap the fish in over the newspaper.

'Come over here and give your poor mother a kiss and a hug. I've missed you for the past two weeks'

'Ah Janie Ma, don't be doing that out here on the road with everybody looking'.

But she grabs me by the shirt collar, throws the two arms round me, and before I get the big suck on the cheek, she shouts; 'Jesus, Mary and Holy St. Joseph what's that awful smell? Did you wash yourself at all? What or where were you sleeping in or on over the last two weeks?'

I managed to avoid the question: 'Is Pop home?,' I ask, but before anyone can answer I'm in the room. Nan is there as well. Sure she's never any place else. She's looking at me with her nose twisted to one side. She takes a handkerchief from under one of the sleeves of her cardigan, puts it over her nose and mouth; then utters the words; 'Jesus, where has he been for the last two weeks?' Pop is looking at me strangely. Jetta and James come running in off the road, they know I have something for them.

'OK, I have presents for everyone', I shout. 'And the best one's for you Pop'. So I reach carefully into the haversack, take out the two sticks of rock for James and Jetta.

'Now Nan, look what I've got for you'. She's nodding away with the handkerchief still over her nose and mouth. Her eyes are looking over at Mam asking 'where's that awful smell coming from?'

'Now Mam, this is for you'. Not hearing anything Mam might have said by way of thanks, I say:

'OK Pop, close your eyes, put out your hands, I'm going to put your present into them.' I'm right in front of him taking the Pollack out; still in the old newspapers after I managed to take away the shirt that Mam gave me, without her seeing me. I put the paper into Pop's outstretched hands. Nan and Mam can see the shrunken head and tail sticking out of both ends. Nan cries: 'Oh Mother of Divine Jesus, look what he's after taking out of the bag!' I'm looking straight into Pop's face, while pulling away the newspaper. I say, 'OK Pop, you can look now'.

I want to see the shock of surprise on his face, when he sees the size of this fish and in perfect motion our heads go down together.

'Look what I caught for you.' Our heads come back up again together. There's shock in both his eyes and mine. Nan is saying 'Jesus, Mary and Holy St. Joseph, look at what's he's after bringing into the house'. Mam is speechless. She can't believe what I've brought home. We're all standing except Pop. He is sitting down looking into the paper. It's crawling with maggots.

'Where's the fish gone?,' I shout.

'What fish?,' says Pop.

'The part that was in between the head and tail', I answer.

'Where did you get it?,' asked Pop.

'In Dunmore East', I said.

'WHEN did you get it?,' he says with the shoulders going up and down.

I'm thinking how the hell did this happen? This isn't turning out the way I planned it at all.

'Two weeks ago,' I answer and Nan goes again 'Jesus, Mary and Holy St. Joseph, he caught it two weeks ago'. I wish to God she'd stop saying 'Jesus, Mary and Holy St. Joseph' and repeating everything I say. She's driving me mad. Pop's shoulders are getting out of control. He's trying to ask me where I kept it for the last two weeks. Mam knows what he's trying to say and says it for him.

'I kept it in my haversack and slept on it for the last two weeks in the tent'. Pop falls off the chair. Nan starts howling with laughter and off she goes again 'Jesus, Mary and Holy St. Joseph, he kept it in his bag and slept on it for the last two weeks'.

But Mam isn't laughing. She can see how hurt I am. She knows how much this meant to me and what my intentions were. She tries to console me, but I'm deeply hurt. I shout, 'I hate you all, I hate you!' The laughing stops. There's a long silence. If this was another occasion, another time, I'd be on the floor now, my neck would be broken, and there'd probably be an ambulance on its way for me. I ran upstairs. I'm left alone and the two best weeks of my life now seem to be the worst. But like life, I get over it. We would talk about this days and weeks later and laugh at it. And then I could see the funny side. And yes! It was the best two weeks of my life.

It's coming up to Christmas time again and Loughy will have the collapsible stage rearing to go. The rehearsals will start. Our patrol will do *The Monkey's Paw*. It's the play Fonsey's Patrol did last year. We'll be on the Saturday night, Loughy and Billy Madigan will provide the entertainment during the interval. There'll be days and weeks of intense rehearsals. We'll be at home, each one of us going over our lines, trying to make sure we don't forget and embarrass ourselves and the Patrol as well. Billy will keep the crowd happy with a good sing-song outside the curtain while Loughy gets the stage ready.

Loughy will have a large white sheet covering the entire front of the stage. There'll be a good sized light behind the sheet at the back of the stage, casting shadows on whatever passes in front. The audience can see a shadow of a Nurse, she's talking to a shadow of a Doctor who's sitting on the shadow of a chair in front of a shadow of a desk. The Nurse tells the Doctor there's a patient in bad pain who wants to see him right away. The shadow of the patient comes, he sits on the chair. The Doctor puts a stethoscope to his chest and stomach and shouts: 'It's an emergency, we have to operate straight away. Get the anaesthetic Nurse!'

Nurse leaves the stage. Doctor puts patient on desk. Patient tells Doctor he doesn't like knives or needles. Doctor assures him there'll be no needles. Patient is sitting up on desk. Nurse comes in with large mallet. Doctor says to Nurse; 'Apply the anaesthetic'. Nurse hits patients on the head with large mallet which really is only a stick with a large sponge but looks like the shadow of a mallet to the audience.

Patient falls back on desk unconscious. Audience screams with laughter. Doctor asks Nurse for knife. Audience sees shadow of Doctor raise his hand with pointed knife. Doctor sticks knife into patient's tummy. Patient raises body upwards while screaming his head off. Audience jumps with fright, then laughs. Doctor asks Nurse to administer the anaesthetic a second time. Audience roars laughing again. Doctor is handed the knife again, cuts open the patient's tummy. Audience screams as Doctor pulls away what looks like patient's skin. Doctor uses a saw to cut through ribs. In the background Gerry Buckley is cutting a piece of wood to the same momentum as the Doctor. Doctor takes out ribs, rolls up his sleeves, puts hand down into patient's tummy. He's got a box by the patient's body at the side of the desk that can't be seen. He's got a bucket of water, puts his hand into the water and makes a splashing sound. Then he pulls all kinds of things out of the box, there's a shadow of a string of sausages on the screen, a shoe, a frying pan, a sock, a scissors, a phone. The audience are screaming with laughter. Then he starts to sew up the patient and the audience jumps again as the patient shouts and raises himself erect on the desk, only for the nurse to give him another thump with the anaesthetic. Then the patient will wake up feeling great, the big bulb will go out. Across will come the screen to cheers and huge applause. Loughy was the Doctor and he's done it again.

The following night will be Seán Carey's time to entertain the crowd at the interval. He'll be the Great Houdini and I'm going to be his assistant. I can't wait. I'm in the limelight again and Pop has a great saying which says, 'opportunity only knocks once.' But that's all I need. It's payback time for Seán.

The curtains open. There's a large brown box that Seán has put together. It looks like a coffin. It's resting on the table that has a cloth draped around it to cover its legs. Seán asks for a volunteer from the audience and before anyone has a chance Gerry Buckley is on the stage and the lads from the Fifth Troop are shouting 'fix, fix'.

Seán tells the audience that he is going to put this volunteer into the box and then cut him in half. Gerry pretends to run away and is forced back on stage to continue. Two large lads lift Gerry into the coffin. When the coffin is closed, Gerry's head and legs are sticking out at both ends. Seán gets a saw; he starts to cut his way down. The whole place jumps when Gerry lets an awful roar out. He shouts 'stop, stop' but Seán keeps cutting away. Gerry looks like he's in trouble, but it's all part of the act and Gerry is lifted out of the box still in one piece. There's a huge roar of applause and cheers. They take a bow and now it's time for the second trick.

The curtain is drawn again. Gone is Gerry's coffin. There's a round coloured tin box resting on the table. Seán opens the lid of the box and shows the audience ten coloured pieces of chalk. He tells them he's going to give the box to his assistant, me, to give to one member of the audience. They are to take from the box whatever amount of pieces of chalk they want while he has his back turned to the audience. When his assistant returns with the box closed and placed on the table he will tell how many pieces were taken or left. Seán has the numbers one to ten wrote in pencil on the top of the table. He has shown me a small mark he made with a junior hacksaw blade on the tin. He has told me to place the mark to the number of chalks that are left in the tin. Four pieces of chalk were taken out by a young girl and I've shown my hand to the audience with the four fingers, making sure everyone can see what is taken out of the box. I place the box back on the table, making sure that the mark on the box is pointing at pencil mark number seven. Seán mumbles some sort of foreign magic formula over the box with his eyes closed and then shouts:

'There are seven pieces of chalk left in this box which means there were three taken out'.

Everybody shouts, 'No, you're wrong'.

When Seán opens the box, to his horror there are six pieces left. Seán looks at me. I have to look totally surprised so Seán says 'OK, let's try one more time'.

He hands me the tin box with all twelve pieces in it and gives me a look that would kill. I look back like I haven't a clue what's gone wrong. So back I go to the audience, repeat the same thing while Seán is turned into the wall. A young lad takes one piece of chalk out and I'm showing everybody one finger in the air. I place the box again on the table making sure the box is by the number six. Then Seán shouts; 'there are six pieces of chalk left in the tin, someone has taken four pieces' and while Seán is opening the box to show everyone, the audience are shouting 'no, no, there are nine pieces left'.

Then Seán shouts, 'ah well, it just goes to show you can't be right all the time'.

And I have to get out of here as fast as I can because Seán is like a dog and I have to miss at least four meetings waiting for him to cool down. But it was well worth it!

This is only a small portion of the years I spent in St. Joseph's Scouts. I can look back at this time of my life with great affection for all those people who loved scouting and the help they gave to young boys who wanted to become good men, like the Deegans, the Careys, the Madigans, O'Keeffes, the Downes, McGraths and many others.

To those who are no longer with us today but left so much of themselves behind a big thank you from all of us; Pat Jones, Dick Penny, Hugh McGrath Willie Loughlin and many more.

from left Noel Grace, Gerry Buckley, Tim O'Keeffe, Fonsie Meade, Myself, Billy Madigan, Pat Madigan, Niall Carey and Tommy Deegan.

Chapter 11

Mary says that our rubbish collector Mr. Binman wants all their customers to collect new plastic recycling bags from their office in St. John's Square starting next month. They want us to separate the clean stuff, put it into the bags and leave it alongside our bin every Tuesday. When next month comes there they are outside our gate, full to the top with all the other neighbours' bins and bags as well. 'It means,' says Mary 'That our bill for the rubbish will be smaller every year as everyone is charged according to the weight of their bins and no charge for the plastic bag that has the empty milk and bottle containers, pea and bean tins, newspaper, cardboard, plastics and God knows what else to be re-used and maybe find their way back into our homes in some shape or colour in the near future.' I'm wondering how two people can acquire so much rubbish in only seven days. So off my mind goes to Carey's Road again and the small battered bucket that was big enough to hold the morsel of real rubbish from a family of five every week. I'm asking myself how come we had so little rubbish then. But it doesn't take me long to figure it out. I'm wondering if we ever heard that word 'recycle' and if we did would we know what it meant, or even be able to pronounce it properly?

We had another expression back then for anything that looked like it was worth keeping. 'I'll use that again' and we did. The biscuit tin, large or half sized from Jacobs the people who make better biscuits better every day, or Boland's. Every house in Ireland had a good few of those tins, and they were treated like gold dust. We had three from the previous Christmas' that Pop brought home from a job he might be lucky enough to have around that time of the year. Mam might give Jet and myself two biscuits each on Christmas Day, and keep the rest for the odd visitor we might get over the holidays if Pop was off the drink. If there were any left by the end of the month, Jet and myself would scoff the lot because if Mam kept them any longer they'd go soft from the dampness that never left our house, even in the summer.

Pop has one he always keeps under the bed; it's a full-sized tin. It has every kind of nail and screw, new and used. He'll come home after work and empty all his pockets that always contains leftovers from the day's work, or if he's walking anywhere and sees a nail on the ground even though it's bent or rusty, it's into the pocket, then it gets a couple of belts of the hammer to straighten it when he gets home and it's into the biscuit tin to join all the other nuts, bolts and washers of all sizes. Parts belonging to old clocks, hinges with years of paint disguising the good quality brass they are made from, thumb tacks, one-sided blades, there's even an old shaving brush and when that tin is full he will have another one ready for the next lot that might take years to fill.

Mam's one can be found in the bottom of her kitchen cabinet that contains cutlery and food for the table. It has odd socks, sewing needles and thread that she has out on her lap every night by the fire, sewing a hole or two in a sock that she stuck a 60 Watt bulb into to help keep its shape while she sews away for the second or third time around. When the sock can't be put on the foot because it's been darned too many times, is beyond repair and going nowhere, it can be seen a couple of days later on Mam's hands washing the windows or even the floor. Other nights she'll work on a frock, maybe a dress that arrived in a parcel from the States or from her sister in Northampton months ago. She has only found the time now to do the alterations. If there was a trousers from Uncle Dave in the States, Mam might have a bit of work to do on that too. Pop will be at one end of the table with the glasses at the end of his long nose and the tongue out, trying to fix a lamp, clock or radio he's brought home that might be better than the ones we have at the moment.

There's a tin too for Jetta that she keeps under her side of the bed. She doesn't have much in it but the novelty makes her feel she's grown up. Then there's the shoebox; the few times that new shoes saw the inside of our house gave us another cardboard box to put under the bed, maybe to give other things a home. And the string that's wrapped around it four times has its knot carefully undone and folded tidily away into Mam's kitchen cabinet drawer with others. The brown strong paper too gets folded neatly and put away with the snow white soft paper that was wrapped neatly around the shoes.

Next is the jam jars, when their contents are empty Mam will have these gleaming after a good wash to join others she has put away for the housewife in Rathbane who makes the homemade jam and wants to buy good clean jars at thruppence each to fill and sell to the shops. The empty pea or bean tins Pop will use to make a savings tin, to collect the pennies, half pennies and if we're lucky the odd thruppence or sixpence. And that's the green light for my next subject - pocket money. An expression we never heard in my day, and if we did, we'd say 'where else would you put it?,' We called it whatever we wanted it for, like 'Can I have money for the pictures Mam?,' or

'Pop can I?'

Pop says 'No'.

'Pop I haven't finished what I was going to say'.

And he'll say, 'Are you looking for money?'

And I'll say, 'Yes Pop'.

'Well the answer is still No'.

'But you haven't heard what I want it for Pop'.

'What you're wanting it for won't change the fact that I haven't got it'.

This is often the case so Jet and myself have to think of different ways to earn money to get ourselves down to the City Theatre where we get a lolly pop when we pay the four pence each for the Sunday matinee. If we don't it will be the usual hanging around the corner across the road from Dinny McGrath's house waiting for Pop to appear over the iron bridge after coming home from the snooker room overhead Cavendish's or the cards at Maureen Faye's, and if he's won we'll get the money. If not we'll be the only ones on the road who aren't going to the Pictures and it gets awfully embarrassing when the lads come home that evening. They'll want to know what cinema we went to but we'll have to find out where they went first, so we can tell them we went to a different one than them. Jetta and I have to make sure we get our stories right of the film we didn't go to; otherwise we'll get found out and look like right clowns.

Right across the road and a few doors down from Ford's pub next door to Fonsey Meade is Christy Davis. Mam says it's OK to call him by his first name as well as Nellie with the sticks because they're not married. When Christy comes out of his house every morning, he'll have the birdcage in one hand and a walking stick in the other. He'll hang the cage on the same nail every day and take it in again before it gets dark. This is where our daily supply of a penny comes from. Out the back of his house Christy keeps four or five pigs and in the six years I lived on Carey's Road I never saw one of them, but could hear them every day. He used to breed and kill them for himself. When it was a pig's turn to get the knife to the throat, the screams coming from Christy's house over his roof could be heard all over Upper Carey's Road and was hard to bear.

Because Dinny was five years older than me, I asked him one day what happened to Christy's leg and why is he always limping. So Dinny said Christy was trying to catch one of his pigs out the back around the yard, to cut its throat when Christy tripped over the root of a tree and fell hitting his knee off a sharp stone and has never been able to walk right since. But in spite of being in constant discomfort Christy was a lovely man. When it was brought to our attention that Christy needed the leftovers from everybody's dinner; mostly potato skins, and that we would get a penny for our trouble, Jet and I are taking turns every second day with the plate of scraps.

When we knock on his door he'll come out and make a great fuss. 'Ah good man', he'll say, 'sure the pigs out there are making a great racket looking for their dinner'. So he'll take the plate and wipe every bit of whatever is on it into a bucket and use the same hand to put into his pocket to take the pennies out. He'll say 'thanks very much young man,' while putting the greasy penny into the palm of my hand. His pennies will always be old and very smooth. Sometimes they are jet black and they will be more than a hundred years old.

So that's nearly four pence each every week for Jet and myself. But we need more to keep the pea tins topped up for the presents we look forward to buying every year. After two and a half weeks I went down to Woolworth's on O'Connell Street by myself to see what I could get for the shilling I had saved. It's time to put on the sad face, the innocent voice and the 'Isn't he lovely?,' act.

'Excuse me, can you help me please?,' I wait until two of the ladies are together having a chat, because there's no one to serve and that will be the time to strike.

'Yes darling, what can we do for you?,'

Great, it's working already!

'Tomorrow is my mother's birthday', which is a downright lie, 'and I want to buy her something'.

'Ah isn't that lovely?' one says to the other and I'm on a winner here.

'Have you anything in mind pet?,' says one of the ladies.

'Well no, not really, I need some help please'.

'Of course my love, that's what we're here for; isn't that right Eileen?,' she said to the other assistant.

In the meantime there are other customers waiting to be served, but I've got these girls' complete and total attention.

'What about a nice brush and comb with a mirror? It's a lovely set. She'd love that I'm sure!'

'How much is that please Miss?,' I ask.

She turns to the other assistant and says, 'Isn't he a grand mannerly young man?'

And I'm thinking - this is going better than I thought.

'Two and six pence darling'.

'Oh I'm afraid that's too much', I answer.

OK love, how about a set of pens, a writing pad and envelopes?'

'How much are those please?'

'Oh they're one and nine pence ha'penny love'.

'I'm very sorry but that's too much as well'.

'How much have you got Pet?'

'One shilling, Miss'.

'Ah sure God love him' says the two ladies and there's a big crowd waiting around to be served. And they're all going 'Ah isn't that lovely?' as well.

'I'm afraid my love that all we have for that amount of money are some plastic roses'.

'How much would one be please Miss?'

And the crowd go 'Ah' again.

'Here love you can have one for the shilling and everyone goes 'Ah isn't that lovely? Isn't he a grand lad? I bet his mother is very proud of him'.

She puts the single rose into a brown paper bag and I'm off.

When the morning comes I'm up before Mam tip-toeing into the kitchen trying not to wake her or anybody else. She'll walk into the kitchen, jump with the fright, shouting 'Jesus, Mary and holy St. Joseph, Paddy you're after putting the heart cross-ways in me. What the hell are you doing up at this hour of the morning, are you sick? I tell her I have a present for her, she seems to be speechless for a moment, then says, 'You have a present for me? Sure it's not even my birthday'. I tell her I know. 'I just wanted to buy you a present Mam'. She's gone all emotional and wobbly on me asking what kind of a present is it and now I'm thinking she's surely expecting something more than the stupid auld plastic flower I bought, I wish to God I never saved the twelve pennies over the last two and a half weeks. She's going to be awfully disappointed any minute now. So I reluctantly hand her the brown paper bag, saying, 'It's not much Mam, just a stupid plastic auld flower' When she takes it out, her face has an expression I've never seen before. Her eyes have gone bigger, huge! There's a big smile on her face. She asks me where I got it, and when. I tell her where and now she's all over me with hugs. 'Oh isn't that a lovely thing to give your mother'. She runs into the bedroom, gives Pop a dig in the shoulder that disturbs his heavy snoring. She's shouting into his ear, 'Look what your eldest son saved for over the last two and a half weeks and went down to Woolworth's and it's not even my birthday. Why can't you do something like that she says, then shows it to Jetta and James. She's leaping all over the place. Boys! If I had known I was going to get this kind of result I'd do it every two and a half weeks. She'll stick it on the mantelpiece beside the black marble clock and tell anyone who comes to our house that her eldest son bought that and it's not even her birthday. While there was always a close bond between Mam and the rest of her kids this was a special day for the two of us, a day when a plastic flower brought us that bit closer.

Mam was the glue in our family, bringing anyone back into line that went astray, had the most gorgeous smile, was very kind to everyone except dogs of course, abounded in generosity, and would take on any neighbour in Carey's Road who tried to bully or make a fool of any of her children. Mam was a woman of simple needs. Her family came first in everything and herself last. She is forty years gone but never forgotten.

Another form of pocket money came by way of the waste paper at so much a ton. It's down to Todd's, Roche's Stores, The Limerick Leader, Cannock's and every shop in town looking for and collecting the waste paper, any colour, shape or size will do. It has to be packed into a couple of borrowed sacks given to us by the Limerick Waste Paper Company in Sexton Street where Uncle Peadar's girlfriend Maureen is working. And when Jett, James and I drag the three heavy sacks into her office, she tells the lads to throw the bags onto the weighing scale, puts her foot on it to get a better reading and we'll get six pence each. Then there are the empty Guinness and Bulmer's bottles, to be washed. They will fetch a good two pence each as well. There's lead, copper, brass, cast iron and if you get enough of it will put a right few pound in your pocket. But if a neighbour asked you to go around to O'Holloran's shop for a few bits, there'll always be a ha'penny to buy some sweets, like the time Mrs. Mullane asked me to go when I was about five years old.

She gave me a shilling telling me to get half a pound of sugar, a packet of tea, a half loaf of bread, and a ha'penny for myself. So I'm off up around the stone wall of Dinny McGrath's house tossing the shilling up in the air with my thumb and every time it comes back down I want to get it higher next time. This happens about five or six times until it isn't coming down anymore. It's gone over the wall of Dinny's house and down into the big garden, the part that's full of weeds and has a twenty foot drop as well. I am running back around the corner, through the entrance of Dinny's front gate, down the concrete steps, my mind is on Mrs. Mullane's table, about what's not going to be on it for Mr. Mullane when he comes home for his supper and it's all my fault. And I'll have no sweets either!

I'm walking all around the dog-leaves and nettles looking for the silver shilling. It's the middle of summer; if it was winter I might have some chance, but I'll never find it and Mrs. Mullane will be out at her front door wondering what's keeping me. Mam will kill me as well. Now I'm running back up McGrath's concrete steps. When I get to the door in the stone wall and run down the road, there's Mrs. Mullane outside her door with the arms folded wondering where her supper is, and I'm screaming my head off. The screams are so bad that every mother on Carey's Road is out looking to see who is making all the noise?

Mam is running up to meet me. And Mrs. Mullane looks very worried now because when Mam finds out she'd sent me down to the shop and got hurt there could be blue murder. There are mothers all around me asking 'What's the matter?' Mrs. Mullane is telling Mam how she gave me the shilling to go down to O'Hollorans' for the few bits of groceries for the supper. Mam is asking me 'What's wrong?' and I'm trying to tell her gesturing with my thumb and hand, but she says she can't understand, and every time I look at Mrs. Mullane my screams get louder and louder. Then Mrs. Mullane puts one arm around me and says something kind and it works. I am starting to get calmer now. So I say,

'Mam'.

She says, 'Yes love'.

'Mrs. Mullane gave me a shilling to go get a half pound of sugar, some tea and some bread and I was to keep a ha'penny for myself'.

'Yes love, we all know that, now tell us what's wrong?'

'I was going up the hill around Dinny McGrath's house',
'Yes, yes. Go on love, take your time'.
'I was flicking the shilling up in the air and trying to catch hit when it came down',
'Yes love, go on, go on',
'And it flew over the wall of Dinny's house and now I can't find it'.
Wallop! 'Jesus, Mary and holy St. Joseph are you telling me you lost a whole shilling belonging to Mrs. Mullane?
I'm after getting a box in the ear and the bawling starts again.
'Ah don't be hitting him Mrs. Taylor; sure it could have happened to anyone', says Mrs. Mullane.
Mam is putting her hand into a pocket she has in her bib, as we used to call it. Other people call it an apron.
'Now stop that Mrs. Taylor', says Mrs. Mullane as Mam counts out the twelve pence and gives them to Mrs. Mullane.
'Get in there you, and let that be a lesson to you, whenever you're asked to go to the shop, you'll be more careful in future'
But I wasn't asked again because all the mothers are there looking on and I'm not to be trusted with their money.
But there's always the black babies to make a penny or two. Brother Rice in Sexton Street C.B.S. has loads of leaflets with a picture of a rosary bead and if I can get one person to stick a hole in every head of the rosary, and give me money, I'll have enough (two and six) to buy a black baby, get him baptised and save him from Purgatory. There's enough space to write the name you want to call him. I get a penny for every card I fill and after one year I own seven black babies. They are all boys and they're all named Patrick.
Another way to make a few bob as I get older is to visit all my aunts to see how they are or if they are flush. It would be the usual, 'Hello young man, and my goodness look how you've grown. Sure I'd have never known you if I passed you on the street. What class are you in now? It won't be long before you'll be working with your Dad'. I've heard it all before and I'm thinking, 'Will you go and look for your bag and get the purse

out?,' but they don't. There's nothing happening. It's just a few sweets, a cake or a drink. I'll have to change my tactics if visiting the aunts is going to be a profitable journey. So when I go again I have to wait for the usual, 'What are you going to be when you grow up?' I try, 'A priest Auntie Kathleen'. There's a reaction.

'A Priest?'

'Yes, Auntie Kathleen'.

'And why do you want to be a priest?' She sits down on a chair with one hand under her chin.

'Well when I become a priest, I can go out to Africa and baptise all the black babies, so if they die they won't go to Limbo, but go straight to Heaven instead'.

'Sure won't that be marvellous to have a priest in the Taylor family? We've never had a priest in the family' says Auntie Kathleen.

'And what will your poor father say when you tell him you're not going to help him in the painting, decorating and building?'

'I don't know Auntie Kathleen, but saving the poor black babies is more important isn't it Auntie?'

'It is indeed Paddy, it is indeed'. She rises from the chair and starts to look for her bag. Everything is going according to plan. My aunt Kathleen gives me a two bob piece and I'm off to all the other aunts, telling them the same story and I'm richly rewarded.

Then there's the Sunday morning to look forward to. Pop would go to a huge snooker hall overhead Cavendish's Furniture Store in O'Connell Street. Mam will tell Pop again to take me along for the usual reasons. He's doing great without the drink. The more he enjoys the snooker and the fishing the better the chance he'll stay off the drink. All I have to do is sit down and be quiet, swing the legs in and out under the chair and wait for the comments.

'Jesus, Harry Taylor, but that's a grand young fellow you have there', while the hand is going into the pocket to look for a bit of change. And when one starts they'll all have to follow suit.

There's always plenty to do on Saturdays except the Saturday Dinny, Fonsey and Noelie kicked me out of the gang again and I can't remember why. I'm sauntering over the Iron Bridge down Roxboro Road pussing, sulking and kicking an auld tin can looking for something, anything to kill the time. I could have gone down under the bridge to The People's Park or over the bridge to Rathbane or Janesborough. My legs all on their own without my brain took me down by the school yard and boy did they take me down the right road! The yard that normally has the legs with the short pants running all over it five days a week is full of cars and ambulances today.

Now my brain decides to get involved and takes my legs into the yard to investigate: there's men and women in all kinds of grey, black and brown uniforms huddled together in groups of four. My head is jerking left and right, helping my eyes and ears to see or hear what's going on. My ears are taking in a language, I think it's English. There's a lot of "wee" this and "wee" that. Is there an opportunity to earn a few bob here? My head keeps turning, looking for a sign when someone puts a hand on my shoulder and takes the living senses off me. It's a man in a uniform; he wants to shake my hand while he talks away. I have my hand in his shaking it up and down in response, but I haven't a bull's notion what he's talking about. This could be the great opportunity to earn a few bob. I'll have to put on my best manners, so I say, 'I'm very sorry Sir, I don't know what you're saying'. He smiles and calls over another. It's a woman. She's nice and easy to understand. 'Have you got a wee moment young man?,' she asks and tells me they're a team of four all the way from Donegal, wherever that is, to take part in the All Ireland Part Time Medical Association Final, and that they need a volunteer for an hour. I interrupt and say 'Of course Miss'. My brain is telling me talk about being in the right place at the right time, don't mess it up. And where are we heading for only the stone building where my class is. It's one big floor now because all the partitions have been folded back against the main walls.

We're all in a huddle together. There's a guy talking to me again in a strange accent. I can only understand one or two words. He's talking to me all the time and keeps looking at me while taking his hat off, scratching his head. One of the ladies says,

'I don't think he understands you Will, do you love? Do you understand what Will was trying to explain to you?'

I have a big problem here; if I say 'no' they might go looking for somebody else and the bit of dosh won't be coming my way at all. If I say 'yes' they'll want to know why I'm not doing whatever it is he's asking and I'm going to look like a right amadán altogether. So I better risk it and tell them that I haven't a clue what he's talking about. Sure who else are they going to get anyway? So I shake my head from side to side putting on my most innocent face and best manners.

I say, 'I'm very sorry, but I don't understand what the man is saying. What country is he from?,'

There's a lot of laughter and the two ladies are saying,

'Wisha God help us William, he thinks you're from another country. We're from the North of Ireland love', says one of the ladies explaining that I am going to have to pretend that I have been injured in some kind of an accident. 'It could be on a road or a roof of a house, I might have fallen off a ladder, there will be bones broken here and there, cuts and bruises, we don't know until just before the competition starts. The judges will tell us then. You'll be lying out there on the floor with the other volunteers and we're going to arrive on the scene to fix you up, when we have you all bandaged up the judges will come along, look at what we've done to you, ask you some questions like 'is the bandage comfortable, is the splinter too tight 'and if what you say is OK along with what we've done, we might get first, second or third place'. Boy is this an opportunity to earn a decent few bob! I'm loving every minute of this. I'll have all these people around me, I'll be the centre of attention and have an enormous responsibility placed on my shoulders that I know I can handle. So it's just a matter of waiting to be told what to do next.

Then after about fifteen minutes a man at the end of the large room calls everybody to order. He asks for the volunteer patients who came to take their positions on the wooden floor. The lady tells me where to lie down. When I do, the man says to the teams waiting to go into action, 'Your patient has been knocked down by a car. He/she has a broken collar bone'. I'm looking over at my team from the North of Ireland. They're all in a huddle again. One of them has a notebook in his hand. He's writing down everything that's being said. The announcer continues, 'the right leg is broken, there are three fractured ribs, a broken thumb and a bad cut on his forehead. You have forty minutes to treat him; starting, now!'

My team are all over me on their knees. The two ladies start work on my head and I like this. They have lovely perfume and I can look at their pretty faces all the time and I think I'm falling in love again. There's someone at my right leg, another at my thumb. 'We'll leave the collar bone 'til last' says another. The ladies are asking me lots of questions like, 'Are we hurting you Paddy?' 'Of course not', I say. There are judges walking around watching every move and action the team are making and my right leg has gone numb.

They've taken my shoe and sock off and I hope my feet don't stink as it just might put the two ladies I've just fallen in love with off me. For the first time in my life I'm glad Mam gives me a change of socks every day.

Now William, the guy with the funny accent is talking to me again. I hope the ladies will tell me what he's talking about. They say, 'He's saying we're going to turn you over and open your shirt and then strap your chest with some bandages for your fractured ribs'. They're asking me 'does this and that hurt, is that too tight', all over again. They've finished with the bandages around my ribs and it's hard to breathe.

'Is that OK love?,' asks one of the ladies. 'Are you able to breathe with these bandages?' It's hard to talk, I nod my head and I think my leg doesn't have any blood in it.

They're working on my thumb now. That's gone numb too. Now they're all working on my broken collar bone. They're lifting up my arm and wrapping more bandages under it and around my neck across under the armpit until I think I'm going to die from lack of air because I can't get my chest to move anywhere. I can't get the air down my throat because it's nearly blocked and I'm completely exhausted. I'm glad this lot is from the North because if I got a belt of a car I'd hate them to be looking after me and would probably do more harm than good.

Now the whistle is gone to signal 'Time's up!' I'm saying 'thanks be to God'. Now I have to wait for the judges to come and ask me all the questions and lie through the skin of my teeth, because if I tell the truth this crowd from the North won't be showing any kind of appreciation or gesture for that kind of honesty. But the judges have started at the other end which means I'm going to be last and I hope I'll still be alive when they get to me, because I'm no good to anyone dead. When they do get to me they're all apologies for taking so long. I don't know where any parts of my body are, I'm so numb. The back of my pole is killing me from resting on the hard wooden floor and I've so many pins and needles from the lack of blood, that's not able to travel around my body at all.

'Are you in any discomfort young man?,' a judge asks.

I shake my head sideways several times.

'Good man', he says. 'What about your leg, is that OK?'

I nod again, up and down this time.

'Your thumb, is that OK too? And your neck is that alright?'

More nods.

I'm glad I don't have to try and speak; otherwise the game is up. I'm looking over at the team to see if I'm doing OK and they're all smiles and giving me the thumbs up. If they're not happy, then it's all over. So the judges go off into a corner to consult and the team come over and bring my body back to life. They're all thanks and hugs from the girls I've fallen in love with. They're saying how well I did as they take off the splints and bandages. My chest slowly starts to do what it's supposed to do and that is to give me air. Then it's time for the cups to be presented and there's no sign of any dosh coming my way for nearly winding up in Mount St. Lawrence's Cemetery.

Third place is announced and it's not my gang, second place doesn't go our way either. But there's blue mayhem when all my pain and suffering bears fruit: the boys and girls from the North get first prize.

They raise me into the air and give me three cheers. They're clapping me and themselves on the back and after their leader is presented with the Cup, then the appreciation is shown. I have managed to collect a total of one pound from the team and I can't believe my luck. I'm tearing back up the road over the iron bridge, round the wall of Dinny McGrath's house; the lads are sitting on the ground playing cards. I'm waving the pound at them saying 'I got this because of ye, ye dirty rotten lousers!'

CHAPTER 12

Pop says the days of the potties under the bed will be coming to an end soon because the Corporation has sent a letter to every house in Upper Carey's Road, except the Lynches, the two new houses below them and Bennett the carpenter's workshop beside the bridge at the bottom of the hill. "They'll be a room for yourself, James and Baby Harry," says Pop as he ruffles my hair. 'That'll be the biggest room in the whole house. You'll have your own room too Jet all to yourself with a window in every part of the house to let the fresh air in and no more standing in the rusty old bath in front of the fire on the cold frosty winter nights. A wash hand basin too and best of all a toilet!' How we'll be able to stand outside the front door of our new house and not get the awful smell from everybody's' toilet waste that's left out on the road every night in buckets for the Corporation truck to come and collect every evening. Sure we won't know ourselves with plugs and light switches in every room; no dampness or musty smells, a garden, front and back. But Pop hasn't told us where the new house is going to be because he says he doesn't know, nobody knows. The only thing we know at the moment is every house up here is going to be flattened very soon. He says they'll be writing to us over the next few weeks to let us know where we're going.

So the rumours start. Mrs. Moloney says it could be Garryowen as her husband Joe 'is working on a block of houses down there and wouldn't it be grand if it was because a new house would have the latest gadgets and you can't beat the smell of a new house'. Mrs. Mullane says, 'Wouldn't it be an awful pity if we were to be scattered all over the city to places like Prospect, Weston, Ballynanty, Thomondgate, or even Rathbane or Janesborough as we're all living up here so long it's like one big happy family'. Nellie with the sticks says she'd prefer if it was a house somebody else had lived in as she has only a small income, no husband and wonders where she'll get the money for paint, wall paper, curtains and lino for the floors and says, she praying every night to The Blessed Virgin not to give her a new house, that the people who live in the house the Blessed Virgin is going to get her might be good clean people and won't scratch the paintwork or walls when they're leaving and might even leave something behind that might be of use to her.

Mrs. Hayes says she hopes it will be a new house with a good sized front and back as her husband Jack loves the gardening, has green fingers and will be in it for the twelve months of the year, no matter what the weather. Mrs. Clohessy who lives on the same side of Upper Carey's Road as ourselves and two doors up from the Mitchell's who left two years ago to go to a house in Weston because they couldn't take the conditions anymore, says she thought the only way she was coming out of Carey's Road was in a box because she's heading into her 80th year and hopes she can be in the house, new or used and doesn't mind what part of Limerick it's in, before the winter comes as she couldn't take another five months of the awful weather it brings and is like her dog Mush, who's still alive, the dirty rotten louser, and crippled with arthritis.

Dinny McGrath's mother and father don't have to worry where they're going because the Corporation already gave them a house under the bridge at the bottom of the hill. We won't be seeing much of him anymore as he's nearly sixteen now, has new friends and wants to chase girls all over the place.

When the second lot of letters arrive from the Corporation it stops the rumours. We're all going to Garryowen. Poor Nellie puts the sign of the cross on her forehead and asks Mary what she ever done to her as it's the first time she's every let her down and says she's worried sick now because of all the expense. But Mr. Moloney who works on the site in Garryowen tells her that all the ceilings, doors, frames and skirting in the new houses are painted. There's even lovely new tiles on the floors of the hall, kitchen and bathroom. Nellie puts the sign of the cross on her forehead again and asks Mary to forgive her, how she didn't let her down after all and says she knows Mary will look after the curtains as well. But nobody's going anywhere yet says Pop.

We all want a guarantee from the Corporation that when the new houses are finished up here we can all come back and poor Nellie is putting the sign of the cross on her forehead a third time and asks Mary what is she doing to her at all? Isn't it bad enough that she's been a cripple all her life with no husband or children and now she's going to be moving house three times in two years? It's only a few days when the Corporation promises to let us all come back again when the builders move in to Upper Carey's Road with their big cement mixers and dumpers. There's great excitement up here now. Pop says they're going to start in Lynch's field first and the Corporation will be giving the keys to the new houses in Garryowen at the end of the month. I will leave this wonderful road in a month's time and not give it a second thought. The orchard at the back of our house that belonged to Nan Ferguson two doors up from us in the two storey house that we skinned every August and September; the bonfire nights that had every occupant in Upper Carey's Road out on the street in their chairs across the road from Dinny's house and the sing-song that would last long into the night. The dobber season when it came, when we would drag the heel of our shoe backwards against the mucky kerb to clear the way for the dobbers we would throw into it on our way to school and had Mam pull her hair out as to why one of the only pair of shoes we had that she polished every night could be so filthy and half the heel worn away. The spinning top with the whip that we belted up and down the hill, during the conker season; the two bolts with the gun cap between the nut to see whose would go the highest will only be memories when we leave. I'll drive up and down this road, over the next forty years and never give it a thought until now and can't figure out why. Maybe it's because I had a future to live and couldn't wait. Well the future has come and gone and all I have now is the past.

But one memory never left me; the memory of what happened a week after the builders moved in and brought the sand with them in one great pile, two doors down from our house. We'll be on it every night after the builders go home. We'll be on it every Saturday and Sunday too and all the mothers in Upper

Carey's Road will be calling down the holy family every night saying there's more sand in their houses than what's out on the road.

Our first Saturday with the sand on the street brings two people up the hill who knock on the first door on the other side of the road. I'm on top of the sand playing away, when I hear a shout, 'Look out here come the Jehovah's'. I turn around and everyone is gone. The mothers who were out on the road talking to each other are nowhere to be seen. Fonsie, Noelie, Mary Hayes and Carol Lysaght are all gone too; even Jet and James. All the top halves of the front doors are shut now. There's complete silence when I look across the road at Mrs. Gallagher's house, there's a man and a woman knocking on the door. He has a case and she's got a handbag. They've got some kind of magazines in their hands. But Mrs. Gallagher isn't answering her door and I'm wondering why, because I know she's there. She was there sweeping the footpath just a few minutes ago. Now they're knocking on Christy Davis' door and he won't answer either. After that it's Fonsie's door and that won't open at all. I look around and our door is open, well the top half and I'm starting to get frightened. They knock on another door, that's four doors now that doesn't answer.

Then they knock on Mickey Fitz's door just after Ford's pub. He works in CIE down at the bus station. He opens his door and starts shouting while waving his hands all over the place. I can hear every word he's saying. The whole road can hear every word he's saying. He's pointing at something in his house. He's saying, 'Do you see that picture on the wall in there. That's the picture of The Most Holy Family, Jesus, Mary and holy Saint Joseph'. Then he catches the man by the arm, starts pushing him and shoving him violently. He's telling him, 'We're all Christians here on this road, everyone in this city and the whole country are Christians', He's pushing the man very hard and now he's saying 'Why don't you and that one you're with go back to Russia with your Communism?' He's trying to shove the man up the hill and out of Carey's Road. I'm looking at Mickey Fitz and wondering who's the Christian here? I'm ten years old and I'm looking at a man and a woman who haven't said a word or raised a hand in their defence, even though they don't believe in God, they're acting more like Christians to me. But when Mickey Fitz goes back into his house, they carry on down our side of the road and I'm wondering why our front door isn't closed like all the rest. After they have finished knocking on all the other doors and getting no answer, they smile at me and knock on our door.

When Mam comes out and sees who's there the man says something about The Bible, and Mam slams the top half of the door in their face. Then they carry on to Mrs. Storan's.

I've never seen Mam so cross before and I know that if Jet, James or I closed the door on someone's face like that she'd give us a right thumping. They're off down the hill towards Sheehan's house now, and I'm back in the house asking Mam who those people were.

'They're Communists, people who don't believe in God. The priests are always telling us to have nothing to do with them'.

'But why did you have to slam the door in their face? Isn't that very rude Mam?'

'Not when the priest tells you, it isn't' she says. 'They want to turn us away from God'. But I can't get it out of my mind how Mam would do something like that just because a priest said it and I'm trying to understand why a priest would tell people to do something like that. I'm asking myself surely Jesus would never slam a door in someone's face. So I make myself a promise which I won't forget, that if I ever meet any of those Communists I'm going to show them what real Christians are like.

As the days and weeks roll on, Pop and the residents of Upper Carey's Road have to meet at the Town Hall to draw a key for the front door of their new house. There's great excitement waiting for Pop to come home. He's hoping to draw one of the eight houses that has a side entrance. Mam says it would be great as we wouldn't be bringing the dirt into the house on our shoes. And with Pop's luck at the cards and other things he's bound to get what he's looking for. So when he comes home we're all surprised when he tells us that he didn't draw the key to an end house but Noelie Grace's father had no use for an end house, so he swapped keys with Pop and we're going to be living at No. 36 and Noelie will be living at No. 35 Claughaun Court, Garryowen for the next two years.

Pop will bring us down to Garryowen to see our house. It's a long walk and Mam lets Jet push Harry's pram all the way. When we get there our house has a front and back garden. There's a wall all around it too.

We have a concrete shed to put lots of coal and other things into it. When Pop opens the lovely green front door, there's a hall with grey tiles on the floor and an upstairs there with loads of rooms and an echo in everyone. It's like four houses in one.

'Janey Ma, its huge', says Jet.

She gets a room all to herself, just like Pop said. Mam and Pop will get the small room. James, Har and I get the biggest room in the whole house

'When are we moving in Mam?,' we all want to know.

'As soon as Uncle Peadar can get the truck to bring all the furniture down for us,' she says.

'When will that be Mam?'

'Next Saturday, I hope', she replies and we're all jumping around the place with excitement.

When I reached the age of 45, Pop told me how he used to lie in bed every night, weeks before we moved to Garryowen worrying about the ten shillings and six pence rent that would be due every week. How the only good thing about living in Upper Carey's Road was never having to pay rent after the five pound he gave for the key. How Mam had to go down to Cavendish's to buy a table and four chairs, three new beds on the weekly and while it was exciting for us kids, it was a huge worry to Mam as well. She needed curtains, lino, and bedclothes. I'm wondering now was Pop still paying for the lovely pearly red accordion on top of all that as well.

There's great excitement when Peadar comes to take what little furniture we're keeping, that doesn't have the woodworm, to Garryowen. Pop gets ten or twelve wooden chests from Halpin's Tea Company to pack up all our bits and pieces. When they're emptied we use them for furniture until Cavendish's arrive with the new stuff. It's our first night in Garryowen, we can't sleep. We're talking most of the night. It's great that we can leave our beds against the wall and not have to worry about the dampness. We're in the bathroom flushing the toilet, turning on the taps in the bath and wash hand basin all night. When Mam comes upstairs for a minute, we're asking 'When can we have a bath? Where do we get hot water from?'

James wants to know if the bogey man from the small dark room at the end of the kitchen in Carey's Road came down with Uncle Peadar on the truck to live inside in the new coalhouse. Mam says that we're not to turn on the lights when it gets dark, as we don't want people looking in because we have no curtains.

We are only down in Garryowen four months and coming up to Christmas when Mam and Pop get word from his sister, the source of all the parcels, Aunt Eileen in America that she's coming home to Ireland after twenty five years. There's never anything in the parcels for Jet, James or young Harry because they have a son around my age called Tommy. So I get shoes, shirts and jackets that Tommy used to wear and they're a great fit for me. In the 1950's there was a huge difference in the style of American clothes compared to the European brands. Aunt Eileen sent over a smashing jacket that could be zipped up the middle. On one side it had a map of America in shiny studded gold brace, and when you turned it inside out, there was a large eagle also studded. It was a winter jacket but it arrived to me in the middle of summer and I put it on straight away and went out on the road to parade it around. When Fonsie or Noelie looked at me, I'd quickly take it off and turn it the other way round. I could see they were mad jealous. I kept it on the whole day even though the sweat was flying off me.

On a recent visit to the States, Tommy's brother Dave told me how he saw his mother getting a parcel ready to Ireland. He said his mother was always very conscious of how difficult things were back home for her baby brother Harry and if there was anything she could do to help even though it was small, she knew that Harry and Bid would appreciate it. Dave told me he might go to the wardrobe for a shirt or sweater and find his mother had sent it to Ireland in a parcel, so he had to hide his favourite ones in case they would wind up here also. Then he told me a lovely story about a brooch his mother was putting into one of those parcels. When he said to her;

'Mam what are you doing with that?,' as he held it in his hand.

'I am sending it home to Ireland, to your Auntie Bridie. It's only a costume brooch I found on the floor at work'.

Aunt Eileen worked in the Waldorf Hotel in New York as a cloak lady. She made enquiries and waited a few months to see if anyone would come and claim it. They never did because, as she thought, it was only costume jewellery. But Dave said, 'give it to me and I'll see if it's worth anything'.

When he came home Aunt Eileen was surprised when he told her it was very valuable. He said married men would give gifts like this to their mistresses. They would never be marked for record keeping in case their wives found out. So Aunt Eileen got some of it melted down for a ring and with the rest of the money that she got came home to Ireland for a holiday in 1977 on her own.

Anyway back to Garryowen. The next eight months will see great activity at number 36. Pop will be bringing home more bits of paint, wallpaper and wood, odds and ends for the bathroom, hall, sitting room and kitchen. The front lawn will have to be dug and grass planted. He says we can't have bare windows and floors when his sister comes to visit us, that moving back to Carey's Road in another eighteen months is not an excuse to have the house the way it is. Jet and I get the garden job. We can only start in spring as the ground is too mucky. When we do get going, there's lumps of concrete blocks that's all shapes and sizes coming out of the ground and takes nearly four weeks to finish.

Pop starts on the hall. He's got one roll of very expensive wallpaper left over from a job. It's bright red with a green leaf and long stem. Mam wants to know where he's going to put it and says she's glad he's only got one roll as it would look terrible if the entire hall had it on every wall. But Pop has a good idea. There's just enough paper to make a large square on two walls. He's finished the edges in a small wood frame, mixes all his bits of paint together and the hall gets two coats of a light grey emulsion. Another night he'll come home with an end piece of mahogany table and one leg with two lovely brass casters. When he's finished working on it, we have a lovely small hall table screwed to the wall in one of the red paper squares, and a mirror screwed above it at face level. After two nights he has a three foot wide roll of carpet on the bike. It looks old, when it's rolled out and Mam says;

'Sure that's all worn away; it must be twenty years old. But it was a nice carpet in its day'.

'Sure we can give it a wash', says Pop.

'A wash won't bring that thing back to life or cause the wool to grow where the patches are,' says Mam.

Well Pop's got an idea for that and he says he's going to try it out.

'You take it outside first,' says Mam 'and give it a good beating to get the dust out of it, before you bring it into this house or anywhere else', says Mam.

After Pop has beaten the living daylights out of it, he's back on the stairs rolling it down the steps and it's great watching to see how he's going to get this woollen yoke to look good and that's exactly what he does. He has the worn bits that used to be on the edge of the stairs, it just came off for God knows how long in against the corner of every step. When he puts on the brass bars and straps that came with the carpet to hold them down, and cuts off the waste of both ends, he calls Mam and she can't believe it's the same carpet.

It's green with red roses and works in very well with the grey paint and tiles on the floor. Everything is progressing very well and finished for the mid July arrival of Auntie Eileen and Uncle Dave.

It's a big occasion. They arrive in Shannon or Rineanna as it was called then. The Mayor of Limerick is there to greet them as he is a personal friend of Uncle Dave's. He puts on his May-oral Chain of Office to make the event even more special. There will be an official picture of their arrival being welcomed by the Mayor of Limerick in the Limerick Leader three days later. Pop is the only one from our family to greet them as there is only enough room for him in one of the three cars that arrive with all the relatives to bring the Yanks back to their home town.

The following day Pop and Mam tell us we have to go down to our Auntie Mary's in Clare Street to say hello. Pop says that they brought their young son Tommy home as well and that I was to look after him while he was here.

He will be staying in our house most of the time, which would be almost six weeks. So we have to put on our best clothes and make a good impression when we arrive in Auntie Mary's. She opens the door and gives us a cheerful welcome.

'Oh it's the Taylor family coming down to see the Yanks from the USA, and they've got a lovely young man for you to look after while he's here Paddy. You will have to give them a few minutes as they were up late last night and still haven't got used to the time difference'.

So while we're waiting it's the usual, 'how old are you now Jet, Paddy and James? How are you getting on at school? You too James?,' and we're all acting shy and giving the one word answers, 'Yes' 'No' to Auntie Mary and so on. It's the same questions that all the aunts and uncles ask you every time you go and see them.

Aunt Eileen comes down. 'Now who have we here?,' she asks in a lovely accent. 'This must be Jetta'. She's rubbing her hand through Jet's hair. 'You're the eldest Jet, have I got that right?'

'Yes, Auntie Eileen,' answers Jet.

'And this must be Paddy. You're the guy that gets all Tommy's clothes, have I got that right?,'

'Yes, Auntie Eileen, and thank you very much Auntie Eileen; they're great and I still have everything you sent over Auntie Eileen'.

Good manners are very important now because I could be well rewarded with a few Dollars any minute.

'Gee golly! Hasn't my baby brother reared you very well?'

'Great' I'm thinking. 'The good manners are going to turn into bucks any minute now'.

'And this young man here has to be Jim, right?'

James says, 'Yes, Auntie Eileen'.

Then Auntie Eileen says the magic words as she lifts her bag off the floor, has a root around in her purse.

'I know I have my purse in here somewhere. Say hello to Harry's kids Dave; they've come down especially to see us'.

'Hello guys', says Uncle Dave.

Jet, James and I all say together, 'Hello Uncle Dave'.

He hasn't a clue who we are, and when he sees Auntie Eileen taking some money out of her purse, he starts rooting around his pockets. I think he wants to give us money as well. When Auntie Eileen takes a pound note out of her purse I'm thinking 'Janey we're getting a whole pound between the three of us!'

Then she says to Jet, 'There you are love', puts her hand back into her purse, takes another one out and gives it to me. My gob is wide open with the shock and Jet has to give me an elbow into the side to say, 'Thank you very much, Aunt Eileen' which I blurt out after getting the elbow. 'Now we have to give something special to James'. So she's rooting around her purse with her fingers and takes out three half crowns, a couple of two bobs, five or six at least, there are some pennies and thruppenny bits and says, 'Hold out your two hands James, I've got a lot of cash for you'. James' eyes are bulging out of his head because he's got so many coins, he thinks that he's got more money than Jet and I. 'Now I've got a new name for you James,' says Aunt Eileen. 'It's small change, that's what I'm going to call you'.

Then Uncle Dave comes over to give us some money. He has only a ten bob note in his hand. I think he's drunk.

'What's one of these things called?,' he asks Auntie Mary.

'That's half of one pound'.

'I guess it would be alright to give this young lady one of these, right?'

'Yes Dave', answers Aunt Mary.

'Now I don't have another one for this guy here', pointing to me and I'm thinking 'ah Janey that's lousy, here we go again'. I'm asking myself who is it that makes all these decisions. Is there someone up there looking down at me all the time trying to make life miserable for me?

'But I've got plenty of these silver things', says Uncle Dave. 'So how many of these do I have to give so they won't think I'm a skinflint?'

So Auntie Mary takes four half crowns from his hand and gives it to me, and I'm off with the good manners again. I hope Pop has more sisters in America and that they'll come over to see us anytime they want and bring plenty of bucks with them. They can stay at our house if they want to.

Aunt Eileen shouts up the stairs, 'Tommy, come down and meet your cousins, what's keeping you?'

Then she turns to me and says, 'Did you know Tommy is going to be staying with you for most of the holiday Paddy?'

'Yes, I did, Aunt Eileen'.

'Well you take good care of him now, do you hear?'

'Yes, Aunt Eileen'.

I can hear light footsteps coming down the stairs. I can't see who the footsteps belong to because Aunt Mary has a wall instead of a banister rail, so when he appears at the bottom of the step, I can see a sight that I'm instantly jealous of. He's wearing long pants. They're jeans and I'm looking down at my bony knees, I know he's looking at them as well. I wish I had long pants like him. I feel really stupid with my white legs and bony knees sticking out like a sore thumb.

'Say hello to your cousin, Tommy', asks Aunt Eileen.

I can barely hear him. He has the head looking down at the ground most of the time. Jet, James and I say a very quiet hello in return. Aunt Eileen gives Tom a parcel;

'That's your pyjamas and a change of clothes', and gives him a pound or two pocket money.

Tommy asks 'What's a pound worth?'

'Three dollars', answers Auntie Mary.

'Go on off with you now.'

So we're walking back to Garryowen. Tommy still has the head down, kicking the odd stone or tin can on the road as we walk up the Long Can lane by The Good Shepherd Laundry. James is counting the coins Auntie Eileen gave him and asks Jetta 'what comes after six?,' When she tells him, 'seven', he wants to know what comes after that? Jetta tells him to shut up because she's trying to think what she is going to buy with her thirty bob. Tommy is still kicking stones along the road and isn't saying much. In fact he is saying nothing at all. So I ask him when he started wearing long pants. He shrugs his shoulders and doesn't say anything. Then he says as long as he can remember and says,

'You guys wear funny trousers over here. Nobody in the States wears trousers like those weird things'.

I wish he hadn't said that. It was bad enough before he said that, now I'm worse. Now Tommy wants to know how far it is to our house from Auntie Mary's. He has a smashing hair style called the crew cut, hardly any hair at all. I'm going to ask Mam when I can have long pants and a hair cut like Tommy as well, when we get home. Mam gives Tommy a big hug. She's all smiles and talking very strange, asking Tommy very stupid questions but he doesn't seem to mind.

We're telling Mam that Auntie Eileen gave us thirty bob each to spend. I want to know if I can go back down to Aunt Mary's again tomorrow.

'You'll do no such thing!,' says Mam.

Then she gets all nice to Tommy again, with the 'Would you like this Tommy?' and 'would you like that Tommy?'

I want to ask Mam how much a long pants would cost. 'Would it cost more than thirty bob?

'For whom?,' she asks.

'For me,' I answer.

'What do you want long pants for?'

'To cover my legs Mam.'

'What do you want to cover your legs for?'

'Because they're all white Mam, that's why'.

'You'll get no long pants 'til your fourteen', and she's back talking to Tommy again.

In our house there was always plenty of bread, butter and jam. Tommy is getting his first taste as Mam lays the table for supper.

'Will you have something for the supper Tommy?'

Tommy looks confused and wants to know what the supper is.

It's like Mam is speaking in tongues, she says, 'I'm sorry love, I forgot you're from the States. Supper is your tea love, what would you like for your tea?'

Tommy is more confused now and looks like he's in great difficulty so he shrugs his shoulders and tells Mam he's never had tea only coffee.

'Oh goodness', says Mam, 'We don't have any coffee at all in this house. We've never had coffee'.

Poor Tommy thinks he's in trouble and says, 'It's OK Auntie Bridie'.

'Oh no, don't worry. I'll get you coffee tomorrow. After all you are going to be staying here a good few weeks; we're not going to have you saying you got no coffee at Auntie Bridie's. Sure you can show me how to make it tomorrow and in the meantime, you'll try a drop of tea instead'.

Mam was talking away while she gets everything ready. Tommy puts his hand out to get a slice of bread from a plate on the table and asks for a knife to spread some butter. Jet and I are looking at one another in surprise.

'What's wrong Tommy?,' asks Mam.

'Nothing', says Tommy. 'I just want to spread some butter on this slice of bread please'.

'You'll do no such thing', says Mam and takes a slice of bread back, puts it on her own plate and starts to spread the butter for him. In our house Mam does everything, she washes our faces, brushes our teeth; she'll comb our hair, milk and sugar our tea, spread the butter and jam on our bread. We don't have to do a thing except shove it down our throats. And when we get to our twenties, we won't be able to wipe our own backsides. So Tommy has to get used to doing the same, while he's over here at number 36 for the duration of his stay with Mam saying every day, 'Jesus, Mary and Holy Saint Joseph, that young man from the States has a ferocious appetite'.

When Pop comes home for his supper, he makes a fuss of Tommy. He shows Tommy his big seven inch distemper brush that he uses to paint ceilings. He's telling Tommy that there's a tin of green paint in the coal shed that he bought specially for his visit to Ireland. And before he goes back to the States he'll have to get his arse painted green. Tommy is all confused and asks 'Why?'

'To prove that you've been in Ireland, that's why', says Pop. The day before Tommy goes back to the States Pop will follow him around the house with the big distemper brush, shouting 'Come here you little fecker till I paint your arse green'. We'll all be killing ourselves laughing but Tommy is scared stiff until we convince him that Pop is only joking.

It's time to go out to the two big greens that split Garryowen in two. Fonsie, Noelie and I have new mates since we moved down here. There are a lot of fellows our own age here wearing the short pants as well and Tommy is going to make friends with them all. There's Ray and Tommy Leahy, Billy, Michael and Eric Noonan, Leo Fitz, Joe Kenny, Austin Desmond and the Ryan brothers. Tommy will have us playing baseball; we'll have him playing hurling and soccer over the next six weeks. Tommy will go down to Aunt Mary's every morning for the spending money and now I know why he asked how far it is from our house. His mother gives him a whole pound every day and tells him to make sure and share it with me. James will always want to come along and he's a right pain, crying when we're trying to get away from him on our own to go down to Aunt Mary's. He knows we get money and he wants some of it. So he'll be running to Mam to tell her to take him with us, he's behind us all the way down to Clare Street crying and pussing because we keep running away from him all the time. This will be the best school summer I've ever had; ten shillings every day to spend on anything I like.

Tommy has never seen Double Decker buses in his life, so he wants to go on one. When we get one, he wants to go on top up at the front. It takes us out over Sarsfield Bridge, its scary looking down at all that water, as the bus waves from side to side if there's a wind. It's out towards the Gaelic Grounds to turn left at the Hotel and up around the North Circular Road. It comes back again over the bridge, and up William Street to stop for five minutes before heading off to Janesborough where Aunt Angela lives and the whole trip costs only six pence each. So Tommy and I decide to spend all our money on the bus up front until the money runs out. We're on it for the whole day. We take one seat each up front pretending we're the drivers. We know every turn and twist. We imagine we have the steering wheel in front of us and its great fun.

I'll take Tommy to Upper Carey's Road to show him where we used to live. I'll tell him about the time the Double Decker bus went down the hill and the huge bang that was heard everywhere when it hit the bridge and wedged itself between the road and the massive steel girders that took the weight of the steam trains it supported several times a day. How every mother in Upper and Lower Carey's Road were drawn to the bridge to see all the excitement and the driver with the big gash on his head and blood everywhere, who forgot he was driving a Double Decker, and not the Single Decker he was used to driving down the hill every day for the last five years, how he had to be taken away in an ambulance before work could start to free the bus from the bridge, and when it did, couldn't be budged an inch, and the young fella who was jumping up and down shouting at all the men in their trucks that he knew how to get the bus out in one piece. If they'd only listen the way he kept asking one of the guards that's telling the crowds to keep back and give the workers a bit of room to work to let him go over and tell the workers how to get the bus out without doing any more damage but his pleas were falling on deaf ears. When the policeman's back was turned he ran over to the workers to tell them to let the air out of the wheels and when they did, he got a huge cheer from everyone.

It's only been a week now. The quiet guy from the United States is a nutcase now. He's never had so much freedom before. He'll come in and out of the front windows of the living room in Garryowen and if Nan is in from Cappamore, he'll have her in an awful state. But Tommy never looks at anything long enough to concentrate on what's going on. There will be the usual 'Jesus, Mary and Holy St. Joseph' from Nan, 'look he's coming in the bloody window again' or 'Sweet Jesus have they any doors in your house in America', or 'don't you believe in closing doors or windows at all?,' He'll always have a slice of bread and butter in his hand when he's in the house.

Tommy loves fishing and we can fish at the Canal right alongside Auntie Mary's house. I don't have a fishing rod but that's no problem. We're able to buy a bamboo stick and all the bits and pieces needed to get going at Nagle's Fishing Tackle near the bridge at the bottom of Broad Street, and there will be hours and hours where Tommy can stop being a lunatic for a while and we can talk about anything we want, like girls!

'Do you like girls Tommy?'

'They're alright, I guess,' he says.

'But do you like them Tommy'

Tommy says, 'No'.

'Why not?,' I ask.

'I don't know, I just don't like them, they're stupid. They're always crying and screaming for nothing at all'.

I say, 'Yeah Tommy, you're right'.

He wants to know what school is like over here, and when I tell him the teachers have a leather with coins or lead in it to beat the daylights out of us, he is shocked. He says that in the States the teachers are not allowed to touch anyone. They get to write lots of lines and stay back in school. I'm wondering what I did to God that he made me be born in a rotten place like Limerick where the teachers are killers, and why couldn't I have been born in the good old US of A?

Other days we go to the cinema. We'll be up at Eddie Donnelly's butchers in Lower Gerald Griffin Street. He always has two pictures on one side of his shop window;

if there's cowboys with guns on horses that must be a good film. Then it's up to the City Theatre to see what pictures they have at their front entrance. After that we're over to the Royal to see what's on there, if they're in colour that's even better. Then there's a run down to the Carlton, Savoy and Grand Central to have a gawk there. Then it's decision time. But it doesn't really matter because we go to see every picture in every cinema every day of every week with the spending money. We know all the good pictures and we'll go and see whatever else is on that takes our fancy; like the time we went to the Savoy to see Louis Armstrong in a film called Jazz in a Summer's Day only because we saw every other bloody film in town that week. And boy was it boring! We were the only ones there and we spent the whole time crawling on our hands and knees playing hide and seek between all the seats. When we got sick and tired of going to the cinema every day we went back on the bus again or down to Garryowen with all the lads, or fishing.

Then there's Tommy's birthday down in Aunt Mary's. Tommy sings a song for us all; a song I'll never forget as it's in French. That's the only bit of the party I can remember because he sang it so beautifully. Some days Tommy doesn't come to Garryowen. He has other relatives to go and see, and I don't know whether I miss Tommy or the ten bob he gives me every day. But I never stop and think that this great cousin and friend I've made will be gone soon. It just happens and it's here, he's going away today. I'm left go to the airport to see him off because we've become such good friends. I don't want to talk to him and he won't look at me. I have saved some of the money he gave me and bought him a special hurley to take back to the States and when I give it to him he hands me back a ten bob note. A relative gave it to him at the airport. He's starting to cry and so am I and all the relatives are going, 'Aw isn't that lovely? They've been stuck to each other for the last six weeks and become good friends'.

Tommy and Family
Note: Presentation made to Uncle Dave and Aunt Eileen by
their friend the Mayor and surviving members of the Buccaneers
Rugby Football Club with Cousin Tommy on far right.

But that's not true. It's more than good friends. What happened over the last six weeks was something special. The clothes that will come in the parcel from the States from now on with Tommy's clothes will have different feelings for me now.

Everyone is waving goodbye to a plane that's heading off to America except me; my best friend and pal is gone. It's like I've experienced the death of a loved one for the first time and it's not a nice feeling. It would be forty years before I ever set eyes on Cousin Tommy again but I'll never forget him or the great memories of a quiet, shy guy who became a lunatic in the space of forty eight hours.

'Jesus, Mary and Holy Saint Joseph when are you going to stop pestering your father and me to get you a long pants and a crew cut? I told you you'll have to wait like every other boy to get your long pants'.

But two weeks later Mam gets Jim and me to go to Bobby Cleary's in Carey's Road to get the crew cut like Tommy and we can't stop rubbing our heads with our hands. It's cold on top all of a sudden but I won't leave Mam alone about the pants. She eventually gives in and offers to take me down to Moran's to get the long pants. It's great; they have the turn-ups in the end. But I'm given clear instructions as to when I can wear it and when I can't.

'Only on the weekends', she says.

'Ah Janey Mam, why is it only on the weekends?,'

'Because you'll get it destroyed playing football, fishing and everything else you get up to'.

So I have to sit and look at the lovely green pants with the turn-ups at the end, hanging over the back of the chair every weeknight and I can only feel like a man on Saturday and Sunday and for the other five days I'll have the knobbly knees and white legs again.

About eighteen months later we get a letter from Limerick Corporation informing us to prepare ourselves to go back to Carey's Road. So Jet, James and I are all excited again about another move to another new house; only to be told by Pop and Mam that we're going nowhere. And when we ask why, it's because they put so much money into the house, they just can't afford to do it all again in Upper Carey's Road. James doesn't mind too much, but Jet and I are devastated. Fonsie and Noelie are going back to Carey's Road and over the next six years I'll have to make my way to Carey's Road and back to the other friends I have made in Garryowen.

I am now spending one half of every week in Carey's Road and the other half with the new mates in Garryowen. There's a gang of lads I've fallen foul with that live at the other side of Garryowen, near the hill and for the life of me I can't remember why. But what I can remember is going up to Carey's Road by the Jail Boreen and home again by the Market's Field looking around every corner for these guys; they're always together and if I run into them I'm in big trouble. It goes on for three years and I get sick and tired of it. I thought if I could just get one of them on their own I'd take him on and one day I got my opportunity.

I'm walking through Rossa Avenue just off Mulgrave Street and there's two of them about twenty yards in front of me with their backs to me, walking in the same direction into town, so I'm thinking if they turn right into Mulgrave Street, I can run back down Rossa Avenue into a gap in the wall, get into the paddocks which is just before The Horse and Hound Bar and I'll be able to head them off. When I get to the entrance next to Hayes' garage which is now Leonards, I look around one of the two stone pillars that has the entrance into the paddocks and I can see them, they're on their way down towards me and I'm thinking of one of Pop's sayings: 'Opportunity only knocks once'. So I look around on the ground of the paddocks for a good sized rocker, a nickname we gave to a decent sized stone. When I find one, all I have to do is wait as they pass by the entrance. I'll jump in front of them with the rocker in my right hand held up high.

I've got all the shapes and talk of a real tough guy, this is better than I thought. They look really scared. They're wondering which one will get the rocker between the eyes first. But I don't have the killer instinct, I know that if I throw this rocker and miss, the advantage that I have now will be gone. So I do the usual routine in all these situations and that's talk before I think. I invite one to fight me hand to hand if I throw the rock away. He instantly agrees and when I throw the rock down, real cool like, it rolls right in front of the other guys legs.

Not only have I thrown the rock away but also the advantage. They can't believe their luck and I can't believe how I could be so stupid again. I can feel the bravery flying out of my body wondering what the hell it was doing there in the first place. The other guy bends down, picks up the rock and says,

'Go on Martin get him and I'll effin brain him with the rocker'.

I've got my hands up like Rocky Marciano and so has the first fellow. We're out in the middle of Mulgrave Street dancing around like two boxers in the ring. I don't know it, but this guy belongs to one of the local boxing clubs and knows when to throw a dig and how to duck one. I'm trying to concentrate on landing a dig on this guy but it's very hard with the small guy behind me shouting all the time about braining me with the rocker and before I know it I get two thumps into the right side of the gob. I think I've got blood running down my nose, and any minute I'm going to have it running down my pole when that small guy lets go of the rock. But the day is saved when a passer-by intervenes and pulls me away.

What a relief I'm feeling on the inside but on the outside I want to show I want to brain this guy. I'm making all the struggles trying to break free and then get another thump from the man who's trying to stop us. He's telling the other two to get going and if he sees us fighting again, he'll call the guards. I suppose I should have thanked the man for saving my skin but that wouldn't be macho would it? So I had to make it look as if I was hopping mad as I walked away. I was feeling really pleased with myself that I stood up to the bullies and I would do it again if the situation called for it and it did, just two weeks later.

There's a new bean-Gárda in town, we used call her 'the first woman policeman in Limerick' because the last thing she looked like was a woman. She was like a German panzer with legs. People said the lumps under her jacket weren't breasts, but muscles. Only for the fact that she wore a skirt she would pass as a man and a very big man at that. The scene is Bedford Row. I'm looking at the four coloured pictures in the glass case on the wall outside the Grand Central Cinema trying to make up my mind if I want to go in and see what's on, when I get a dig on the side of my face which brings me back to reality. I immediately look to my right to see where it came from, drawing back my hand to let fly at whoever gave it to me. After I landed my fist in his face we both get into a scuffle. I'm lifted off the ground by something behind me. I can see the deliverer of the punch, another one of the gang from Garryowen. He's got two others with him and he can't believe I hit him back, especially when they were with him. I think he said, 'here's the guards', as we were struggling together. But I said 'F the guards'. But whatever is holding me off the ground by the scruff of the neck speaks. I recognise that voice. It belongs to the panzer with the legs and it's talking to me.

'What are ye fighting for?,' he asks or she asks I should say.

I'm trying to tell her I was minding my own business looking at the pictures on the wall when this guy gave me a dig into the face. But when she asked the other fellow, he's got two witnesses who lie through their teeth and say I threw the first punch. They get to go free but I have to give my name and address and they're up at the corner making faces at me. But the episodes of standing up for myself paid dividends. I never had to look around corners again.

CHAPTER 13

Pop is four years off the liquid now, and before he puts another drop to his mouth seven years will have passed. It will be an all time record. He does it without any help from anyone except of course his love for Mam. Her headaches are very few and far between now and only come when Pop will go to a funeral or the odd wedding. So our last Christmas in Carey's Road Pop decides to treat himself to a six by three Joe Davis snooker table. It's a reward he gives himself for doing so well. There is great excitement when he takes it out of the cardboard box on Christmas Day and puts it on the kitchen table. It comes with all the colour balls, two cues, an angle frame, chalk and four small rubber legs to adjust the table and make it level. There isn't enough room to play on every side of the table. Pop makes a fool out of me when I ask him is the room too small for the table?

He says, 'No, the table is too big.'

So we can only play on two sides at anytime. Pop says, 'It won't be long as we'll be going to our new house soon and we'll have plenty of room to play on all sides of the table'. Pop has made five of what he calls 'skittles' four white and one black. He makes a mark on the table in black biro for each one and puts the black skittle in the centre. He's got numbers 4, 3, 2 and 1 beside each of the other four skittles. He explains the rules to me. 'The score has to finish at 31, not 32 or 30. It must be exactly 31. And every time you knock the black skittle, you have to put a penny into a saucer, and start again if you go over 31 you have to start again as well. There's a red, black and white ball only to be used and I won't bore you with anymore details as the game can last for hours and the pot can grow to reach a pound or two'. Pop is very good at it; in fact he's very good at everything.

When we get to Garryowen Auntie Nora and Uncle Jimmy will visit every Sunday after dinner. Uncle Jimmy is a small, jolly man with a great big tummy and a huge belly laugh. Nan will always be sure to be in Garryowen on Sunday in the afternoon to be part of the whole arrangement. I didn't know it then, but on reflection I now realise it was to encourage Pop to stay at home with the family and give him something to look forward to instead of being tempted by the demons to go down to Bedford Row.

When he comes to Garryowen every Sunday, Mam will have the table cleared for Pop to put the Joe Davis on top of it. Nan and Auntie Nora will occupy the two fireside chairs that Pop brought home from a house shortly after we moved down here. Mam will be all business with a smile on her face, because she doesn't get the headaches as much and everybody is home where they should be. Marie, Uncle Jimmy and Auntie Nora's daughter is playing with Jetta and things just couldn't be better for Mam. Pop and Uncle Jim will play the skittle game all afternoon and anytime the cue ball stops near the corner where Nan is sitting by the fire, Uncle Jim will stick his big fat bum into her head and she'll get into hysterics laughing. The whole place is cracking up with laughter. I can't remember happier times in our house than those days in Garryowen. Pop will let me play one game with them every week and when six o'clock comes, the game finishes. The snooker table is back in the cardboard box and might come out midweek when I will get the chance to play with Pop and I love it. Uncle Jim and Auntie Nora are coming for almost twelve months now, never missing a Sunday and Mam is in great form. But the hiding I dreaded getting from Pop is coming my way very soon.

I'm about twelve years old at the time and after the table is cleared of all the cutlery for the snooker to start with Pop taking the level out to make sure the table is straight on all four sides; Nan, Uncle Jim and Auntie Nora arrive. It's the usual fun and laughter. Auntie Nora takes her usual place by the fire and Mam is in and out with the teapot every few minutes, topping up the two girls by the fire. The spotted dick is on the go as well.

And I'll be worried like I am every Sunday that one of the two spotted dicks that Mam bakes every Sunday might be eaten by all the mouths and I'll only have the one left for the rest of the week. And if I run out of spotted dick by Wednesday I don't think I'll be able to last until Mam makes more the following Sunday. She has the usual beaming smile. Nan is cracking up with laughter as Uncle Jim keeps sticking his backside into her face every chance he gets. But Pop isn't his usual self today and whatever is bothering him is going to rise to the surface very soon. Everything is the same as it has been every Sunday and when Pop and Uncle Jim finish their game which takes about an hour and a half, I get to play next. That lasts about an hour and as they get on with their next game I'm upstairs playing with Jim in our bedroom. We start doing what any normal kids do, and that's messing around. Now we're having a wrestling match and we fall onto the bed, then off it onto the floor which makes a big bang. Pop shouts, 'What's going on up there?,'

'We're wrestling Pop', I shout down.

I can hear Mam saying the usual, 'Jesus, Mary and Holy St. Joseph what's going on up there at all?'

The wrestling that James and I are doing and the noise we're making is bad enough, but the comments that are coming with it from Nan and Mam makes the whole situation much worse for Pop. James and I of course think it's very funny and we're at it again. But when we fall on the floor a second time we can hear the door of the room where all the entertainment is going on opening quickly. Mam is shouting, 'Will ye be quiet up there for goodness sake?'

There's heavy steps coming up the stairs and I can hear Nan still at it, with the Holy Family being called out again.

Pop is at the top of the stairs with the snooker cue in his hand and boy does he look mad. He's got the right hand with the forefinger right up against my nose, not James'. He's telling me that if he has to come up again a second time, to the two of us, that I will be very sorry. 'Do you hear me now?' Down he goes; James and I sit on the bed. When Pop closes the door James looks at me and when I look back at him we start laughing our heads off. We can't stop. But when I fall over from laughing so much I manage to hit the bedroom door that's halfway closed with my shoulder. It slams shut causing a terrible sudden bang. The laughing stops and I know I'm in big trouble. I can hear Pop's loud voice in the hall saying,

'Jesus Christ, I warned him, but did he listen?' The vibration from his heavy feet landing on every step as he comes up the stairs is coming in along the floorboards of all the bedrooms and up through my legs. I can feel a tremor like I never felt before. He's on the landing just outside the door. I jump with the fright as the handle snaps its way down and the door swings open.

Sheer fear has stuck me to the floor. I can't move anything and before I know it I get the full force of his giant closed fist into the mouth, bursting my top lip wide open and putting me on my back in the bed. James is up against the wall kneeling on the bed, unable to move as well. Pop is shouting at me, 'Didn't I tell you what would happen if you didn't keep quiet?' He's got one knee on my stomach and his other leg on the floor. He raises his fist into the air again. I'm getting another one. If he hits me again like the last one, I'll surely be dead and before he strikes, he says, 'you'll remember the next time to do what you're told.' And he hits me on the right side of my face. I can hear Mam screaming as she runs up the stairs. 'Jesus, Harry, stop you'll kill him.' She's in the room trying to pull him off me but she can't. She shouts down to Uncle Jimmy not knowing that he has followed her up the stairs with all the commotion. Now Uncle Jimmy and Mam are trying to pull Pop off me and there's blood spatters everywhere. Pop is out of control. Mam and Uncle Jim, have a hold of him. He's breathing very heavily now.

Mam and Auntie Nora take me downstairs from the bed that's now in tatters because of the weight of Pop. I'm being washed down by Mam and Auntie Nora in the kitchen. Mam is hugging me while I'm crying. She never does that. Mam and Auntie Nora are crying. Nan isn't; she's looking at me as if it's all my fault. Uncle Jim is trying to talk to Pop. He's got both hands around Pop's face trying to calm him down. Pop is trying to light a cigarette and when he can't because his hands are shaking so much, Uncle Jim lights it for him. There's a silence that's eerie and Nan still has the stare at me. The snooker table is still out, the coloured balls as they were before Pop's temper took him up the stairs. I have the hiccups and I'm sobbing my eyes out with a cry of injustice. I'm trying to tell Mam that I fell against the door by accident. She's trying to hush me while holding a wet cold cloth to my eye and lip which are badly swollen. My teeth are loose and I can see Uncle Jimmy just sitting there with Pop and Nan. Pop is still shaking and tries to light up another cigarette but he's looking at Uncle Jim to help him again. Uncle Jim is as white as a sheet as Mam and Auntie Nora whisper to one another in the kitchen about maybe going over to St. John's Hospital for that awful expression again 'a stitch or two'. This causes me great distress and I break all the terrible silence with a loud,

'No! I don't want to go down there to the nurse with the funny walk and the thick glasses and get more injections and stitches; No please Mam not again.'

Mam reassures me that she won't take me anywhere today that we'll wait until tomorrow and see how I am, which helps to settle me down.

I'm wondering why no one especially Mam isn't giving Pop hell for what he has done. Mam always lets Pop know what's on her mind. Surely she can't be in agreement with what he has done to my face. After another hour of that weird silence and whispers, Uncle Jimmy, Auntie Nora and their daughter are saying goodbye and we never see Uncle Jimmy or Auntie Nora at 36 Claughaun Court, Garryowen again.

I don't think that in all her years of growing up Uncle Jim and Auntie Nora's daughter Marie ever had a hand raised to her. It must have been a huge shock to Uncle Jimmy and Auntie Nora to see what Pop had done to me. As I write this story, looking back, an older, hopefully wiser person, having raised my own two children, I can see Mam's difficulty back then. Pop had great willpower. He had been off the drink for more than three years. He would have had a great excuse to break out and drown his sorrows, but he didn't. He held firm. Had Mam laid into him like she can, it might have been the straw that broke the camel's back. She knew that. She could see that Pop knew he had gone too far and nothing would be accomplished by giving him a mouthful.

Another aspect of this story is how it's not high on my list of memories. I think it should be and I wonder why it's not. Is it because it's the only bad memory of my childhood? I hope so, or did I see in Pop a strength of character that I admired?

Anyway, the Sunday afternoons would never be the same again. Nan's visits won't include Garryowen on those Sunday afternoons. And the snooker table won't see as much daylight either.

Uncle Jamie, the accordion player, my mother's baby brother was my favourite uncle; a small, happy hard-working painter all his life, who gave me great time and attention. 'Jez Boys' were the first words out of his mouth every time he walked through our front door in Carey's Road and Garryowen. He always included me in his early odd jobs like delivering the papers every Sunday morning from a collection point at the Dublin Road in a black Volkswagen car to go to the shops around Limerick city. I would have to do the running in and out of the car from seven in the morning 'til ten with the papers for nothing just to be in the front seat of the car.

Then in the autumn months Nan would give Uncle Jamie the money to go and buy 'an orchard' as he called it. 'An orchard' of apples to bring to the shops and sell; this was great fun and a chance to earn some good spending money for Jet, James and myself. We had to help pick the apples, put them in boxes and then help Uncle Jim to take them to the shops. Then one year while in an orchard I put one of my feet into a hole in the ground and was immediately attacked by a swarm of bees or wasps, I can't remember which. They're everywhere! Uncle Jim has his shirt off because of the lovely sunny day and every one of us is running in all directions. But it doesn't matter. We can't get away from them, and because I was the one who stuck my foot into the hole, I'm getting the most stings, especially on my head, with the new crew cut I got with Jimmy down at Bobby Cleary's in Carey's Road. Uncle Jim keeps shouting at us to get into the van and when we managed that, some of the bees got in as well. But Uncle Jim manages to see them off before they can sting anyone else. Jet, James and I are bawling our eyes out from the pain and Uncle Jim is giving us chocolate to try and keep us calm. When we get home Mam tells Uncle Jim that there won't be anymore apple picking from now on. Poor Uncle Jim has to go and get other volunteers before his apples rot on the trees. Uncle Jim will not be around for much longer. He will leave for England shortly, like thousands of others, because there's no work anywhere to be found, not just in Limerick but the whole of Ireland.

After two years he'll be back again, married but Uncle Peadar, the quiet Uncle, the man of few words and complete opposite of Uncle Jimmy is getting married in a house in the country just outside Limerick. Jet, James and I can't wait, as we've never been to a wedding before. Mam says that there will be lots to eat and drink for all the kids that will be there. But we have to go through the boring bits first like the Mass and the photographs before we get to sit down for the goodies. It's all the children together, out in the back garden, while all the adults sit in a big room eating and talking away. Then the priest talks forever and ever. The father of the bride stands and he's talking for ages too.

Then the floor is cleared for the dancing and that's great. Uncle Jim is blasting away goodo on the accordion. People are jumping and leaping all over the place. There's a big bang, a twenty stone woman has dropped dead on the floor and now everybody is on their knees with the rosary beads in their hands praying for the next hour and the whole blooming day is ruined.

Telefís Éireann has come to Limerick. It adds another station to the dirty rotten lousers on the east coast of Ireland who already have the BBC network and has the likes of Denis O'Sullivan who lives in Rossa Avenue on his knees in front of the radio with his hands clasped together praying that his beloved Manchester United won't be beaten no matter who they're playing every Saturday, and if they're playing in the European Cup Denis knows someone who has a car that knows someone in Waterford who won't mind the four or five guys that will come from Limerick and sit in his living room on the Wednesday evening and look at the snowy picture for the hour and a half.

TV shops will grow like mushrooms overnight in William Street, O'Connell Street and along with the Shannon Industrial Estate that's giving jobs to hundreds in Limerick, Ennis and other counties will slowly increase the volume of traffic on the streets of Limerick. The good life is on its way and the evidence of this can be seen on the roof of every house with TV aerials sprouting out of every chimney in Garryowen. Vans of all shapes are on our roads every day from R.T.V. Rentals in O'Connell Street, now the home of Empire Music, Rentel next to Todds, Irish TV Rentals in William Street, Telefusion and others, with the new TVs like everything else available on the weekly. Some will come with a box at the side that takes a two bob piece and gives you two hours of viewing. You'll forget all about it until you're half way through a suspense thriller and bang goes the TV. Everybody is on their feet searching for a two bob piece, shouting 'hurry up or we'll have to wait until next week to find out what happened!' And if one can't be found it's out to Mrs. Hogan next door, who moved in after Noelie went back to the new houses in Upper Carey's Road, who takes ten minutes to find her purse and when she does, tells me she has every coin in it except a two bob piece, so it's up to the shop at the corner. There's four people before me and only one person serving and by the time I'm back down with the two bob the blooming thing is over and I have to listen to Pop, Mam and Jet giving out to me because I took so long.

My sister Jet is nearly seventeen now and has a job with the Limerick Leader; the girl that used to play hurling and football in Upper Carey's Road, who'd beat the living daylights out of Dinny, Fonsey and Noelie or anybody else who laid a hand on James or myself; who climbed walls, skinned orchards, played rugby with all the lads and was very good too has gone missing and someone else has taken her place. It's like it happened overnight. She's gone all posh now and won't go outside the door unless she's wearing high heels, perfume, nylons, lipstick, hairspray, carrying a handbag and isn't interested anymore in coming to my assistance if I get a dig. Mam says she can keep most of her wages because girls need to buy things for themselves every week, but tells me when I go to work with Pop I'll have to hand over half of what I get and here we go again! I'm telling her that's lousy and its' the only time in my whole life that I ever wanted to be a girl.

There'll be fellas calling to the house every night, dressed in their best suits looking for Jet. She'll be at the door talking for hours with a voice and a stupid laugh that she only has for the fellas like Paddy Gleeson who drives a van for Clancy's in O'Connell Street delivering bottles of gas to people who have the latest Calor Gas cookers and heaters. He's very decent and gives me two bob every Friday night. I think he likes me, but I'm too stupid to realise I'm only getting the two bob because of my good looking sister. He'll call every night and after an hour of talking at the door will come in for the cup of tea and clear four or five slices of one of the two spotted dicks. I hate him, six nights of the week when he takes most of it out the door in his stomach with the five or six cups of tea Mam will give him and love him on the Friday night, when he gives me the two bob. When Jet tells him to 'feck off' because she's gone off him, I'm totally confused because I'm happy six nights of the week with the spotted dick all to myself and miserable on the Friday night without the two bob.

But the latch on the front door will be banging away every night with more fellas that won't be parting with money on any night because Jet is a real stunner. It never dawns on her that she could have looks like Pop and if she had, no amount of make up plaster would improve her looks or hide the big ears, even if it was put on with a trowel. Pop will come out to the fellas and ask them questions like, 'Who's father are you?' 'What's your surname?' and no matter what their surname is, he'll ask them, 'Is that your mother, the big fat one with the bust like a tank who sells the second-hand knickers and bras down at the market every Saturday morning? or 'Is that your father who has the disease the doctors say a cure will never be found for?' and the poor fellas will look at Jet to see if Pop might be joking and Jet will just stand there straight-faced and they'll swear on all that belongs to them dead or alive that he's in no way connected. Pop will turn around and walk towards the living room door and mutter the words, 'Good, I don't want my daughter down at the market every Saturday next to that dirty old one selling the used knickers or living in a house she might catch something out of'. When he gets through the living room door his shoulders are on their way up and down. Mam and Nan if she's there are killing themselves laughing and when the laughing stops Nan will say 'Jesus, Har you'll have every young fella that calls to the door frightened off and your poor daughter will never get a husband'. Your man is still out at the door swearing his life away to Jet that he has nothing to do with any of the people Pop named before Jet puts him out of his misery and tells him that Pop does that to every fella that calls.

The days when Pop lies in bed with one hand behind his head and a fag in the other worrying into the early hours have gone. His nephew, a tall skinny handsome young man of eighteen and a son of his deceased eldest brother of the same name Frank is working with him now. Pop says the time has come for me to go working with him after school and the Saturdays that I'll get some spending money too. It's hard to believe the days I used to dream about working with him have come. I'm going to be working with my Dad and getting paid for it too. Sure I'd do it for nothing. Dinny, Fonsey and Noelie can go to blazes. I'll have much more interesting things to do now.

I won't feel stupid either. In fact I'll feel intelligent and clever every day because I'll be good at it and every house he'll take me to, there'll be the usual comments like, 'Is that your son Harry, isn't he a grand strong young man, not a bit like yourself Har. And I'm thinking, 'Thanks be to God'. They'll be asking me 'Do you like working with your Dad?' and when I say 'I do', they'll say 'Sure we can see that the way you're watching your father all the time'. Pop will explain everything to me because I'll have him pestered to let me have a go. One week we're papering and painting, another week he's doing some plumbing; after that we might be out in Corbally building a wall or up on a roof, another time we're in O'Connell Avenue hanging a new door. There's people wanting the iron weights in the sash windows looked at, in the centre of town, mostly the Georgian houses and I can't get enough of it. Some people will give me a pound or a ten shilling note because I'll always have the good manners. Pop will tell every customer how I'm up every morning waiting for the sun to come up so I can go to work. They'll laugh and tell him to leave me alone, that I'm a grand lad. But I'm loving every minute of it.

The summer holidays are on their way and Pop says there'll be no shortage of work. There's a house at the bottom of Henry Street that has a narrow lane separating it from the Franciscan Church. 'We'll be there for the whole two months of your holiday'. And because of my constant pleas he will let me try my hand at every trade. He'll be sending me across the road to James McMahon in Bedford Row four or five times a day for screws, nails, cement and paint. Other times he'll ask me to get something I never heard of. I'll come back without it. Then he'll take me back over; show me what he wanted and where he got it. McMahon's shop is a funny auld place. Pop says it used to be a couple of old houses years ago, how they only changed the ground floor into a large shop, that all the houses in Bedford Row were just like the Bedford Hotel and Mrs. Fay's House.

'Come up here', he says. 'I want to show you something'. He takes me up four flights of stairs that's above the shop floor. There's only enough room to walk on half of every step that has boxes of all shapes and sizes stacked several feet into the air. Each room on every floor is filled with paint tins and electrical goods, the walls and ceilings full of cracks and old paint, the banisters old and bockety on every row. We keep climbing 'till there's no more stairs. The landing has a room on each side. He looks at me and points to one of them and says, 'this is where you were born'. I'm confused and say 'I thought I was born across the road in the hospital'. 'You were', he answered. 'This is where you lived for four years after you came out'. 'I used to live here when I was your age'. I'm full of questions like 'Were you born here too?' He tells me how his father owned a tailoring shop in Taylor Street up near the Royal Cinema that had two stories overhead. 'That's why we were known as Taylor by name, Tailor by trade and lived in Taylor Street'. I'm asking him how come he lived in this house then. 'Your Granddad sold the building in Taylor Street and bought this one when I was ten years old'.

'Why?,' I ask.

'I don't know', he replied. 'Maybe he wanted a bigger house'.

'So ye were well off then?'

'Oh indeed we were,' he answered.

'How come McMahon's own it now Pop?'

'Because they bought it', he says and the shoulders are moving.

'I know that', I answer. 'Did your father sell it to them?'

'No,' he answered. 'Frank sold it to them'.

'Who gave the house to Frank then?' I'm asking totally confused.

'I did', answers Pop.

There's silence, he's looking at me waiting for me to ask the next question like he knows what I'm going to say.

'How do you mean you did, where did you get it from?'

So he starts to tell me his mother died when he was nine and when he reached the age of sixteen he was left the house because his father passed away. He hardly has the last few words out of his mouth when I hurriedly ask him 'How much did you get for it?' He answered me back just as quickly with the word 'nothing'.

I laugh and say, 'You're having me on, come on tell me, how much did you get?'

'I'm telling you I got nothing'.

I'm asking him how he could own one of the most expensive properties in Limerick city centre and just give it away.

9 Bedford Row

Family Photograph
This family portrait was taken while the Taylor Family
was still residing in Taylor Street, with Pop, four years old in
the centre.

'Because I didn't want the responsibility that's why; Rates had to be paid, repairs, gas and ESB Bills. Sure I hadn't a bean to my name so I gave it to Frank'.

'How much did Frank sell it for?,' I ask.

'Seven hundred pounds', he answered.

'Is that all? I thought it would be worth more than that'.

Pop says seven hundred pounds was a lot of money in those days.

'So how much is it worth now?' I'm asking.

'About seven hundred and fifty thousand pounds' he answers.

WHAT? I shout. 'Janey Mack that's a fortune, why the hell didn't you keep it? We could be living out in the North Circular Road now or Castletroy with a car and a posh accent?,' I'm looking at the Dad I adored, the perfect man that never made a mistake in his life except take the odd few drinks every couple of years and all I can see now is a total amadán who gave up a three storey house to his brother for nothing and wound up years later paying rent for a room of a house he once owned and now I know that being a total idiot isn't my fault at all. I got it from him.

I'm totally depressed for the next few days. But like everything else I'll get over it.

The rest of the school holidays will be the best I've ever had because I'm working with my Dad. Before I know it September is on its way and it's back to C.B.S. Sexton Street for the sixth class and my last year there.

CHAPTER 14

There's a rumour flying around the school that 'the gut' is retiring. He's being replaced the rumours say by a guy who is ten times worse. We don't have long to wait to find out. It's lunch time, most are out in the yard playing when a large, a very large black figure enters the scene. Play gradually comes to a halt. It's him, the new guy. 'Janey he's massive,' says Jackie Liston. A giant, he'll walk around the yard with the hands behind the back just like 'the gut', but this one is like King Kong. He's big everywhere. He's like a lion browsing around the yard telling everyone 'I'm the boss around here!' He's making sure we all get a good close up.

We won't want to cross this guy. The rumours were true. This is Brother Kenny, enter the fear hunter. If he can see the terror in our eyes we'll be ok and it's not too long before he's making changes, big changes.

A message goes out to every class. Anyone interested in sport is to meet him at the end of the play yard after school. There's a big turnout. I'm there because I think I can run. He tells us all there's going to be a sports day at the Gaelic Grounds in eight weeks time between all the local boys in Sexton Street, and other schools in Limerick city. He continues, 'I'm going to call all the events and if you think you can perform in any of them, put your hand up'. The hundred yard dash is called and up goes my hand. I think I can win this because of my Uncle Paddy being the Munster Champion in that event for several years. And sure didn't they name me after him? The last event is the big event of the day, five times around the field of the Gaelic Grounds, a race for everyone. There's only one hand up for this event from all the lads that turned up.

'Who owns that hand?' says Kenny, 'I can't see who it belongs to'.

A small figure appears from the back of the bunch. Kenny looks down in amazement.

'Are you telling me you can run around the field out in the Gaelic Grounds five times?'

The small guy just says, 'Yes Brother'.

I know this guy, he's from sixth class.

'Show me your hands', says Kenny. He puts his hands out. 'Turn them around' says Kenny. 'Your hands are all brown, do you smoke? Is that nicotine?'

'Yes Brother'.

'Aren't you an awful Eejit to be smoking at your age?' says Kenny.

'Yes Brother'.

'Do you really expect me to believe that you can run around the Gaelic Grounds five times, the size of you and you're smoking?'

'Yes Brother'.

'Very well', says Kenny, 'seeing as you're the only one who wants to run in that event, but I think you'll be on your knees after twenty feet'.

So the day arrives and when it's my turn to run the hundred yards first heat, I'm glad my uncle Paddy who was the Munster Champion in the 100 yards for several years is dead and in his grave and wasn't here or alive to see me make a holy show of the Taylor name, and being called after him because I came last in the first heat of the one hundred yard dash. But it's down to the last event; our school is way down in the medal list. They're lining up to start five times around the field, and there's our guy. He's the smallest one of the whole bunch of twenty. There are four or five lanky guys, they'll surely be there at the finish and off they go. And there's our guy in the lead straight away and Kenny is shouting 'Go back, go back, take your time', but maybe he can't hear because he's still out in front and very far away. He's half-way round the track now and Kenny is down to meet him and as he passes Kenny is shouting, 'Fall back, slow down, you'll run out of steam', but he's still out in front. Our school is in the lead. All of us should be shouting our heads off encouraging him. But Kenny is shouting to this guy what he'll do to him when he falls down from exhaustion. Here they go round again, it's one and a half times and our guy is still out in front. He's passing Kenny again and Kenny says, 'Do you hear me talking to you, I said slow down'. But our guy just steps up the pace instead and Kenny is walking around in circles talking to himself. There are other teachers asking Kenny where he got that little fellow from and Kenny isn't answering and here comes our guy again. They are now two and a half times around the track, and he has increased the lead again. Now we've forgotten about Kenny and what he's going to do to this guy. And we're shouting, 'Sextons, Sextons'. Kenny is waving his fist at our guy as he passes the third time. The field is starting to thin out. There are five behind our guy and when they come around again for the fourth time, our guy is still in the lead and Kenny is jumping up and down waving everything at our guy, saying 'If you conserved your energy you could have won, you Eejit'. There's one round to go and our guy is still in front. Can he do it? Surely a guy of his size can't, how can anyone who smokes run like that, but instead of slowing down our guy increases the pace to screams of applause. We can't believe it. Now Kenny has changed his tune, he's jumping up and down and shouting 'Come on, come on, you can do it' and by the time he comes around the final bend he can't be caught. He looks back and instead of slowing down increases the pace again and crosses the line to a hero's welcome. Kenny is slapping him on the back saying, 'I knew you could do it, well done' and he's the talk of the school for months, and is hero worshipped for the rest of the year. What would have happened to this guy if he couldn't have kept going after four laps we'll never know, but the fear hunter is going to come very close to stopping my heart from beating the flow of life to my body very soon.

And so another year of learning nothing comes and goes. The summer holiday has been and gone. It's September again, and the next teacher to be driven around the bend by my class 6D is Brian O'Neill or Chuckser as he was known. I've no idea why he was called this but of all the teachers who tried to teach me anything, Chuckser is the one I will learn the most from. I will leave Sexton St. CBS with great affection for this man.

We're on the top floor of the stone building. This is the Primary Cert year and if we don't pass it, a good job will be hard to come by, so the teachers say. But I'm not worried. I'm going to be working with my Dad. I don't need a stupid bit of paper for that. It's our second week and there's no sign of Chuckser. We only had him for half of the first week and hardly know him yet. The large partition that folds like an accordion dividing all the classes from a long corridor, has glass half-way on top that distorts the human frame as it passes along and there's a huge one coming into our classroom. The door opens and in walks Kenny. There's instant silence. We all have a look on our faces that asks 'what the hell is he doing here?,', and out he comes with a dreaded announcement. 'Mr. O'Neill is going to be out sick for the next few days, so I'll be taking his place'. And I'm thinking 'Oh Mother of Divine Jesus, we're all going to be killed'.

He opens the roll book, he's calling out the names, there's no answers' because we're all in shock. He shouts 'are ye all deaf in here?,' We jump from our seats with the sound of his voice. 'I'll start again,' he says. There's lads' clearing their throats' as they call 'present' or 'anseo' when the roll is called. Lenny Holman's name is heard, there's no answer because he's not there. After he calls his name again and getting no answer, he calls Cyril Meade, he's not there either; he calls it a second time. Then there's another six or seven names mentioned the answer is again 'present' or 'anseo'. Jackie Liston's name is called, there's no answer. It's called a second time, there's still no answer. He's finished now.

'I see from the roll-book that Holman, Meade and Liston have been missing for three days of last week and today as well. The long holiday was enough for them to be missing. Does anyone know why these boys are not in school? But who's going to put their hand up and say 'I know Brother?'

We all know they're walking around the town 'on the go' as we called it back then, so no one is saying anything. Then I am taken completely by surprise with the fright when I hear him call my name. I jump to my feet in shock, there's all kinds of things running around in my head. What does he want me for, am I going to get pucked for something I'm going to do or say?

'Do you know where Cyril Meade lives?,' Kenny asks.

Sure everyone knows where Cyril Meade lives. He's just down the road from here, you could throw a stone there, it's so close. His father has a small cabinet making shop and they live overhead. The dogs in the street know where Cyril Meade lives. I know why Kenny is asking me, he wants me to go down to the house and find out why Meade is not in school, but I don't want to go anywhere near Meade's house. There are lads in the class that will give me a right thumping if I go anywhere near his house and tell his parents their son is not in school.

'No Brother I don't'. I'm shaking; I'm after telling a dirty rotten lie. I'm frightened, I know I'll say or do something that will give the game away. Then he shouts, 'Brosnan!'

Brosnan is up in the front row.

He jumps to his feet and says 'yes Brother'.

'Do you know where Meade lives?'

'I do Brother', answers Brozey'

And I'm saying to myself, 'oh thanks be to God, I'll be alright, I'll be safe now'.

Then I hear Kenny shout, 'Well tell Taylor where he lives' and my heart is back up in my throat again. The blood has gone from my head and I have to fall back into my seat because I'm not able to stand. Brozey is telling me where Meade lives but I can't hear a word he's saying. How am I going to get out of this? Then Kenny tells Roger Browne to find out where Lenny Holman lives. He has to come back tomorrow with news from Lenny's parents and Wacker Noonan has to go to Janesborough to Jackie Liston's house.

Now I'm in another mess. It's after school, the class is gathered outside. Roger Browne and a couple of other lads are telling me and Wacker Noonan not to go anywhere near Meade's or Liston's houses. It's agreed we'll all make excuses tomorrow, but they'll have to be different, we can't all give the same excuse or we'll be caught out straight away. I know the whole thing is going to go pear-shaped at some stage but I'm thinking if I don't go along with this I'll risk several thumping's from all the lads in class. I'll be branded a tell-tale against being mutilated or killed by Brother Kenny, not if he finds out but when he finds out. I don't get a wink of sleep that night, practising my lies. I know that I'm going to make a mess of it when I stand up to tell the lie.

Mam is asking me that evening why I never ate my supper and left my dinner after me when I came home at lunchtime. She keeps feeling my forehead to see if I'm coming down with something. The following morning Mam says: 'You're fine, there's nothing wrong with you'. She's got her hand on my forehead again, I try to pretend I'm sick but Mam's not falling for it and I can hear my heart pounding out my ears.

I've forgotten the excuse, here's Kenny coming in the door to class. He's calling the names from the roll book again, the pounding of my heart and the blood around my body is unbearable, I can hardly hear him calling out the names. He's come to Cyril Meade, Lenny Holman and Jackie Liston. Then he says 'take out your exercise books and copy what I am going to write on the blackboard'. He's forgotten - I can't believe it. He's forgotten, the pounding out of my ears has stopped, there's a smile back on my face, life is great again, to think I went through all that worry for nothing last night. But there's Brozey in the front row, he's standing with his hand in the air, he's trying to get Kenny's attention but Kenny is writing on the blackboard with his back to Brozey. So Brozey starts with the 'Brother, Brother' bit. What the hell is wrong with him? He's all excited.

'What's wrong Brosnan?,' asks Kenny.

And Brozey opens his big gob with the words, 'you forgot to ask Taylor, Browne and Noonan why Meade, Holman and Liston aren't at school Brother'. And the heart is back in full throttle again. My whole life is flashing before me, that dirty rotten louser, I'll brain him! He wants to hang Noonan, Browne and myself. There's one of his kind in every class.

'Well done Brozey, well done,' says Kenny while looking down at the class. 'Who was to go and see Cyril Meade's parents?,'

I have to raise a limp hand.

'Well Taylor', he shouts 'did Cyril Meade's parents tell you why he hasn't been at school, since the holidays finished?'

'He ah, they ah, I mean he ah, I ah, he ah, they ah, has am, he has ah,'

'For God's sake Taylor, he has what?,'

'He has Brother, he has the chicken measles Brother'.

Kenny's face changes from anger to being confused. 'What the hell is chicken measles?,'

I knew it, I knew it, I just knew it, I've made a hames of it.

'Is it chicken-pox or the measles or has he got the two?' asks Kenny and I think he's smiling a bit.

'Ah the first one, Brother'.

'OK very good'.

It's all over, thanks be to God, the blood is coming back to my head and feet, I can sit down while Roger Browne and Wacker Noonan are telling their pack of lies. I'm dizzy and exhausted. The heart is beating much slower now. Kenny is talking away and I'm not listening. I haven't the energy. I'm sitting by the glass partition, I've my head in my hands and when I raise it up, there's movement on the other side of the partition. It's hard to tell if they're adults or young boys from another class on the same floor. The silhouettes get closer to the glass, there are two of them. I think one of them is a woman. They're stopping at our door, they're moving closer. There's a hand going to the glass to knock on it. Mother of Jesus I know who they are, my heart goes bang again. Its Cyril Meade's mother and father, I see them every week when Mam asks me to go down to Carmody's shop for the sour milk to make the spotted Dick. Their shop is across the road. I stand outside their door every Saturday morning with the sour milk can in my hand for an hour, watching him making and shaping all kinds of wood. He knows me and I'm sure he expects to see me every Saturday. He'll smile. I know he doesn't mind me standing at the door watching him. But maybe it's not Meade's mother and father; it might be somebody else that looks like them. There's a sharp knock on the glass. My heart has stopped. The door opens, Jesus I was right! It's them! I'm for it now. Kenny goes out of the class, closing the door behind him.

I'm in an awful state, stuttering out the words to Wacker Noonan and Roger Browne that those two people outside the door are Cyril Meade's parents and they go snow white. My heart is at it again and I don't know how much more it can take. I've never heard of a thirteen year old boy dying of a heart attack but I think I'm going to be the first. Kenny's silhouette is towering over Meade's parents. Cyril Meade will tell us tomorrow how his parents caught him walking around the town with Lenny Holman and Jackie Liston. It seems like they're out there in the corridor for hours.

He's coming in. 'Oh sweet Jesus I think I'm going to die, please get me out of this and I'll never lie again'. How can I be still alive the way my heart is beating. Look at Kenny's hands, they're getting bigger and so is his body. The fear hunter is on the war path, look at his face.

'Noonan', shouts Kenny,

'Yes Brother',

'Get out by the wall'.

'Browne',

'Yes Brother Kenny',

'Get out by the wall'.

I'm next 'oh dear God, I am heartily sorry for all the sins I have committed, please keep a place for me in heaven and look after my poor mother and father when I'm gone'. Kenny reaches down into his gown for the leather. We've heard all kinds of stories about his leather, how he had it specially made, that there's a strip of lead in the middle or a row of pennies. He grabs Noonan's hand, places it high above the right ear and brings the leather down as hard as he can; he raises the leather a second time and gives the same hand another wallop. Then it's two more on the other hand. Wacker looks like his head is going to explode. I'm looking and thinking I should have told

Kenny the truth. I don't think the beating from the lads would have been as bad as this. Roger Browne has the hand out and every wallop he gets means I'm closer to getting mine. I didn't think my heart could beat this fast but it does. He's finished with Roger Browne, now it's my turn.

'Taylor,' he shouts. I stand up and I start to walk to the top of the class and when I'm half way up he shouts, 'I'll deal with you after school'. I stop in my tracks confused. 'Yes Brother,' I answer. I'm trying to understand why he is doing this to me. I did the same as Wacker Noonan and Roger Browne. Why have I got to wait until after school? When lunch time comes the lads are asking me why he wants to see me after class. Some of them are saying he doesn't want any witnesses to see what he's going to do to me, others are saying he'll give four wallops on each hand and they're having great fun all through the break but I can't eat a thing. There's all kinds of things going through my brain, and as I look at Roger and Wacker they're playing away. It's all over for them, I want to run away but I can't.

We're back in class, all I can do is watch the clock all afternoon; when 4.15 arrives all the lads are walking out the door, they're making all kinds of gestures at me and my heart is at it again. They're all gone now. There's just Kenny and myself. He's at the desk writing, he's finished now. He raises his head, looks down at me, I'm worn out from praying, saying Acts of Contrition, sweating and shaking, I can't do anymore.

'OK Taylor, come up here'.

'Yes Brother'.

'Can you swim?,' he asks.

Oh sweet Jesus he's going to drown me.

'Well young man are you going to tell me if you can swim?' I'm totally confused and manage to say 'no, Brother'.

'Would you like to learn?' Again I don't answer.

'Well, would you?,' he asks. My brain is on auto-pilot. It opens my mouth and shouts out the words 'Yes Brother'.

'Right then, I want you to lie across the desk here as soon as I clear it'. My brain is doing everything for me now.

'OK lie on your tummy so that your legs and arms are out over the top and bottom of this desk. I want you to think about the frog, the way it swims. First move your hands in and out just like the frog'.

He's holding my hands together and moves them for me. He says:

'Keep doing that now. Very good, very good, while you're doing that I'm going to move your legs like the frog does' and after several movements with his hands holding my legs and shoving them out he says 'keep it up now, keep it up'. After five minutes I have my hands and legs moving just like the frog. I thought I was going to be dead. I haven't noticed my heart is beating normally; the sweating and shaking have gone. So is my promise to Jesus never to lie again. This man has me convinced I can swim. He's smiling all the time. I'm wondering where the nearest river or body of water is that I can throw myself into it, clothes and all.

'OK young Taylor, off you go now'.

'Yes Brother'.

And as I open the classroom door, he says

'Taylor!'

When I turn and say 'yes Brother'.

'Your classmates are outside the school gates waiting for you, tell them I beat the living daylights out of you and I want to see your mother and father' and he winked at me.

Coming out the yard the lads are asking 'Well Taylor what did he do to you?,' I said exactly as he told me. They can't figure out why he did this to me and most of all I can't tell them I can swim. But it would be years before I realised what this man's vision and foresight was like. How did he know I was bullied into lying, the way he made me suffer without the physical pain? This was a unique man, a great motivator and nothing like the reputation that preceded him. He would start the CBS Pipe Band, a massive sports day in the Gaelic Grounds every year, a born leader and teacher, and not as I thought, the Fear Hunter.

Cyril Meade's father's house and workshop (above) in Wickham Street and Carmody's milk shop across the road (below)

The next day sees no sign of Chuckser. Kenny is still with us and is losing the rag because he says we're unteachable. He walks out the door, his silhouette tearing down the corridor, he disappears for two minutes until we hear the heavy thumps of his shoes hitting the worn timber floor on his way back, until his silhouette appears again through the glass partition, followed by another smaller one behind. He's back in the room with a guy from the super-intelligent class. We all know him. He's like the rest of them down there all brains and no beauty! Kenny shouts, 'I want ye to watch and listen.' Kenny asks the brain box several questions in quick succession and hardly has each question finished when an answer comes flying back. Then it's a half dozen questions in Irish again the brain box answers back in Irish without blinking an eye. Kenny tells us this is what we should aspire to be. I want to put my hand up and ask what does aspire mean but I won't. He says we all have a brain just like the brain box but we're too lazy to use them. But I don't want to be like this guy, I'm not able. I hate his guts. What the hell is the use of talking in Irish? Sure we all hate it. Kenny tells the brain box to go back to class and says he hopes Mr. O'Neill will be back tomorrow, because he doesn't think his patience could last another day, and wonders how Mr. O'Neill will manage to keep sane over the next ten months with a shower like us.

The next day Chuckser is back. Fonsey had him last year. He fills me in on what to look out for. If you're in the yard when he comes in go over and ask him 'Will I bring your bike down to the shed sir?' ask him again before he goes home'. 'Why would I want to do that? I ask Fonsey, to get into his good books'. 'OK' I'll have some of that Fonsey'. Then he tells me Chuckser loves music and he's the choirmaster in St. John's Cathedral, he'll be looking for volunteers from your class, he made a lot of blokes from our class join last year, and they won't be going back this year so he'll be asking for more volunteers to fill the gap. 'When he asks for some volunteers put your hand up straight away', again I'm asking Fonsey 'why?' He says he's got a gorgeous look-ing wife living out on the Ennis Road, it's a good two hour walk there and back, she'll have chocolates and buns to give whoever he sends out with the packet of fags he'll want delivered. So I'm telling Fonsey, 'I'll have some of that as well.'

I have the bike assignment, I'm waiting for the volunteer's job to come up but I don't have long to wait. When he does ask I have my hand up like a shot, just like Fonsey told me. 'OK Taylor', asks Chuckser, 'do you know where?'

'I do sir,' I answer.

He's surprised, 'I haven't finished yet Taylor, and you say I do'.

'You do what?,' he continues.

I know where the Ennis Road is sir.

'Very good,' he says smiling.

'Do you know?'

'I do sir', I answer.

He's still smiling, 'OK what was I going to say?'

'You were going to ask me do I know where your house is sir?'

'And do you?,' he asks.

'I do, sir'.

'I hope you're going to be as clever in class for the next ten months Taylor'.

So he hands me a packet of fags and says 'take these out to my wife'. 'Yes sir' and I'm going to be missing for the next two hours and all the lads are looking at me, mad jealous. I'm sauntering down William Street trying to think of the longest way to Chuckser's house. Maybe I can stretch it to three hours. When I get there, Fonsey was right. There's this gorgeous woman talking to me, she's pleased to see me, she must be gasping for a fag, because she's throwing all kinds of stuff at me.

'Would you like a piece of this, here have a bit of that!' Then it's 'you'll have a glass of orange juice' and as I'm leaving she's shoving a handful of sweets into my pocket, and I think I'm in love. I'm thinking about her all night. He'll send me out every week, sometimes I'll have a ten shilling note with the fags and I'll wonder all over town on the way back day-dreaming about her and that beautiful smell when she bends down to shove the sweets in my pocket. I'm wondering if I was married to a woman like that I'd stay at home and look at her all day. Now I'm wondering when Chuckser is going to ask about the choir, I'm telling all the lads about this gorgeous woman that Chuckser is married to, that I've never seen anyone like her. And I only have to wait until tomorrow when he asks the whole class, 'who wants to have no homework every Friday night for the rest of the year?' Every hand in the class is up including mine. We're shouting 'Sir, Sir, Sir'.

Then he says: 'Who would like to join St. John's choir?' And now my hand is the only one still in the air.

'So you think you'll be a bunch of sissies if you join the boys' choir, come on now boys, surely there's three of four of you who wants to have no homework every Friday night. Imagine no worries on Monday mornings if you're going to get a box in the ear or a wallop of the leather if it's incorrect.'

The offer was too good for Eejits like me and up goes another four hands. I know I can sing but I don't know what he's going to do with the four who put up their hands. They can't talk, never mind sing.

'Why did you join the choir Taylor?,' asked some of the lads after school.

'Because of what I'll get', I answer.

'Like what?,'

'Well twice a year we get to go up to Knock by train to sing at High Mass, we'll get our dinner in a hotel and in the summer months some of the priests will take us all down to Ballybunion or Kilkee in their cars and we'll get dinner there as well'.

Now they want to join the choir but Chuckser will tell the ten who want to sing, it's too late, he has enough. The choir is full. I have never been in a train before and was only in my Uncle Peadar's truck once. So getting a spin in any kind of a car or train was a huge incentive for my generation. There'll be practice after school for two days every week at St. John's Cathedral for the couple of high Masses that will take place every year which we'll have to sing at. Then there's a game of football in the churchyard for an hour or two after practice. I really love singing in the choir, watching Chuckser play the huge organ with all the pedals under his feet, the three layers of piano keys around his hands and the mountain of pipes of all shapes and sizes trying their best to touch the ceiling behind us amaze me. The way he would keep his hands and feet going in different directions while watching the music sheet, keeping an eye on us, taking the right hand away from the keys to conduct our singing, all of which made him a master craftsman of the sound of music.

Our trip to Knock, when it came, happened only once, but it was the bees' knees. The spins in the priest's car came and went but not in the summer, more like October with the wind and rain howling and the dinner in a hotel was a bottle of Coke and a stale bun, but I wouldn't have changed it for anything. After our third week with Chuckser I'm in for a shock. There's a dark side to him when it comes to the leather. He tells us he's going out of the room for five minutes, if he comes back and finds anyone talking we'll all get two of the best, but one minute after he's gone out the door, the talking starts, a few try to hush the rest quiet but it only gets worse. The clock on the wall says it's been ten minutes since he left, there's a right din going on. I could get walloped for something I'm not doing and it's driving me mad. So I'm on my feet telling them to 'shut up, or we'll all get killed' when in walks Chuckser.

'Right I told you to be quiet and what do ye do? Taylor you're going to be the first'.

Why is this always happening to me? I'm like a magnet to disaster. Chuckser has long fair hair, he's always running his fingers through it, fixing it back to one side of his head and as we're all lining up to get walloped his hair is falling down with every stroke of the leather. He'll flick his head back every time.

There's a couple of lads in class who react in strange ways before and after they get the belt from the leather. There's Tom O'Brien. He has the premature withdrawal reaction. He'll be as stiff as a poker while waiting his turn and when it is, Chuckser will tell him to stop pulling his hand away. But Tommy can't help it. He's a bag of nerves and he's going to get worse. Chuckser will tell him again and again, shouting 'keep your bloody hand still' while he makes three or four swipes and misses every time. And the madder Chuckser gets, the more he'll shout at Tommy. In an effort to concentrate on Chuckser's hand with the leather as it rises into the air Tommy will open his mouth as wide as he can get it while lifting his left hand and leg up and down in keeping with the right hand that keeps going in and out. And there's Tommy standing on the classroom floor on the one leg with everything else moving in all directions. Chuckser grabs Tommy's right hand in frustration while Tommy holds his ear with the left one and gives him two wallops on the right hand that should have only got one. Now Tommy is jumping around like a jackass with a big hand that he doesn't know where to put and a red ear as well.

Then there's Lenny Holman or Lenny the levitator. When Lenny holds out the hand, he has the idea that when Chuckser's leather goes into the air his hand should follow it. The least distance between Chuckser's leather strap and Lenny's hand the better. It's like there's a string tied to both. But Chuckser keeps pulling Lenny's hand down and Lenny keeps putting it back up again. Lenny is holding out his hand but it won't stay still, so Chuckser will grab it with his own hand to keep it down. That doesn't stop it either. Chuckser is loosing the rag. He's shouting at Lenny to keep his hand down, as Lenny gets his two wallops on the same hand but they're weaker than the rest of us get. In the months to come Chuckser will try Lenny's other hand but it makes no difference.

There's Jimmy McQuane the wrestler. He starts out like Tommy O'Brien but when Chuckser's hand rises he'll manage to wrap himself around Chuckser's legs. Chuckser will say 'get off me you clown'. He'll start again but it makes no difference. So McQuane gets two half-hearted slaps just like Lenny when Chuckser unwraps himself.

After Jimmy McQuane it's big red-ear Murphy, he has one big ear on the right side, he got it from the two years with the Christian teacher, because of the way his body twists when getting the leather. Chuckser holds Murphy's hand which will wind up under his right ear. Murphy's ear will get the full wallop of the leather on the way down to meet the hand and he won't know which to hold first, the ear or the hand.

There's two other types, like the cool lad, he'll just walk up, put the hand out, it will be as steady as a rock, take the punishment, go back to his seat and look at the wall for five minutes and show no emotion whatsoever. Guys like Gerry Buckley, some of the lads will say 'he has great guts', others 'that he can't feel the pain because he's so thin and has no fat under the flesh of his hand'. His mother says, 'he's anaemic' but never told him what it meant. But we don't need any name for what he has, we've seen people before who look like that, they were laid out in a box down in Cross's Funeral Parlour. He has loads of room on the long timber desk that's supposed to have six bodies in it. His doctor is the same dirty, rotten louser as mine, and told his mother to give him a pint of Guinness every day with his dinner. Chuckser has to give him a note for his mother that asks her to know if she could give him a half pint at dinner and the other half when he goes home for the supper as he comes back to school after the dinner well and truly scuttered and is asleep for the rest of the rest of the day. And if it lasts any longer her son will learn nothing and won't pass the Primary Exam that's coming up at the end of the term. But the shy, sick looking Gerry that we think might die any day now is going to get better on the Guinness. He'll grow into a good looking man with a great personality. He'll run marathons here, there and everywhere and it's hard to imagine he was the sickly, pallid child from CBS Sexton Street.

And last of all there's the howler. He'll be roaring on his way to get the belt, scream his head off when he gets it and bawl his eyes out for twenty minutes after. We didn't realise it then, but it was as hard on Chuckser to wallop the whole class as it was on the rest of us.

When the blockbuster movie Ben Hur comes to Limerick everybody's talking about it. There are rumours spreading like wild-fire that every school in Limerick is going to get a day off to go and see it. The Ten Commandments came to Limerick three years ago and every school got turns to fill the Savoy Cinema in Bedford Row. It was two bob a head but Mam couldn't afford to give me the money to go and see it, and the same blooming thing happens again. I'm one of twenty who can't get the money to go and worst of all we have to stay in class with Chuckser. But he decides to have no lessons today and tells us the whole story start to finish and boys, can he tell a story. He leaves out nothing, he's pacing up and down the classroom floor talking, and minutes after he starts, I'm gone, lost in the story. I got to see the movie five years later and was amazed at Chuckser's detail. It was just like I saw the movie before.

Chuckser is back on the fags again. He gave them up six months into Fonsey's class last year and after five weeks with us he needs them to calm his nerves. We've never seen him smoke before and we are in for a shock. Chuckser loves books, he reads while we're swatting away in class, at lunch-break, he'll walk up and down the yard with his nose stuck in a book that's inches thick, and God help anyone if you run into him accidentally. He can read and speak Greek, Latin and God knows what else, and look who he's teaching!

What the hell did he do to get to teach us? While he's reading he'll smoke but when he sat down at the class room desk for the first time after starting back on the fags, this man is going to mesmerise the lot of us.

He'll put one hand into a pocket of his jacket and take out a packet of Carroll's Number One cigarettes. At the same time the other hand will go into another pocket for the box of matches. He lights up and takes an almighty drag that sees the fag reduce in size by at least a third; the top part shining red like a beacon from a lighthouse. Then he'll open the mouth, let a large portion of the smoke out and then as it leaves, suck it back as it heads its way up his nostrils and down his throat and what happens next has us all speechless. As he exhales there's smoke everywhere, on the second exhale there's more smoke on its way down his nostrils and out his mouth as well. The same happens again on the third exhale and the only place the smoke isn't coming out is his ears. Chuckser will only get four drags from one cigarette and I want to smoke like Chuckser.

The whole class wants to smoke like Chuckser. He's a man. A real man, and if we can smoke like Chuckser we'll all be real men too. So it's across the road from our school to the small sweetshop on the corner. It's owned by an elderly couple. They sell one square of Cleeve's Toffee, a bun, a bottle of the cheapest orange you can buy, bulls eyes, ice cream, milk and the best all time seller, one fag, tipped or untipped. This couple must have known that if the parents' of all the guys that bought the one fag from their shop every day found out they were selling cigarettes to their darlings, they'd be liable to be thumped regardless of their age. Every summer this couple would think they were going out of business during the eight week holiday break because the passing trade was passing. But because of Chuckser's smoking powers this shop's business is going to boom. Two pennies would buy you a Woodbine, two and a half pennies a Carroll's Number 1. Everyone wants to buy a Carroll's Number 1 just like Chuckser. I'm in the shop with all the lads, and half the school outside on the street, as there's no room left in the shop. I want to smoke like Chuckser but I don't have the two and a half pennies to buy the fag.

Roger Browne, Bobby Allen, Jackie Liston and Leo Murphy have enough money between them to buy one Woodbine and a box of matches and I'm standing there in the middle looking on at them. Leo Murphy lights up first and tries to take a drag just like Chuckser. The skin of his jaws are halfway into his mouth with the print of his teeth showing and when he can't suck anymore, has a go at letting some of the smoke out under his nostrils the way Chuckser does. That part he manages OK. Now he tries to take the whole lot down in one go and when he does, finds himself in an epileptic fit. He has his two hands around his throat. Then he starts pounding his chest, there's nothing going in or out. I think he's trying to tell us he's choking. He has dropped the fag and Roger, Jackie and Noel are trying to find it between all the shoes that won't stand still. They're shouting at everyone 'mind the fag, mind the fag'. When they do find it, it's quenched and all flattened out. We've all forgotten about Murphy who was on his knees and somehow managed to get air into his lungs. There are tears running down his face. Now it's Bobby Allen's turn.

After seeing what happened to Murphy he's a bit nervous. He managed to get the cigarette back into a round shape again. So he lights it up, shoves it into the mouth, takes a drag just like Murphy, forgets to let some out under his nostrils and sucks the whole lot down his throat. His eyes are rolling around his head and after three seconds he passes out. He's on the floor in a sit-up position alongside Murphy who is still trying to breathe normally. Jackie Liston manages to take the fag out of Allen's hand on his way down, and sticks it into his mouth real macho like! Takes a drag, lets the smoke out under the nostrils exactly like Chuckser and hands the fag to Roger Browne. Roger is waiting to see what happens to Liston before he takes his turn.

Liston exhales just like Chuckser, then puts his hand to his mouth, runs to the door and throws up all over the street. 'I'll show ye crowd of sissies how to smoke like Chuckser,' says Browne as he puts the fag to his mouth, draws the smoke into the mouth goes through the whole routine but can only get smoke from one exhale. 'Here Taylor,' he says handing the fag to me. 'You have a go'. I don't think any of the other three will want another drag of this thing. I'm looking at what he hands me. It's a bit of a fag, all limp and full of spit. Browne wants me to put this into my mouth, I want to try and smoke like Chuckser but will I put this limp soggy thing in my mouth that's full of spit?

I can see Mam's finger wagging away in front of my face. She's always telling me 'never put anything into your mouth after it's been in somebody else's do you hear me?,' When I ask her why she says because 'you don't want anybody else's germs, you have enough of your own?,' I ask her 'what about Jet or James' germs?,' She'll tell me they're OK when I ask her why she says: 'They're family germs and friendly'. She said the same about the water fountain below in the People's Park. It has a heavy metal cup with a long chain, 'you're never to drink from that dirty, filthy thing. It's been in every mouth in Limerick, you'll get sick', but I took no notice and drank away and wound up in

Barrington's Hospital for several days after. She'll tell me 'never comb your hair with someone else's hair brush' and keep away from Babsey Nealon's house'.

'Why Mam?,'

'It's full of fleas that's why. I don't want you bringing those things into my house. Before we know it the place will be walking with them. Keep away from that fellow'.

'Why Mam?'

'Because there's a smell off of him, I don't think he or his mother ever saw a bar of soap in their life'.

She never stops washing me, combing my hair, spitting on a towel and wiping this and that off my face. She'll wash me the seven days of every week, polish the step in front of our door every day, her whites will be the whitest ones on the road. I'll never be left go to school looking dirty or untidy. 'Pull your socks up, take your hands out of your pockets, that habit is for corner boys, wipe your nose, use your handkerchief not your sleeve, don't come to the table unless you wash your hands, don't use public lavatories'.

'Why Mam?'

'Because you never know whose backside was on them, that's why?,'

'Don't pick your nose in public. Always wash your hands after you use the toilet!'

'Why Mam?'

'Because that's the why'.

'Yes Mam'

But Browne is waiting for me to take this damp yoke out of his hand. If I take it I'll probably be dead in the morning from Liston's, Allen's and Murphy's spit and germs. So I put my hand out to take it. Then a voice says, 'He's not getting that.' It's Murphy, he's back on his feet again, looking for another drag and his mouth is full of mucus. There's always a snot hanging out of his nose, when he talks bubbles appear from both sides of his mouth and I'm out of here. If he hands that yoke to me after he puts it in his mouth again I'll surely be ready for Cross' the Funeral Undertakers to come and take me away in the box in the morning. I'm not going to share a fag with anyone. I'll have to have one of my own. They'll be in there every lunch time sharing their fag, other lads will be able to buy their own and it will be a Carroll's number one too. Their father's have full time jobs. They get thruppence every day for a bottle of milk. They'll be spending that on a fag now.

I don't want to share my germs with anyone, I better think of something fast or I won't be able to smoke like Chuckser.

There's a bus depot on Roxboro Road just by our school. It's where all the buses go at the end of every day to be cleaned out and washed for the following morning. Sometimes I'll go there to look for money or the small roll of paper the conductor uses for taking money and giving tickets. I only ever found a penny once. Now I'm desperate and it's the only thing I can think of at the moment. It's no use going there now. I'll have to wait until the morning when all the buses are gone. There will be a large pile of fresh rubbish, so I'll leave ten minutes earlier tomorrow morning to give myself plenty of time to sift through everything. I'm here twenty minutes now, if I don't get moving I'll be late, there's not a sign of anything. There's a fair pile of junk here, but the solution to the problem has been staring me in the face all the time. Why didn't I see it before? There are fag ends here by the dozen and best of all there's ones with lipstick on them. They're the best. Women throw away a decent fag end or nobber compared to men. They'll suck them right down until they're nearly burning their fingers. Pop's fingers on both hands are dark brown, Mam's hands aren't. She won't even smoke in the street, because she says it's not lady-like. So if I look for the longest fag end with lipstick on it I might even get two or three. But the problem is they're all flattened out from being walked on. But it doesn't matter. I can roll them back into shape again, I don't have to worry about germs. If the women that smoked these fags are like Mam sure there won't be any germs on them at all.

And off I go to school with three decent smokes in my pocket but I'll have to practice first. I'm not going into that shop and have to be carried out like Liston or get a convulsion like Murphy, I don't want to pass out like Allen either. But if I can smoke better than Roger Browne, even the same as Chuckser, then I'll be best in the class at smoking. So it's into the lavatory at the side of the school yard. I light it up and take a big drag, but instead of taking it down to the lungs I swallow it, it's gone into my stomach I don't know the difference yet. There's no dizziness or falling into a convulsion. I don't even feel sick, I feel great but there's no smoke coming back out of my mouth like Chuckser.

There are red spots in front of my eyes, they seem to be on the wall, there was a sound like a spatter just before the spots. Then I see the wall is full of vomit. I'm after throwing up, how can that be? I never felt sick at all. It's just as well no one's around to see this. I don't want to be like the other three Eejits who couldn't hack it, so I give it another go taking a much bigger drag this time and if I empty my intestines against the wall again so what? Getting sick from fags is a doddle. This time the smoke goes down the way it should have gone the first time and Mother of Divine Sorrows I can't stop coughing. How the hell is that? I'm coughing so much I should be getting sick but there's nothing down there so I'm spewing nothing four or five times. I'm on the lavatory seat, I don't know where the ceiling or floor is, my hand is resting on the part of my stomach I left on the wall, it won't keep me steady 'til I get my bearings because my hand is sliding all over the place. It takes me ten minutes to recover. Do I want to have another drag now that I've recovered? Yes. The desire to succeed at this is much stronger than giving in. But the fag is gone, it's down there somewhere in the vomit and I'm not picking it up to put it in my mouth.

I have another two anyway in my pocket, plenty of matches and an endless supply of fag ends from good old CIE so I light up again, take another drag and I move away from the vomit into another lav. Sure there's about fourteen of them here. The coughing isn't as bad as before and by the time I get another three drags down my throat there's no coughing at all. It's time to get back to class. I've run out of fag ends but I have to practice the exhale and get it just like Chuckser.

So the next morning I'm back in the CIE rubbish tip. It only takes a few minutes to get another four or five butts which gives me enough time in the lav. to crack the smoke and get a good strong exhale on the first drag. It's going to take a good few days to get the hang of it, but I'll get it if it's the last thing I do. It's been a week now and I've got it down to a fine art, but only on the second exhale. I don't know it yet but I'm addicted. But it's not costing me a penny as long as CIE keep the front gates of the garage at Roxboro Road open and after another week of practice in the school lav. the best I can do is to see smoke on the second exhale. Now I can nearly smoke like Chuckser.

So I'm ready for the corner shop. I have six good-sized butt ends in my pocket, all rounded out as well. I got a small scissors that's borrowed from my mother's sewing box that helps me cut the burnt ends off. I can stick that part in my mouth and burn the end with the lipstick. Browne, Allen, Murphy and Liston are there still trying to smoke like Chuckser. They can only get smoke after two exhales as well, so I'm not going to be the best. They're all addicted too. I'm in between the lot of them puffing away. Tomorrow they won't have any money and they'll be asking me for a drag on mine. But I'm not having their mouths all over my fag ends, especially Murphy's mouth, so I give them a butt each.

'What's that red stuff at the end?,' they ask me.

'My mother's lipstick, use the other end'. Now I'm the most popular guy in the corner shop every day. I have to make sure there's enough butts in my pocket to go 'round any day they need one and this is what causes the next problem.

Mam is fixing my tie on before I go to school. Mam does everything for all of us. We just have to stand upright. She'll comb my hair; my shoes will be polished every night. When I'm at the table she'll butter my bread, pour out the tea, put the milk in, then the sugar, give the spoon a couple of turns and all I have to do is shove it down my throat. I'm not lazy, it's just the way Mam does things, fussing and cleaning from one end of the day to the next. She's putting a handkerchief into one of my pockets. She's got a puzzled look on her face, now she's saying, 'what on earth have you got in that pocket at all Paddy?,'

'I don't know Mam', I reply.

When she takes her hand out there are two butts in it. There's silence for a few seconds. I'm in shock because I forgot all about them. Mam's in shock too because she can't believe her Paddy would be smoking and before I get a chance to think of the consequences, Mam starts to wallop me across the face, she's using both hands, the wallops are fast and furious. I've never seen her like this before and of course the Holy Family are brought into it.

'Sweet Jesus, Mary and Holy Saint Joseph, what are these things doing in your pocket?'

There's another left and right to the face. She's screaming at me looking for an answer. I can't think of one.

'Do you hear me talking to you? Where did you get these?'

Pop is gone to work and it's just as well. I had only ever got the odd box from him. Mam's wallops hurt even though she's small and light, but if Pop were to loose his temper with me, I can only imagine the damage he'd do to me, but I won't have to imagine much longer, as Mam will surely tell him when he comes home, and there'll be no shoulders going up and down this time. I'm trying to think of an answer quick. If I tell her I got them down at the dump at CIE she'll be saying 'what did I tell you before about going into these kinds of places?' She'll surely say, 'you've been in the dump in CIE for cigarette butts that people throw away on the ground, that half the shoes of Limerick have walked on, shoes that have been in dog piss and sugar, every known germ in this world and you've been putting those things into your mouth, and bringing them here, into my house that I'm working morning, noon and night to keep clean'.

She's shouting into my ear, 'answer me when I'm talking to you'. I still haven't answered her because I can't think of anything and it's making her worse. So I get another box across the face. I have to get away from her because she's frightening me. So I run into the bedroom, she's in after me; my back is against the bed. She's trying to hit me again and she's saying: 'Wait 'til your father comes home, this evening, you'll answer to him my boyo!'

I fall back against the bed and raise my legs in the air in an effort to stop her beating me. I'm so frightened I can't cry. Jetta is behind her looking on. She's frightened too. She hasn't seen Mam like this ever before either. Mam is still trying to hit me in the face but can't over my legs. She's still saying, 'you'll tell me where you got these bloody things or I'll break your bloody neck, do you hear me talking to you?,' Then in a moment of pure madness, without giving it any thought, I start hitting out at her with my legs.

She stops dead in her tracks. There's shock on her face and for one very long second there's no sound, no movement of any kind, just a facial expression of horror. Then Mam starts to cry. She walks away from me, out of the room. Boys! I've really done it this time, what happened, why did my legs do that? I never told them to do that, not to my mother. What am I to do now? Mam is saying, 'I never thought I'd see the day when my thirteen year old son would raise his hand to me'. I'm saying, 'Mam I didn't raise my hand to you at all Mam, it was my legs Mam, I'm sorry Mam, I don't know what happened Mam, I'm really sorry Mam. I never said it in my mind that I was going to do it, honest to God Mam, I swear Mam it just happened'.

She says it's out of her hands now, 'your father will deal with you when he gets home'. I can see Mam's headache is coming back because she has her hand on her head. Jet is telling her that I didn't mean it and I hope she'll keep saying that to Mam because I need all the help I can get. I have my hand around Mam's shoulder, I'm telling her I'm sorry and will she not tell Pop when he comes home? She says she has to because it's too serious. 'But Mam, I didn't raise my hand Mam, I'd never do that to you Mam, it was my legs Mam, honestly Mam, it just happened'. Jetta is still telling her not to tell Pop, she is frightened of what Pop will do, if he looses his temper, and there'll be no one there to pull him off me. I'm dead, I have to leave home and run away if Mam doesn't agree not to tell him, I've only got another two hours before he comes home.

I just kept on keeping my arm around her, telling her all the time I was sorry, that it would never happen again. It was a once-off. Jet kept saying, 'he won't Mam, you know he won't, he didn't mean it and if he does it again Mam, I'll tell Pop for you'. Now she's saying she'll think about it, but she doesn't have much time. I'd better stay alongside the front door when Pop comes, so I can make a fast getaway if Mam decides to tell him. I'm asking her does she want me to go down to O'Holloran's shop to get her a Cullen's Powder. She says 'no'.

'Is there anything I can do for you Mam?,'

She says 'no' to that as well. Five minutes later I'm asking her again.

'Have you thought about it yet Mam, are you going to tell him Mam?'

She says she doesn't know. I tell her I love her, I don't think I've ever told her that before. I'm surprised I said this because we don't say this very much. There's no need, we all know we love one another here. What's the point of saying it? Then Mam says she's decided not to tell Pop tonight. She wants to sleep on it and she'll have a decision made tomorrow. I'm thinking at least I'll be able to sleep in my own bed with Jet tonight, and not on the side of the road, or worse still a derelict house which there are plenty of in Limerick. But Jet and I know that Mam is very soft and easy to get around.

Telling Pop would surely cause another problem. She wouldn't be able to control him in her house. I had committed the ultimate sin - I'd raised my hand to my mother. It's an expression commonly used in those days for any child who'd physically used force against his or her parents. We were never allowed to back-answer our mother. When we tried on the rare occasion, one wallop from Pop was enough to bring us to our senses.

It was never mentioned again. In the days and weeks ahead it would be like it never happened, because I show Mam the healthy fear she thought she'd lost. And Mam's family is her life. With hindsight and having the experience of raising two children of my own I can now understand her dilemma. What would I have done in the same situation if my daughter or son showed some form of resistance by way of physical confrontation or defence? On the few occasions I had to use force with my kids I know I'd be devastated. There would be a feeling that I'd lost something, respect maybe. I might feel that they hadn't the fear of displeasing me anymore. After all everything in those days was about fear. In school - your teacher, any teacher, the local priests, any priest, grown ups, the Guards. They all knew you feared them, but it was a healthy fear. We benefited from that way of life. It made us what we are today, so I can understand now Mam's devastation, her dilemma and what she was going to do about it. I still frequent the rubbish tip at CIE on the Roxboro Road every day. I'll make sure the pockets are empty before I go home every day. I'm the most popular guy in class, they all think Mam wears red lipstick and is a heavy smoker.

It's the autumn of 1961; the Fianna Fáil Government goes to the country looking to get back in power. It's Wednesday, the school is closed and I'm off on the prowl looking for an opportunity to earn a few bob. I bump into one of the lads from class. He tells me that Ted Russell is looking for men to stand outside the Polling Stations and hand out leaflets to people coming in to vote. He says 'you have to be sixteen to get the job. You'll have no problem, Taylor you're big enough to pass for sixteen, I'm not'. So I'm gone like a rocket up O'Connell Street to the address he gave me. I don't even know who Ted Russell is or why he would want people to stand outside the door of a Polling Station. Sure people must have their minds made up by the time they get there. But who cares. If Ted Russell wants to give me money for doing that I'm your man. I arrive at a shop two doors down from South's Pub, puffing and panting. I'm told by the shop keeper the place to go is upstairs.

I'm on the First Floor, when I walk into a big room there's a guy sitting at a desk.

'Are you here to go to a Polling Booth Station,' he asks and 'hand out leaflets young man?'

'Yes sir', I answer.

'Right, here's a bunch of leaflets and this man will take you to a Polling Station in a few minutes. There'll be a van out to you during the day with milk, sandwiches and cigarettes and at the end of the night around ten o'clock you'll get your ten bob and a lift home'.

I didn't think I'd be out that late. Mam will be giving me grief when I get home, but when I give her half of what I get today that will make up for it. Before I know it I'm out in Farranshone outside a small house with five other guys, they're handing out leaflets too. After a couple of hours the road and garden are full of leaflets as people are throwing them away. They won't even bother to read them. I'm wondering why are we here at all, why is Ted Russell and other politicians wasting their money? But that's not my problem. Then a bread van arrives, it's for me. I get the bottle of milk, two sandwiches and a packet of twenty cigarettes. I can't believe it.

Twenty cigarettes! I'm still going to the bus station everyday for the two butts, now I've got twenty full cigarettes altogether for myself. They're not filtered; they're the same as Pop's, John Player's Please. They're strong. I have to smoke the whole lot in one day because I'm not going to throw away good long clean cigarettes, just for the sake of it. I better be careful where I put these cigarettes. I remember what happened the last time Mam found two butts in my pocket. They also gave me a box of matches. I'm the only young fellow among the five others.

I know they don't have regular work, if they had they wouldn't be here on a Wednesday, so when I get the milk and the sandwiches and the cigarettes I can tell there's a bit of jealousy here.

'How the hell did you manage to wangle that?,' asks one of them. 'I do this every time there's a local or general election and I never get anything like that'. I'm moving away with the milk bottle in one hand, the fags well tucked away in my pocket and the sandwiches in my other hand while telling him 'I just heard from a school mate'. I ask him what time it is. He says, 'two o'clock'. So I have seven hours to smoke twenty fags, that's two and a half fags an hour. So I better get going. The other five look on as I light up. They've been sucking nobbers since I got here and don't like the idea of a fourteen year old with a packet of John Players in his pocket, a bottle of milk and two sandwiches. I don't have to worry about anyone seeing me out here. Sure no one belonging to my family live out here at all. After I finish the first fag I'm wondering how I'm going to smoke twenty by nine o'clock, but smoke I will. I'm not going to throw away or give away some to anyone else here. If I do offer them around they'll be offering me back half a nobber or a drag off one and I had enough of that at the Corner Shop back in Sexton Street. There are very few people coming to this polling station and the time is passing away slowly. The guys are getting tired of me asking for the time every few minutes so I can make sure I smoke the two and a half fags every hour.

I'm into my third fag, I don't feel too good. But it couldn't be the fags. There are people giving out to me as they pass in and out saying, 'Aren't you a silly boy to be smoking at your age? I wish I never started, they're a curse. Why don't you stop now while you've time?,' they say and I'm there with the fag stuck in one corner of my mouth with the eye over it closed, trying very hard to look macho and intelligent. And isn't it amazing that a simple thing like a fag can do all those things just because they're stuck in your mouth or between the fingers of your hand. It's five o'clock and I've gone through eight cigarettes. The other five are telling me that I've gone very white in the face. But apart from a dry taste in my mouth I'm fine. By the time six o'clock arrives I have to sit down for a while just to take a rest. It's just that my head feels a bit light, and there's nine fags left in the box.

It must have been something in the sandwiches that didn't agree with me. Then another bread van arrives. It's a different driver. He's all apologies about not being here at four o'clock. He's saying 'you must be starving with the hunger, so he hands me another bottle of milk, another packet of sandwiches.

'Do you smoke?'

'Yes', I answer, and he hands me another packet of twenty Player's Please.

He thinks no one came out to me at all and I'm not going to open my mouth and ruin everything and I hope the other five don't give the game away either. They might just do that out of jealousy. He's gone and the others aren't a bit pleased. They've had nothing all day and I've got another twenty fags on top of the nine left in the box to smoke in the next three hours. So I stuff the two ham and cheese sandwiches down my mouth and follow with a couple of slugs of milk to help it down. The others are turning away in disgust, I can hear them saying; 'I know where I'll be going, come the next election'. I'm lighting up my twelfth fag, puffing away, it's one after the other now.

When I open the box to count and see how many I have left, there's much more than when I looked the last time. I'm squinting my eyes to see properly. I'm seeing double. When I look up there's two of everything. And I don't feel very well. Now I'm throwing up vomit against the wall, I've never seen white vomit like this before, there's no red bits. Now I can't stand up, I'm like a drunk and the other five are laughing. But a couple of people coming out of the house come to my rescue. It's eight o'clock and a bread van has arrived to take me home.

The driver gives me my ten bob, asks me where I live and brings me home. Mam is waiting at the door worried sick wondering where I was. She's all questions and the driver fills her in, as to where I was. She puts me straight to bed. The following day when I wake up, Mam and Pop are at the end of the bed. Mam has a new packet of cigarettes in one hand and a ten bob note in the other.

'Where did you get this money and these cigarettes from?'

It was just as well I left the others behind me in the packet on the seat of the van. Otherwise I was in trouble.

'They gave me those with the money for standing outside the door with the leaflets so I kept them for you Mam and you can have half the ten bob note'.

'Oh aren't you very good love, thank you very much'. That's me off the hook but ends my visit to the bus depot for another two years at least.

Later that year at Christmas, Dinny, Fonsey, Noelie and I will get battery operated torches. There's a large hut in the garden where Dinny lives. His father has an important job in CIE and they live in a house belonging to the company. The hut is for the workers to come and have their lunch and tea break.

There's a pot belly stove always on the go and because Dinny's father is the boss, Dinny can go where he likes, and the best place for us to go in the cold winter evenings is to that workers' cabin. On Christmas Day and St. Stephen's Day every train and carriage is lying idle. The station, which is only a two minute walk through the back garden from Dinny's house, can have five lines of idle carriages where we can play hide and seek with our torches for those two days and smoke to our hearts' content. Dinny, Fonsey, Noelie and I went through our teens smoking and after seventeen years I would pack them up at the age of twenty five. Maybe I'm alive today because of that. But when I look back at trying to fit in and the things I did try to achieve it, I'm beginning to learn something about myself I never knew before, how I would never grow out of it, even down to this day.

But there's more to tell about Chuckser, his love of apples in the mid-afternoon, how he'd take one and sink his thumb into the middle where the stem is, snap it in two, now we're all trying to do the same, and wind up with sprained or broken thumbs in failed attempts to copy him. The time he gave Bobby Allen a bob and asked him to run across the road to the corner shop and get him a bar of chocolate at 2:00pm and Mike wasn't seen in class for another two days. When he did come back, Chuckser asked him what happened to the shilling he gave him and the bar of chocolate he was supposed to get, saying 'you hardly lost it, as the shop is only across the road'. Bobby stood up and stuttered out the words that he did lose the shilling and was afraid to come back in case he got a wallop of the leather in each hand and asked Chuckser would he mind not sending him across the road again because the responsibility is too much. But Bobby tells us at the break that day how there was a great western showing at the Lyric and when the thought came into his head of going to see it, now that he had the bob in his hand, he couldn't resist the temptation so off he went!

Then there was the day that started something very special which leaves me with precious memories. When Chuckser asked the class with a look on his face that said, 'I don't know why I'm asking this lot this question but I might as well ask it anyway'. He raises his voice and says: 'I suppose there wouldn't be any possible chance that one of you, just one, would know any of the great operas'. I'm up out of my seat like a rocket with my hand in the air. I'm on my toes leaning out over the two lads in front of me shouting: "I do Sir, I do". Chuckser looks at me like he's in shock and shouts 'You Taylor! You know some of the great operas". He says this as he walks down to me. When he stops he looks into my face and says, 'OK Taylor, are you going to tell us some of these great operas then? And I don't want any smart answers, like the answer you gave me last week when I asked you to name the four seasons, like winter, summer, autumn and spring and you gave me the four names of the pop group. So unless I hear the proper names of one or two operas you'll get a box in the ear, is that clear now?" "Yes Sir," I answer and then I say, 'I don't know one or two Sir', Chuckser interrupts;

'Did you not put your hand up and nearly jump out of your seat when I asked you the question and now you're telling me you don't know any?"

"No Sir, that's not what I meant Sir; I know them all Sir".

Now Chuckser has a look of disbelief, like how the hell could I have knowledge of the arts when I'm so bad in class. He plants his backside on one of the desks, folds his arms and says; 'OK let's hear them then". I know Chuckser doesn't believe I could have any knowledge of stuff like this, neither does any of the lads in class. I can see they're all waiting for me to make a total idiot of myself and have a good laugh at the same time. So with a quiet confidence I start. 'Well Sir, there's the Barber of Seville by Rossini'. The smirk has gone from Chuckser's face, his jaw is starting to fall. I continue, 'then there's La Bohéme and Tosca by Puccini', now Chuckser's jaw is wide open and his arms have moved from the folded position, like they've gone dead and just hang there, by his side. 'There's La Traviata, Aida and Il Trovatore by Verdi', Carmen by Bizet, William Tell by,' 'OK, OK' says Chuckser. 'Taylor how the hell can you sit there and rattle off by heart the great composers and the names of their masterpieces?,' Would you like to hear the names of the light operas by Gilbert & Sullivan Sir?,' 'No I wouldn't', he says. 'For the love of God will you tell me how did you come by this information?,'

'From my father, he loves the operas Sir. He locks himself into the sitting room at home every Sunday after the dinner Sir; he'll put one of the big LPs on and stay there for hours Sir'. He asks me does my mother like the operas. 'She does, Sir'. 'Well here's two tickets for an opera that's on tomorrow night at the Coliseum in O'Connell Street, give them to your parents'. 'Thank you Sir'.

He's shaking his head from side to side in disbelief as he walks away. I can see all the lads are in shock but I'm not telling Chuckser that I can't stand listening to that awful noise that's called music. Jet, James and I will always be out of the house after dinner every Sunday and spare our ears from the terrible attempts Pop will make to match the great Jussi Bjorling. There'll be blood vessels doing their very best to escape from Pop's neck as he'll try to match Jussi but Pop is way out of his league here. He's known to sing a good song or two at a wedding or a funeral and does have a good voice. Mam will be out in the kitchen listening away through the hole in the wall with the small door we call the hatch that's used to hand Pop his mug of tea every hour. The cup is the size of half a bucket and sent from Australia by Aunt Tess. The room will be full of smoke from the fags that will be between Pop's brown fingers. Mam is happy because it's coming up to four years - the longest spell Pop is off the drink.

To keep Pop away from the Bedford Bar Mam went to Power and Hogan down in Patrick Street and made arrangements to buy the latest contraption known as a stereogram with legs, made from solid mahogany with a dazzling high shine from the French polishing it got at the factory. A radio in one half capable of bringing us every station across Europe, a speaker on both sides to give the listening ears the excitement of the new stereo sound effect; the other half with a lift off top held a record player able to hold four or five LPs and play one after the other, which meant that once Pop relaxed into his chair he could stay there for hours. It had at one side a small section to hold the ten large black plastic LPs that came with it. The weekly payments will, along with all the others, put an extra burden on Mam's purse, but it will be worth it because the worry of Pop being on the tear would be far worse. He'll have less to do at home by way of fixing clocks, old furniture, holes in the roof or dampness as most things in the house in Garryowen are new. He has far less time on his hands these days as the days of no work seem to be gone and a thing of the past. So his Sunday afternoons are well and truly full. Then after the supper it's down to the Stella Ballroom or St. John's Pavilion for the bingo and with his luck it will be a fruitful night.

But I've got two tickets from Chuckser to go to an opera and boys will Pop and Mam be surprised when I put them in their hands. It's a longer walk to Garryowen from school but I've ran all the way. I can't wait to see their faces when I show them what I've got. It's 12:45, Pop won't be home for dinner before 1:15pm so when I burst in the back door waving the tickets in the air saying to Mam, 'Look what I've got for you and Pop' she puts her hand out with a face that has a puzzled look, and asks me where I got them. So after filling her in, I'm asking will she and Pop be able to go? I'm trying to get her to answer me, but she's too interested in getting the information that's printed all over the tickets. So I keep repeating the question. She says, 'we'll have to wait and see when Pop comes home for his dinner'. I'm asking her is she pleased because I know she likes that awful music too. Sure isn't that where I got all the information about the composers and their operas over the supper table every Sunday evening and I never knew all that information was going into my ear until today. She says she is, and hopes Pop will be able to go. 'Sure what could stop him Mam?,' I ask.

'Well I know he's very busy working for Mr. Whelan, he's renting a room out on the second floor of his shop'.

So when Pop walks in the door after putting his bike against the wall outside, I'm shoving the two tickets under his nose, saying 'Look what I've got for yourself and Mam'. Mam fills him in on where and how I got them, but he shakes his head and says he can't go because he has to have a new hairdressing salon opened on Monday and he has to work the whole weekend, nights and all.

'Sure can't you take Paddy?,' he says.

Yacks! I shout, 'there's no way I'm going to see that rubbish'.

'Well you'll have to go with your mother because she won't go on her own, so you'll do what you're told'.

Mam looks at me and asks, 'Don't you want to escort your poor mother out for a night at the opera? Would you be ashamed to be seen with her Pa?'

'No Mam, I would not, sure I'd go anywhere with you Mam, it's just that horrible sound that you and Pop call music; I don't think I could sit through that for two and a half hours. It's bad enough having to listen to it every Sunday after dinner, but I'll go with you Mam', How could I refuse? I'd do anything for her, she's too good to me, making me those spotted dicks every week and ever since Jet and James went off the currant cake she's making me two and never misses a week even when she has one of those awful headaches. There's the sausages, the ones she buys from O'Connell's in William St. They have a special recipe. She'll cook them on the large black frying pan that came from Tower Hill to Carey's Road and was one of the few items that came to our house in Garryowen in Uncle Peadar's truck. It was the only kitchen implement that never saw a drop of water or soap because it would loose the special flavour of bits and pieces of everything that went into it over a lot of years. The flavour would soak its way into or stick to the pound (1 lb) of sausages she'd do for me every Thursday without fail. She'll tell every woman she meets how I'll eat sixteen sausages in one go along with the spuds, but only if they're done in the big black frying pan. So when the following day comes, it's Saturday I can't get the fact out of my head that tonight I'm going to be stuck in a theatre listening to music for ould people.

We get a bus into town and walk up O'Connell Street. I have her pestered about the opera. 'Oh I think you're in for a surprise tonight Pa', says Mam, and after I ask her what kind of surprise, I'm told I have to wait and see. When we get to the Coliseum there's grown ups everywhere and I seem to be the only young fellow here. There's a crowd outside the main door smoking because Mam says 'there's no smoking allowed inside because of the singing'. So we take our seats inside and wait. There's a small orchestra just in front of the stage. They're all blowing and fiddling away making a right din. Mam is laughing at me because I have an awful face on me. I have my ears covered and I think I should be going now, if she'll let me. She says 'That's not music Pa; it's just the musicians tuning up.' Then the lights fade. It brings the crowd to silence. There's an announcement on the loud-speaker. A voice says, 'Ladies and Gentlemen, will you please put your hands together for our conductor this evening Mr. Brian O'Neill'. And out walks Chuckser. I'm stuck to the seat with my gob wide open. Everybody is applauding. I turn to Mam and shout while pointing, 'That's Chuckser Mam, that's Chuckser'. She can't hear me because of all the clapping. I have to tug on her arm to get her attention. She puts her ear to my mouth. 'That's Chuckser Mam, my teacher Mam; he's the one that gave me the tickets Mam'. She nods her head in response and puts her forefinger to her mouth to calm me down. There's silence and Chuckser raises his hands into the air. He's got a small stick in his right hand and when he brings them down the music starts. It's nice. Mam whispers into my ear, they're playing the overture. And when I ask her what an overture is, she says 'I'll tell you at the interval'. And now I want to know what an interval is? She smiles and says half-time. Then the music stops to more applause. Up goes Chuckser's hand and again he brings the orchestra to life. There's singing behind the curtains, that's nice too and when they slowly open the stage is full of men and women clothed in wonderful coloured costumes.

I'm sitting up with my head stretched as far from my shoulders as I can get it, because of the two big heads that's in front of me, blocking my view. I thought I'd be thrown on the seat with my head in my chest bored out of my skull but I've got goose pimples running everywhere I have skin. I'm starting to have an experience I'll never forget. Mam was right and I have Chuckser to thank. After what seems to be only a few minutes, everybody is on their feet applauding including myself. I look at Mam, she's smiling away. How could she have known I would enjoy this so much? Because I'm loving every minute of it! She says the musical is called The Pirates of Penzance by Gilbert and Sullivan. I said 'I know Mam; sure doesn't Pop have the LP at home? But now that I've seen it, it's just so much better'. She says, 'You know it's by Gilbert and Sullivan don't you? That one wrote the words and the other the music? And the reason you're enjoying it so much is because it's a comedy play as well as a musical, and sung in English and not Italian like the other stuff Pop listens to every Sunday'.

We're out on the street in front of the main entrance, where she joins the crowd for a smoke, and all I want to know is when the second half is going to start. I haven't long to wait before Chuckser is back with the hands in the air that starts the goose pimples rising all over my body again. And then it's all over. My hands are sore from clapping the cast as they take their final bow. But Chuckser will get my swollen hands even hotter when his name is announced to take his bow. I came home that night buzzing with excitement. I couldn't stop talking all the way home. I didn't realise it then but that was my baptism to the arts. And every Sunday after dinner would find me humming away to Figaro, Jussi and others. I'm starting to like it and to this day I will think of Chuckser anytime I hear The Pirates of Penzance and that night I spent with Mam. It will give me a lump in my throat as will Pavarotti if I hear him singing any of the great arias. It will be accompanied with a picture of Pop lying on the couch with the fag in his hand singing along with Jussi and Mam out in the kitchen smiling away.

It's Monday morning and I'm back at school. I have my hands in the air again and Chuckser wants to know what's wrong with me. 'Sir, my mother asked me to thank you for the two tickets to the opera on Saturday night'. Chuckser says, 'She's welcome' and asks 'Did your parents enjoy themselves'. I told him my father couldn't go because of work and that I went instead. Chuckser looks pleased and asks me what I thought of it. I told him it was the best night I ever had in my life and asked him if he had anymore tickets for operas would he keep me in mind. 'Oh and you were brilliant Sir'.

Chuckser smiles, thanks me and assures me if there's anymore tickets he would let me know.

That night gave me a whole new appreciation of Chuckser and his abilities. I will be more attentive to his every word now. The Primary Exam is coming up very soon but my sudden interest in Chuckser's teaching skills, his way of helping my brain to understand and see things I've never seen before, has come too late. Because when I take the exam I am one of twenty who fail. Those that don't will go next door to Secondary School and better themselves. I and seven others will wind up in John the Baptist School in Garryowen and only a stone's throw from my house. I will stay here for four months and leave after the Christmas holidays. But my time at CBS Sexton Street has come to an end. I'll walk across to the other side of the road, turn and face the school that demanded my presence for the last five years, and feel I've been released from jail.

I'll look at my hands and tell them 'there will be no more walloping; the time has come for your creativity to shine'.

But the memory of Chuckser and his gifts, the scouting days and life between the three bridges will never leave me. The next seven years will see many changes in my family. Mam, the glue that kept us all together will be taken away from us and all because of a stupid medical error. History will repeat itself with my brother Harry being left without a mother at the age of nine just like Pop. Jet will marry and have two children. James will continue growing and I will meet and marry the best friend I've ever had. Pop can drink what he likes, whenever he likes. The

'70's and '80's will be harder on him than the '40's and '50's because he will lose interest in all of us including himself. But that's another story for another book. I'll be talking to you.

Taken from the Sextonian School Manual of 1961 6th Grades
Brother Kenny top with glasses,
Chuckser next left with glasses.

Fonsie

Noelie

The Author

*No photo of
Dinny could be
found*

(To The Air of The Boys From the County Mayo)

OLD CAREY'S ROAD OF LONG LONG AGO

I

As an exile of Limerick I travelled the world
And Chiswick in London I made my abode
With friends of old Limerick we sat reminiscing
Of the once happy times in Old Carey's Road.
Good neighbours we had, sure the best in the world
If you were in trouble they would answer the call
For they all stuck together in all kinds of weather
And some of those friends I will try to recall.

II

The Gilligan's the Quilligans the Cooney's and Toomey's
The Halveys the Cronin's to mention a few
The McCaull's and the Farrell's the Gleason's and Carroll's
McMahons and Hannon's each son a true blue
The Sheehy's and Deedigan's McCaffery's and Keaton's
The Barrett's the Stacks of Carey's Road Grand
The Stubbins' and Gubbins, Kiely's and Riley's
Young Munster's team and the Boherbouy Band.

III

When William of Orange invaded our homeland
No mercy at all to the Irish he showed
But he got his comeuppance at the Sweet Walls of Limerick
By the courage of those like in Old Carey's Road.
The Kelly's, the Healy's, the Quinn's and the Kerly's
The Kehoe's the Shanns McGrath and the Ryan's
The Murphy's and Johnsons the Browns and the Benson's
Doherty Nunan's Crofton's, O'Brien's.

IV

In the time of the trouble the famed Irish Rebellion
The Boys from the Road all shouldered the gun
They fought and they died and they bled for old Ireland
They were the boys who made the Black and Tans run.
The Lawlor's and Hourigan's the Buckley's and Horrigan's
Atkinson's Powers the Clancy's and Mann's
The Frawley's and Cowel's the Moore's and Mulrooney's
The Halloran's Flaherty's the Leamy's and Quans.

V

The Hanrahan's the Shanahan's the Meehan's and Whelan's
The Fords and the Daly's all of I.R.A. fame
The Deans and the Keane's Maloney's and Mahoney's
Higgins and Collins each one a proud name.
They would all pull together in all kinds of weather
Never showed the white feather where ever they would go
They loved one another and were just like brother
In old Carey's road of long long ago.

VI

McGuiness and Callaghan's McDonough's and Galvins
Connelly's and Clohessy the names I do tell
The Raleigh's and Wallace the Holmes and the Hennessey's
McNamara's McSweeney those folks I knew well.
The Kennedys the Williams the Morgan's and Elms
Costello's Nashes the Frosts and the Hayes
In London we are sitting and fond reminiscing
Of Old Carey's Road and those wonderful days.